SEX INDUSTRY SLA\

MW01225174

Protecting Canada's ʏᴏᴜᴛʜ

Robert Chrismas

Sexual exploitation and human sex trafficking is a multi-billion-dollar international industry that preys on youth. Written by veteran police officer Robert Chrismas, *Sex Industry Slavery* is an impactful read for anyone who wants to know more about this serious Canadian problem.

Many young women are coerced into oppressive relationships in the sex industry, often starting in childhood. There are numerous barriers and challenges for children who are vulnerable to exploitation as well as for survivors striving to leave the sex industry; however, there are also many opportunities to help them. Based on Chrismas's award-winning research in Manitoba, this book includes gut-wrenching stories from survivors, social workers, police officers, lawmakers, and activists. Representing decades of collective knowledge, *Sex Industry Slavery* presents first-hand perspectives on the problem as well as proposes practical solutions.

ROBERT CHRISMAS has served over forty years in various Canadian justice, law enforcement, and peacekeeping roles and has written prolifically on a broad range of justice-related topics.

Sex Industry Slavery

Protecting Canada's Youth

Robert Chrismas

UNIVERSITY OF TORONTO PRESS
Toronto Buffalo London

ISBN 978-1-4875-0613-1 (cloth)   ISBN 978-1-4875-3572-8 (EPUB)
ISBN 978-1-4875-2485-2 (paper)   ISBN 978-1-4875-3571-1 (PDF)

Library and Archives Canada Cataloguing in Publication

Title: Sex industry slavery : protecting Canada's youth / Robert Chrismas.
Names: Chrismas, Robert, 1962– author.
Description: Includes bibliographical references and index.
Identifiers: Canadiana (print) 20200234439 | Canadiana (ebook) 20200234455 |
    ISBN 9781487506131 (hardcover) | ISBN 9781487524852 (softcover) | ISBN
    9781487535728 (EPUB) | ISBN 9781487535711 (PDF)
Subjects: LCSH: Human trafficking – Canada. | LCSH: Human trafficking
    victims – Canada. | LCSH: Child prostitution – Canada.
Classification: LCC HQ281 .C47 2020 | DDC 364.15/34 – dc23

University of Toronto Press acknowledges the financial assistance to its
publishing program of the Canada Council for the Arts and the Ontario Arts
Council, an agency of the Government of Ontario.

 Canada Council **Conseil des Arts**
for the Arts **du Canada**

ONTARIO ARTS COUNCIL
CONSEIL DES ARTS DE L'ONTARIO
an Ontario government agency
un organisme du gouvernement de l'Ontario

Funded by the   Financé par le
Government gouvernement
of Canada   du Canada

I dedicate this book to my children,
Crystal, Chelsea, Brandi, and Bobby,
and my ever-encouraging and supportive
wife, Barb

Contents

Preface

All the flowers might die, the grass might die, but the thistle will live. That explains women.

– Paige, a sex trafficking survivor,
talking about survivors

In the modern world of internet connectedness, we no longer have the excuse of isolation for our inability, or unwillingness, to participate in the global discourse around fundamental human rights, including what is happening in our own backyards. This book is my contribution to bridging the knowledge gap on one of humankind's most persistent and deplorable social scourges, the sexual exploitation of our youth. For those who want to contribute to change, this is a road map for community-wide engagement around social issues, and a deeper understanding of sex trafficking and exploitation and how to intervene and, perhaps, one day eradicate it.

I am grateful to the many participants who agreed to be interviewed for this research. Sexual exploitation and human trafficking are not easy matters to discuss, particularly for survivors, many of whom have dedicated their lives to helping others escape exploitation and abuse. I thank these people for opening their hearts and revealing their compelling stories for the greater good of preventing exploitation and assisting others to escape the sex industry.

I thank Dr. Sean Byrne, who has been a great role model, mentor, teacher, and source of inspiration and guidance through my educational journey. As a person who left school to join the workforce at fifteen years old, I have a deep appreciation of the life-long students and mentors who have inspired me. One of my hopes for this book is that it will encourage others to continue their education throughout life.

I also acknowledge the influence that the discipline of Peace and Conflict Studies (PACS) has had on my work. As a police officer, and throughout my studies, I've come to appreciate PACS for its focus on social justice, human rights, and peacebuilding, which is consistent with the focus of my life's work, striving to increase community safety and to reduce victimization.

I have saved my greatest debt for the last: I thank my children, Crystal, Chelsea, Brandi, and Bobby, and my wife, Barb, for their years of encouragement through my journey to add to the public discourse on social justice. Without the support of my family and friends, the years of work that culminate in this book would not have been possible.

A Note on Terminology

The definitions of terms such as "sexual exploitation," "human trafficking," and "prostitution" differ in common usage and application. This research uses the following definitions. In the first chapter, I explain the rationale and process for defining these terms.

Low track: The place where street-level sex selling occurs.

Prostitution: Generally the act of selling sex for remuneration, usually for money. This term is avoided, as it implies a freely chosen professional vocation, and this research finds that children do not freely choose to engage in selling sex for money.

Sex Trade: This term, often used in the past, is avoided, as it implies a freely chosen professional vocation or "trade." The term "sex industry" is used instead.

Sexual exploitation: Forcing a person to have sex against her/his will, without consent, for any reason.

Sex Industry: This term is preferred, as it implies an organized, market-driven business in which people are exploited for sex.

Sex Trafficking: Describes any situation where one person controls or manipulates another, using her/him for sexual services or gain.

Slavery: In the context of this research, the same as trafficking.

Survivor: A person who has been or is actively engaged in selling her/his body in the sex industry.

Abbreviations

AMC	Assembly of Manitoba Chiefs
CBC	Canadian Broadcasting Corporation
CFS	Child and Family Services
CSU	Crisis Stabilization Unit
CWF	Canadian Women's Foundation
EIA	Employment Income Assistance
EPPS	Exploited Persons Proactive Strategy
NGO	Non-governmental Organization
MMIWG	Missing and Murdered Indigenous Women and Girls
NWAC	Native Women's Association of Canada
PTSD	Post-Traumatic Stress Disorder
RCMP	Royal Canadian Mounted Police
TERF	Transition Education and Resources for Females
WPS	Winnipeg Police Service

SEX INDUSTRY SLAVERY

1 Introduction

ASHLEY: From a survivor's view, I was first victimized at the age of fifteen. I was groomed and coerced into entering the sex trade, and then to selling myself on Ellice [Avenue] and Home [Street]. All the money I made went to drugs. I was then introduced to an older man who pretended he was my boyfriend, he had me working out of an older girl's apartment who was out of town. I was advertised on the internet and I would see many men a day there. He said he was keeping all the money and that I would get a car, my own condo, clothes, he bought me jewellery, but I didn't see any of the money.

Then I ended up moving from Winnipeg to Vancouver and back to Winnipeg to an abusive dangerous predator and then to Toronto where I was with a very controlling abusive predator who actually sold me. I was in jail, and I had a surety, and I guess he had had enough of me, so he essentially sold me to another predator who ended up being murdered. He was shot in the head, after which I returned to Winnipeg.

Then when I came back to Winnipeg, I was trying to get help for my addictions, and I had ended up getting a big settlement from a lawsuit I had in Vancouver. And I wasn't able to manage the money, and I felt so hopeless, so much guilt and so much shame that I jumped off of the Maryland Bridge. I landed on the ice. I broke my back, and my legs and my feet were crushed. So, I spent six months in the hospital rehabilitating from that, and from then I still was entrenched in the sex trade. That's all I had known my whole teens and adult life. I had been brainwashed by these men into thinking that I needed them, so I had a son and I lost him to CFS [Child and Family Services]. The turning point really wasn't for me until I was pregnant with my daughter.

Ashley's story encapsulates many elements of Canada's sex industry that this book covers. Imagine that your daughter didn't come home last night. She has been acting withdrawn lately, but otherwise nothing has been significantly out of the normal. Desperate for answers, you start checking with her friends and looking on her social media and realize she has been hanging out with some new people in the last few weeks. Eventually, as the police get involved, you realize she has been groomed and abducted into the sex industry. Does this sound implausible? It shouldn't. It happens more often than most people wish to acknowledge, and to people in all socio-economic classes and cultural groups. This book provides insights into how it happens, and what can be done to reduce or prevent it. My background in policing, working in counter-exploitation and then studying the phenomenon more deeply, has positioned me well to produce a book that may save lives; it will undoubtedly improve insights into how society might rally around fixing this persisting scourge. If you are a practitioner of policing, social work, the health care industry, education, or adolescent care, you should read this book. For scholars and students, this book presents a transdisciplinary exploration, with significant insights for a broad range of perspectives.

Living and working primarily in Manitoba, I focused my research there; however, many of my findings refer to Canada at large. I chose to focus on Manitoba because, despite its having one of the most comprehensive, robust, and well-funded provincial counter-exploitation strategies in Canada, in that province women and children are still exploited and hurt in the sex industry. Manitoba has many experts with deep experience in these issues. The people I interviewed for this book collectively represent over one thousand years of experience, either as survivors of the sex industry or as practitioners working with survivors. This vast pool of insights and expertise is brought together in this book, with the aim of reducing the criminal exploitation and sexual predation of women and children. Gathering their stories, I ask how the systems of services are working, and the ways they could be improved to reduce exploitation. Again, while the focus in these pages is on Manitoba, the findings and recommendations are relevant to all of Canada.

A twenty-first-century perspective includes new understanding about sexual exploitation, power disparity, and the affront to human dignity and social justice that they represent. Boys and men are also sexually exploited; however, most sex industry survivors in Canada are female (J. Smith, 2014b). Historically, and even by some in the present, prostitution has been viewed as acceptable entertainment, with little consideration in the public discourse about its exploitive nature

(Hayward, 2014). It is now more broadly understood that many young women are coerced into oppressive relationships in the sex industry, often starting in childhood, and find it extremely difficult and sometimes impossible to escape (Farley et al., 2003). This modern narrative differs radically from those of historical eras where prostitution, exploitive relationships, and human slavery and torture were less understood or recognized, and were more acceptable in many societies.

There are numerous barriers and challenges for children who are vulnerable to exploitation as well as for survivors striving to leave the sex industry. There are also many opportunities to help them. This book illustrates that exploited women and children are among our most vulnerable citizens. Those who escape demonstrate extreme resilience, often going on to dedicate themselves to helping others escape the oppression they themselves experienced in the sex industry. My hope is that this book will be a catalyst for change, building upon the work that has already been undertaken, and taking advantage of the growing awareness and momentum in the public discourse to compassionately intervene in this ever-increasing social problem. Giving voice to the people who have survived, and to those who are dedicated to helping survivors, taps into the wisdom of their experience, and perhaps will close some of the persisting systemic gaps. This work can have a significant impact on communities as well, but if it saves or improves the life of just one person, then I believe it was all worthwhile.

Some information about my background will assist in situating my interest in this work. Being well into my fourth decade of service as a law enforcement officer in Manitoba, I am acutely aware of the risks to children and vulnerable people in the community. I have spent the latter thirty years of my career with the Winnipeg Police Service (WPS), working in many roles that are concerned with developing strategies to protect the vulnerable. In the first half of my career, as a constable and later a patrol sergeant, I worked several assignments as a uniformed patrol officer in Winnipeg's North End, where a lot of street-level sex selling has historically been situated. During those times, I developed a passion for protecting young girls from exploitation, setting up enforcement projects, working the "low track" and patrolling the areas that were notorious for street-level prostitution.

Moving into detective work for several years, I developed investigative skills and a reputation for tenacity and innovation, later working for three years in the Anti-Crime Tactical Unit, a specialized team investigating and taking down organized crime groups. During Winnipeg's arson crisis in 1999–2000, I volunteered for and was selected as a founding member of the Arson Strike Force, a unique joint task force made up of personnel from the Winnipeg Police Service, Winnipeg Fire Paramedic Service, and Manitoba Fire Commissioner's Office. The strike force was recognized nationally for effectively ending an arson crisis in Winnipeg, and it was here that I first started to appreciate the value of multidisciplinary collaborative approaches to social problems.

When the first Integrated Child Exploitation Unit (ICE Unit) was established to investigate internet-based child exploitation, I was invited to join within the first year. This unique new unit was made up of police officers from the Brandon Police Service, the WPS, and the Royal Canadian Mounted Police. Manitoba's ICE Unit was so successful that it became a template for units that were later established across Canada. Within the unit, I developed and practised new investigative techniques utilizing cutting-edge technology, global collaboration, and innovation investigating internet-based child sexual exploitation. In that role, seeing how children were being sold, traded, and abused worldwide, I became fervently devoted to thwarting sexual exploitation and human sex trafficking.

In a later assignment, as a team leader in the Child Abuse Unit, I supervised a specialized detective team investigating child abuse, child exploitation, internet luring, child homicides, and historical sexual assaults. Here I learned the nuances of vulnerable person victimization and investigations, as well as human vulnerability and how predators can take advantage of human frailty and trust. From that role, I moved into behavioural sciences and criminal profiling, learning tactical intelligence analysis through self-directed study and mentorship, online courses, and several training programs at the Canadian Police College in Ottawa. I became a resource for intelligence analysis and major case management for units investigating crimes against the vulnerable, including sex crimes, child abuse, high-risk offenders, vulnerable persons, domestic violence coordination, child exploitation, and other specialized units. While in this role, eighteen years into my policing career, I returned to university to complete a master of public administration degree through the joint program at the universities of Winnipeg and Manitoba.

Drawing on my previous experience, and new skills I was developing through my graduate studies – such as environmental scanning, policy and budget analysis, program evaluation, and a better understanding of government and bureaucracy – I began to see more risks and opportunities for the Police Service and the community. For one thing, news about the serial murders in British Columbia around the Pickton pig farm was unfolding; the disappearance of sixty-three Vancouver women from the 1990s until approximately 2004 was coming to light. Ultimately Robert Pickton was arrested in connection with the murder of twenty-two women (Cool, 2004). As well, the Edmonton Police Service announced in June 2004 that they were investigating the suspected serial killing of nine Alberta sex industry workers over a period of seven years.

Justice Wally Oppal led the commission of inquiry into the serial killing of prostitutes by Robert Pickton in British Columbia (Oppal, 2012). He found that there were likely close to 150 women murdered around the time Pickton was operating, and Pickton may have been involved in many more than he was prosecuted for. Oppal found that Pickton could have been stopped earlier if information had been better shared between agencies in adjacent communities. I recognized these dynamics early on and identified the same issue in the WPS, where we had only a small staff assigned to missing person cases and we had over one hundred long-term "cold cases," some of whom might very well have met with foul play. Police departments across Canada had evolved the same way.

In 2012, I was working as a duty officer, overseeing front-line police operations for the WPS, when Devon Clunis took office as chief of police, with a platform of "crime prevention through social development." I had published one journal article (Chrismas, 2012) and my first book on policing was in press at McGill-Queens University Press (Chrismas, 2013), focusing mainly on crime prevention, community trust building, and collaborative, multidisciplinary approaches to community safety. These matters resonated for Chief Clunis, and he assigned me to work full time on community engagement. For the next several years I participated in numerous community partnership activities, often looking for opportunities to engage police resources in collaborative crime prevention and public safety initiatives.

My earlier passion for protecting the vulnerable led me back to seeking solutions to the growing problem of child sexual exploitation; hence this book. The main question behind the research I conducted for this book is: what we can learn from those working on the issue of sexual exploitation, and from those most affected by it? Some broad questions were asked of several distinct stakeholder groups, with more specific questions posed that were relevant to each of the two broad categories of participants, survivors and practitioners. The subject groups included (1) survivors who have been sexually exploited or trafficked for the purpose of sexual exploitation; (2) workers from government agencies that are mandated with public safety, including police, prosecutors, and social workers; (3) political and Indigenous leaders; and (4) people involved with non-government organizations (NGOs) working with issues around exploitation and human trafficking in the sex industry. The questions used, as suggested by Cederborg and Lamb (2008), were open ended so as to allow respondents to provide subjective observations and impressions about the issues.

The questions elicited answers to the following broad issues: (1) What makes people vulnerable to being exploited, and is there something we could do to reduce this phenomenon and prevent exploitation? (2) What could assist people to exit the sex industry? (3) What strategies have been effective and what should be followed going forward? (4) What barriers and opportunities exist within and between organizations to improve service and collaboration? and (5) What effect do laws have and what should the police be doing? To assist people in thinking creatively, participants were asked, What is the best thing that could happen in Canada concerning the sex industry (Chrismas, 2017)?

Sexual exploitation of youth in Canada is worsening, according to many respondents to this study; it requires urgent attention. In speaking with police and child welfare and health officials in preparation for this research, I heard a consistent and loud call for action. Dedicated professionals in many service sectors reported lack of resources and frustration with the fragmented isolation of agencies that could be cooperating better on these serious social problems. The evidence that opportunities exist to improve systemic approaches is the fact that children and youth are still being victimized, and even murdered (Dehn, 2009; Paperney, 2009). This book identifies and seeks to close some of these critical gaps.

Practitioners working in core service agencies, including police, justice, child welfare, education, and health, tend to view social problems such as trafficking and exploitation as part of one agency's mandate or another, rather than as everyone's collective responsibility. The fundamental challenge, it seems, is to move responsibility for these serious issues into the centre, to be shared by all stakeholders rather than deflected by them. While previous research has explored sexual exploitation, the respondents in this study said new investigation is needed, and they were happy to contribute to this book – to raise awareness and spur further action.

Sexual exploitation and human trafficking are complex topics crossing multiple disciplines. Therefore, to gain the fullest picture possible, this book takes what Johan Galtung terms a "transdisciplinary" approach (Galtung, 1996). Wheaton et al. (2010) have also defined the need for different theoretical perspectives in understanding complex subjects. For example, Schauer and Wheaten (2006) point out that the criminal justice and sociology fields have historically dominated the literature on human trafficking. Some scholars have reported that peer-reviewed journals contain relatively little literature on human sex trafficking, and that much of the information on this topic can only be found in the media, law enforcement records, and government and NGO reports (Clawson et al., 2009; Muftic & Finn, 2013). This book is informed by scholarly literature as well as reports published by government agencies such as the Royal Canadian Mounted Police (RCMP) and the governments of Canada and Manitoba, and from studies and reports from organizations such as the Native Women's Association of Canada and the Canadian Women's Foundation (CWF).

The book brings in other perspectives as well, examining the sex industry as organized crime and as a social justice issue, including lenses of direct and structural violence, economics, law, gender and feminist perspectives, and intersectionality. I also include literature from the field of peace and conflict studies, which ultimately provides tools that can assist in understanding and reducing conflict and improving collaboration in society's response to sexual exploitation. I describe the existing literature and my new findings on patterns of abuse and violence, including a focus on challenges that are specific to Indigenous people. Laws and approaches to preventing sexual exploitation are outlined, as well as how to effect sustainable change through employing collective impact strategies, disrupting the public discourse, and improving community engagement.

I anticipated that I would conduct about forty interviews; in the end the uptake was so strong that sixty-one were completed. The salience of the themes became more apparent to me as the study progressed. For example, most participants mentioned the need for more resources, greater collaboration between agencies, and more education and awareness regarding sexual exploitation. By completing all the interviews myself, I was able to compare and contrast the opinions, observations, and stories that participants offered, yielding insights that are nuanced and informative.

From the outset, I realized that the language we use around sex trafficking and sexual exploitation is critical. It frames the debate around voluntariness and whether people can freely choose to sell their bodies for sex, or if, as most of the people I interviewed for this book argued strongly, it is in fact slavery. In addition, people employ different definitions of terms such as "sexual exploitation," "human trafficking," and "prostitution" in common usage and application. Also, it was necessary at the outset of my research to determine how people who are exploited in the sex industry should be referred to, in order to respect their dignity and most accurately depict the phenomenon being examined. An insightful source of expertise for defining these terms was the group of participants I interviewed, as they are in the field and are sensitive to the evolving discourse around the way that language is used. They all stressed that language is critical, as labels further victimize sex industry survivors. Therefore, I consider their perspectives in defining terms used in this book.

Important distinctions must be drawn, for example, between sexual and general child abuse, sexual exploitation, prostitution, and human trafficking. Sexual abuse and rape involve violence and are generally done against a person's will, whereas sexual exploitation and trafficking also include elements of manipulation that often cause exploited persons to feel complicit in their own victimization (Richardson, 2015). This complicity and psychological manipulation have implications for the effectiveness of prevention, intervention, and support for victims.

Cook and Courchene (2006) highlight that a "prostitute" is someone who sells her/his body as a sexual service in exchange for money or drugs. Sexual exploitation, on the other hand, involves the act of coercing, luring, or engaging a child (for the purposes of Canada's Criminal Code, a person under the age of eighteen) into a sexual act, and involvement in the sex industry or pornography, with or without the child's consent, in exchange for money, drugs, shelter, food, protection, or other necessities (Cook & Courchene, 2006). In this book, I extend the definition of "exploitation" further, defining any persons, including adults, who are manipulated, coerced, or otherwise conscripted into the sex industry as exploited. My rationale is simple: I take the position that a person does not change on the day s/he turns eighteen. Age of majority is a legal construct that does not always reflect a person's social reality: a twenty-year-old suffering from mental health or developmental issues may be operating at a younger age, and so could be manipulated and exploited by unscrupulous predators.

Rose, a senior Crown attorney with Manitoba Public Prosecutions, succinctly summed up the basic definitions:

ROSE: Prostitution is a form of exploitation. It is any payment for any sexual activity. Sexual exploitation is broad and covers any form of sexual abuse including prostitution. Trafficking is a specific form of prostitution, involving controlling someone.

The term "human trafficking" is defined differently in different contexts. For example, O'Brien et al. (2013) and Lee (2011) provide in-depth discussions on the nuances of the terms, the differences between trafficking and human smuggling, and the value-laden debate over whether women can willingly consent to be exploited. Human smuggling differs from trafficking in that smuggling involves people willingly seeking and gaining assistance in crossing national borders, often with the hope of obtaining meaningful employment and a better life (Schauer & Wheaten, 2006). Trafficking differs from smuggling in that it is characterized by "deception, fraud, coercion, force or exploitation" of persons by traffickers (Kluber, 2003). Often people engage in the smuggling process thinking they are going to a job opportunity and a better life, only to wind up being trafficked in the sex industry by predators. A person can be trafficked without being smuggled. For instance, someone who is socially isolated and coerced can be trafficked in his/her own home, without being moved anywhere.

For the purposes of this book, the terms are to be understood in the simplest forms. Sex trafficking is any circumstance wherein a person is socially isolated, manipulated, or forced into acts of selling sex, whether s/he is forcibly moved from one place to another or not. The terms "sexual exploitation" and "human trafficking" are used in the general sense of human beings exploited sexually through forced labour for others' gain, by people who are in positions of power over those who are exploited. In this way, sex trafficking and exploitation results in oppression and social injustice that amounts to slavery.

An ongoing debate exists over the legitimacy of selling sex as a freely chosen profession rather than as the victimization and exploitation of vulnerable women (Meyers, 2014). The term "sex trade" is used by some to indicate their view that selling sex is a legitimate occupation some freely chose. Others argue that no one freely chooses it, but rather is forced into it. Wendy Sheirich, who recently retired after serving as the coordinator of Manitoba's counter-sexual-exploitation program for ten years, defined what the relevant terms mean to her:

WENDY SHEIRICH: In Manitoba, we tend to refer to the issue of "sexual exploitation" across the board because we've gotten used to doing that. In other jurisdictions across Canada, they don't use "sexual exploitation." They say "trafficking." So, we've had people come to Manitoba – some stakeholders – and tell us about "trafficking" in Manitoba, and initially we don't know what they're asking because we're used to referring to it as "sexual exploitation." But there is more awareness now about "trafficking." It is sort of the up-and-coming more politically correct term, and everybody is getting on the trafficking bandwagon these days.

The terms "trafficking" and "sexual exploitation" are used differently in different regions across Canada, as Ms. Sheirich points out. Therefore, throughout the book I often refer to the two together, as sex trafficking and sexual exploitation are similar and mostly interchangeable. I deliberately avoid the term "sex trade" in my writing as it implies a willingness on the part of women and children participating in selling sex. Many women are not willing, and my position, and that of the people I interviewed, is that children do not willingly enter the sex industry.

Diane Redsky is the executive director of Ma Mawi Wi Chi Itata Centre in Winnipeg and also coordinated a two-million-dollar research project entitled "Stories and Strategies to End Sex Trafficking in Canada" (CWF, 2014). The project, an eighteen-month task force in 2013–14, interviewed experts from across Canada and resulted in thirty-four recommendations on how to end sex trafficking in Canada. Ms. Redsky told me that she and her team struggled with the terminology related to the sex industry:

DIANE REDSKY: The first thing that stands out when I look at these [interview] questions is one of the key learnings we figured out with the National Task Force. One of the things we felt was important as we did our work was common definitions and common phrases to describe exactly what we're talking about because it was very different across the country. And it's even very different in Manitoba here. So, we [decided] on some keywords. One of them is to describe the sex industry as a "sex industry." So, you won't hear me say "sex trade" or "sex work" because we decided that the best way is to – because it is an industry. There are so many people who profit from the sexual exploitation of women, and ["sex industry"] just describes it all. "Sex trade" and "sex work" kind of personalizes it, individualizes it into a consenting woman and a consenting man when it's not as simple as that when you actually unpeel what the sex industry really looks like. So, I struggle when I see words like "sex trade." But I can get through this. The other thing is that we also don't call them "sex trade workers" or "sex workers." We call them "sexually exploited women." And that's another language shift that we felt was important because then it really was describing the victimization of it all. And that was really important to us.

Ms. Redsky and her team's decision to employ the term "sex industry" because it better captures the true nature of the issue – as an organized crime "industry" that exploits people rather than an occupation that many people do not freely choose – resonates with the insights of many experts I interviewed; therefore, I use the term "sex industry" throughout this book, rather than "sex trade," to denote the social phenomenon of selling sex. Another term that resonates for me, in light of all of my interviews and research, is "forced prostitution." This term could be inserted as well, to respect the dignity of those it refers to.

The existing academic literature has also documented the shift in language referencing the sex industry. For example, Cook and Courchene (2006) have analysed prostitution in Canada, with a focus on Manitoba. They argue that the terms "child prostitute" and "juvenile prostitute" are now outdated, stressing that the new way of looking at prostitution views involved youth as victims of exploitation, rather than as criminals or business people, as the term "prostitute" implies. There is now general agreement among professionals working in the justice and social work professions, and in academe, that youth involved in the sex industry are sexually exploited and preyed upon as opposed to being willing actors who are merely making a business decision to sell sex.

Another term that is important to define at the outset is how we refer to people who are engaged in the sex industry, being trafficked and exploited, and those who have left or escaped the sex industry. The term used is crucial, as the wrong one could offend and revictimize women. The term chosen also intersects with the essence of this book, answering the question of whether people engage in the sex industry willingly or are generally manipulated and coerced into it. Here again I defer to Diane Redsky and others, including Jennifer Richardson, the coordinator of Ontario's counter-exploitation strategy, who have wrestled with these definitions and are unquestionably sensitive to the impact they can have on exploited people, funders and officials, practitioners working in this area, and the general public discourse.

Diane Redsky and her team refer to exploited and trafficked people as "survivors." This made sense to me at the outset, and later, after I had completed interviews, it seemed the only term that fit the people we are talking about. Ms. Redsky points out that the term "victim" is disrespectful, as it takes away from the person's agency and sense of self-determination. The term "experiential" has been used in social work circles, but comes across as somewhat vague in meaning. In this study the terms "exploited" and "trafficked" are used to refer to people who are actively participating in the sex industry or have left it as survivors, as these seem to best describe them. I asked Diane Redsky how she and her team referred to people who are still engaged in the sex industry, and she clarified:

DIANE REDSKY: Experiential women/survivors will always refer to themselves as "survivors" if they are in it or not. Referring to them as victims is very disrespectful. That being said, there is no consensus in the experiential person's committee [a group of over one hundred sex industry survivors] on this. "Women with lived experience" is the best way to describe them and I only use "victim" when I am talking about [the] law enforcement/justice system where they qualify for benefits.

My intention in this book is to respect people who have endured the sex industry and to provide recommendations that may help them. Therefore, I have chosen to use the term they prefer; they are referred to as "survivors" whether they are currently or were formerly engaged in the sex industry.

A qualitative approach was selected as the best means of completing this study. Semi-structured interviews sought to gather insights and perspectives from survivors of the sex industry, police officers, counsellors, and social workers employed with government and non-government organizations working with sex industry survivors. I also interviewed prosecutors, policymakers and lawmakers, and leaders in the provincial and federal governments and the Indigenous community, with the intention of gaining a full picture of the social phenomenon of sex trafficking, as well as how all the stakeholders interact with each other when addressing the sexual exploitation of young women.

This book draws on a social integrationist view of the environment, meaning the subjective interpretations of my research subjects are considered. Social integrationists view human experience as a reflective and reactive journey in which interactions are interpreted and understood subjectively (Blumer, 1969). While dated, Blumer's perspective is still relevant, as my research sought to gather my participants' personal stories, observations, and recommendations. This approach was inspired in part by previous studies, such as Wiseman's *Stations of the Lost: The Treatment of Skid Row Alcoholics* (1970). In that book, Wiseman reported on her in-depth study of men suffering from alcoholism and a broad spectrum of services, and places that these men spend their time, in the 1970s in an area of Los Angeles known as "skid row." She wrote, "to study human beings in any area of their social life it is necessary to view that area of life in terms of their experience and from their point of view" (p. xii). Through qualitative, story-based narrative interviews Wiseman created an insightful and rich picture for the reader of the social situation around skid row. My intent was to conduct a similar type of multiperspective study around sexual exploitation and human sex trafficking in Canada. My research is a similarly broad exploratory case study, proposing to share the same kind of rich insights into the world of human sex trafficking and sexual exploitation in Manitoba in 2016, through the eyes of the people I interviewed.

A qualitative research approach has been found to be useful in examining local conceptions of coordination in peacebuilding (Ripsman & Blanchard, 2003). Qualitative research is "human-centred," phenomenological, and highlights the perceptions and human agency of research participants (Palys & Atchison, 2008). Mac Ginty and Williams (2009), for example, have written that person-centred qualitative approaches can better capture "local voices and Indigenous solutions" (p. 8).

It was clear from the outset that women and children in the sex industry face numerous intersectional challenges, which were expected to come out in the interviews. Scholars have suggested that qualitative research is ideal for the study of intersectionality because it allows us to explore and capture the rich multidimensional nature of humanity and people in their unique contexts (Hankivsky, 2011; Hunting, 2014; McCall, 2005). Qualitative research is said to be suited to research that has a goal, as this book does, of informing improved social justice (Hankivsky, 2011; Rogers & Kelly, 2011). The sociological term "intersectionality" refers to multiple disadvantages and challenges that some face in society (Grace, 2014; Hankivsky, 2011; McCall, 2005). Grace (2014) writes that intersectionality researchers "consider complex interactions between structures of power and oppression and interconnected aspects of individual and group identity and social location" (p. 1). All of the sexually exploited/trafficked survivors interviewed for this book fit this definition of intersectionality. Children and women in the sex industry face multiple compounded challenges, thus explaining the difficulties that they have in escaping that life.

Robertson and Sgoutas (2012) have further noted that "intersectional analysis," or "intersectionality," has been used in different academic disciplines to describe the challenges that people face as a result of being marginalized due to their sex, gender, sexuality, race, class, and national identities (also see Vidal-Ortiz, 2006). These authors caution that there is a danger in applying labels such as "prostitute," as they oversimplify the complex interplay of gender, sex, and sexuality. For example, Amahazion (2014) notes that the literature as well as society at large tends to label sex industry survivors as deviants, and this does not help them.

Robertson and Sgoutas (2012) also argue that "social science research that relies on normative identity categories can lead to incomplete intersectional analyses" (p. 421). Such incomplete analysis could result from labels being assigned by "dominant members of society" (p. 421). Biases could enter research as well. For example, some scholars have determined that stereotypes held by social science researchers can affect their interpretations of data (Robertson & Sgoutas, 2012; Valentine,

2007; Vidal-Ortiz, 2006). This is a further reason that I settled on the term "survivor" to refer to people who have been trafficked in the sex industry, as it does not detract from the survivor's self-determinism and agency.

An intersectional perspective is applicable to the issue of sexual exploitation. Ferguson (2005) wrote, "In the intersections is where we fashion languages against coherence. Intersections are necessarily messy, chaotic, and heterodox. Why necessarily so? Because intersections are not about identity; they are about social dynamics" (p. 66). Intersectionality theory seems to fit this subject, as people are vulnerable and exploited both in grooming for and introduction to the sex industry and in the socialization, manipulation, power imbalances, and outright physical force that keep them there.

Hooks (2000) also argues that intersectionality that attributes to "sexist oppression, economic oppression, and racial oppression can intertwine to create different realities for women based on their particular location in society" (p. 40). For example, Cullen-DuPont (2009) wrote about how traffickers identify children and women who are desperate to escape lives of poverty, luring them into the sex industry with lies such as the promises of legitimate work. Therefore, exploring interventions and strategies around sexual exploitation requires consideration of the effects and interplay of gender, economic disparity, and the social psychology of manipulation. Intervention and eradication of sexual exploitation calls for collective approaches addressing root problems, many of which are correlated with transgenerational traumas stemming from colonization, early childhood sexual abuse, poverty, and its related effects on lost educational and job opportunities for victims of sexual exploitation and gender and general vulnerabilities that allow children and women to be victimized.

This book highlights people's subjective perceptions; therefore, a grounded approach was taken, utilizing inductive analysis of the observations gathered from the participants (Charmaz, 2005; Creswell, 2007; Glaser, 1992; Glaser & Strauss, 1967). Patton (1980) wrote that grounded theory uses "inductive analysis, which means patterns, themes and categories of analysis come from the data; they emerge out of the data rather than being imposed on them prior to collection and analysis" (p. 306). I asked some structured questions, to gain specific detail on relevant issues that I wanted to explore. The questions were open ended, allowing interviewees the opportunity to provide a story, offering rich subjective insights that could not be obtained in any other way (Senehi, 2009). The stories, I learned, are incredibly powerful and insightful. Taking a grounded approach, I gathered the perceptions, stories, experiences, and comments of participants and then analysed them to ascertain themes that are separately dealt with in the chapters of this book. I was careful to retain the intent and meaning in participants' stories.

The sex industry exists everywhere, yet it differs from region to region. Manitoba is unique within Canada, with issues and challenges that differ from other regions. For example, history, demographics, and economic conditions are different in every province and territory, and therefore should be studied regionally as opposed to nationally (CBC, 2014a; Paperny, 2009; RCMP, 2013; Welch, 2014). About 80 per cent of the practitioners I interviewed work or worked in and around Winnipeg and about 20 per cent mainly in rural parts of Manitoba, yet the findings generalize to people across Canada. The psychological manipulation and coercion of sex trafficking and exploitation that my subjects described are the same whether they occur in the Greater Toronto Area, the prairies, the east or west coast, or the territories. Similarly, the dynamics that keep agencies and people from working better together are the same no matter in what region they occur. Most of my findings will translate to and resonate with practitioners and scholars from every part of Canada.

My research focused on the exploitation of women and girls in the sex industry. While boys and men are clearly also victimized, the incidence is much lower, and different in some ways. Eighty per cent or more of sex industry survivors in Canada are female (Badgley, 1984; Cullen-DuPont, 2009; McIntyre, 2012; J. Smith, 2014b). The Task Force on Sex Trafficking of Women and Girls in Canada (CWF, 2014) concluded that the number-one risk factor to being exploited in the sex industry is "being female." Some research has been done on sexual exploitation and trafficking of males and LGBTQ2S (Lesbian, Gay, Bisexual, Transgendered, Queer, 2-Spirited) people in the sex industry; however, it is limited and is clearly an area for future research (McIntyre, 2012). Practitioners and survivors I talked to in planning this research mentioned that men and boys are victimized as well, but to a much lesser extent. The demographics of those who have been victimized in the sex industry in Canada are primarily female, and a large percentage of these survivors are Indigenous.

Only subjects who were over the age of eighteen and who were out of the sex industry were interviewed. I chose to limit the scope to people not currently active in the sex industry because those who are actively involved could be exposed to significant risks by cooperating with research that aims to reduce sex trafficking. While this research did not focus specifically on Indigenous people, most survivors and many of the practitioners interviewed were of Indigenous ancestry. This is consistent with previous research findings. Cook and Courchene (2006), for instance, found that 70 per cent or more of sexually exploited youth/women in Manitoba have Indigenous ancestry.

The survivors who reached out expressed sincere appreciation for the research and for the opportunity to participate, and some of them contacted me several times after they were interviewed. Their engagement felt increasingly important, from both a community-building and a therapeutic aspect, as the research went on. Participants were selected based on their positions as well as by referral. For instance, in policing I spoke with police officers who currently work or in the past worked in assignments related to counter-sexual-exploitation and human trafficking. I interviewed people who are known to be experts and experienced in the field, and in many cases they referred me to others who are experts in the field. Of the sixty-one interviewees, six were political leaders, twenty-three were social workers, twenty-four were police, and eight were survivors. A substantial portion of the practitioners I interviewed are also survivors. No benefits, financial or otherwise, were provided to participants. They were offered a feeling of inclusion, as I promised that their insights would become part of the resulting published literature.

The instrument utilized in this research is semi-structured interviews recorded with audio equipment. All interviews were conducted at a place and time arranged by the participants, ensuring, as much as possible, that interviews were conducted in private and in such a way that subjects' privacy was protected. In several cases, when interviewing Indigenous Elders, I offered a gift of tobacco so as to respect their cultural position and tradition.

The research was conducted within guidelines established in the 2001 Tri-Council Policy Statement: Ethical Conduct for Research Involving Human Subjects by Canada's three leading federal research agencies, the Canadian Institute of Health Research, Natural Sciences and Engineering Research Council of Canada, and Social Sciences and Humanities Research Council of Canada. An informed consent process was applied with every subject, including questions about whether or not the subject consented to be identified and quoted in the literature that would flow from the research. Most service providers were eager to weigh in and be identified in the research findings; however, some did choose to remain anonymous. Survivors who are not engaged in the field of helping sex industry survivors were not offered the choice of having their responses attributed: pseudonyms were used for all, to protect them from any impacts of their participation.

Some of the service providers are also survivors who now work to help people to exit the sex industry. In these cases, they were offered the choice of anonymity or of being named in the research if they are publicly known as advocates and survivors. No deception was used in conducting the research: information was not deliberately withheld from participants and participants were not deliberately misled in the research.

The potential risks and benefits of participating in the interviews were laid out in the consent for each interview. I also went to great lengths, both in the informed consent process prior to each interview and then again on tape, to emphasize the voluntary nature of the interviews. I laid stress on this until I was satisfied in each case that the participant understood s/he could withdraw from the study at any time either before or after the interview.

The interview process respected all the interviewee's time schedules. They were treated with respect and sensitivity and their privacy was protected. Participants were accommodated, for example, allowing them to have support persons with them during the interview if they requested it. Only one participant chose to do so. Some of the participants were people who have chosen to become involved in public advocacy and support work and therefore have been speaking publicly about their experiences. This research posed no significant further threat of traumatization to these people.

Informed consent was ensured, as I read a prepared script and provided a copy of the consent form to each subject after we went through them together. The form was reviewed verbally with each subject to remove any feeling of obligation or compulsion to participate or be identified in the research. The survivors are not identified in this study, even if they consented to be, if there was any perceived risk of embarrassment, danger, or any negative repercussions from being identified. To counteract the risk that participants would be ordered by their organizations to participate, or feel compelled to participate, because of my positionality, I took steps to ensure every subject understood that participation was voluntary, even if their employer approved their participation.

Practitioners, as well as survivors, were cautioned regarding traumatization potentially resulting from the interview process. There is growing research into and awareness of increasing post-traumatic stress found among service providers (Bonokoski, 2012; Chrismas, 2013; Freeze & Baily, 2011; MacQueen, 2011). Social science researchers are necessarily concerned with the potential impact of trauma-related research on participants. Legerski and Bunnell (2010) reviewed the contemporary literature on potential traumatization of research participants when they are interviewed about their stressful experiences, how to reduce the impacts, and how to consider whether the benefits of such research outweigh the potential harms. The general finding was that a minimal number of research participants of trauma-focused research experience distress as a result, and those who do only experience the negative feelings for a short period of time after being interviewed. Most participants in previous research have described their experience of participating in research on their traumatic experiences as "positive, rewarding, and beneficial to society" (Legerski & Bunnell, 2010, p. 429; also see Jorm et al., 2007; Runeson & Beskow, 1991).

Legerski and Bunnell (2010) also reported that while adverse effects of participation in trauma-focused research appear to dissipate, the positive rewards reportedly increase with time. They write that, according to some studies, most participants experience some level of distress as well as positive benefits from their involvement in the research (Halek et al., 2005). In addition, Yuen et al. (2014) interviewed twenty-three sex industry workers in Hong Kong and found that they used positive psychology to maintain their resilience. They rationalized their role and their lack of control over their situations, and thus could stay optimistic about the future. The authors explored the findings of this research to generate resilience-building strategies that might inform policy recommendations.

During the interviews some respondents did experience mild emotional reactions, but none appeared traumatic. Some participants did mention that talking about their experiences is sometimes emotionally triggering, but none mentioned an intention to seek assistance from the resources provided with the consent forms. Several participants also mentioned that contributing to research like this, as in their work, is part of their healing journey and that they were glad to participate. Confidentiality was protected by physically securing all digital and paper files.

Scholars have highlighted that the position and relative power of the interviewer/researcher versus participants is significant in any study (Hunting, 2014; Jootun et al., 2009; Karnieli-Miller et al., 2009). My research required that I remain cognizant of my own positionality as a white male. At the time of the interviews I was also a serving police officer, and the people I proposed to interview had potential preconceived feelings because of their previous individual experiences with the police. Survivors often have either good or bad preconceptions about the police, as most report having been prosecuted, harassed, apprehended, or helped by police officers. For these reasons, I was careful to consider positionality and the way I influenced the interviews with questions, body language, demeanour, and context. To enhance my awareness of the dynamics of positionality that might influence the interview process, I consulted the existing literature on interview methods (Morris, 2009). For example, Hunting (2014) notes the importance in qualitative research of considering intersectionality and of situating the researcher in relation to the subject. One must carefully analyse the intersections and power relationships that might affect the interview. I was careful to consider these dynamics of the interview process, respecting participants' wishes regarding the place and time of interviews, dressing in a non-threatening manner, and ensuring participants were comfortable.

This research involved two main categories of participants: survivors of the sex industry, and practitioners and community leaders at all levels. These lines became somewhat blurred as the interviews unfolded, because practitioners who work directly with survivors in treatment programs are often sex trafficking survivors themselves. Over half of the practitioners interviewed had first-hand experience in the sex industry. This did not create any problems that I am aware of. In some cases, my participants and I negotiated and agreed upon issues they wished to be identified with and those aspects they wished to have anonymized in resulting publications. For example, some practitioners advised that they would like to be identified with their comments in subsequent literature, excluding those in which they discussed their own previous involvement as a survivor of the sex industry. In some cases, people had put that part of their life behind them and had no wish for people to know about that aspect of their past. I carefully respected these wishes.

Researchers must also be aware of the generalizations they may impose on participants. Phillips (1996), for instance, found that feminist researchers must guard against the tendency to "essentialize," or impose an intrinsic similarity on the perspective of women being interviewed. Indigenous subject interviews also require sensitivity to our colonial past, and the reality that many Indigenous people may see the interviewer as privileged and/or biased in favour of Western views (Wilson, 2008). At the same time, this Indigenous participant perspective must not be assumed, as every individual is different.

My position as a police officer had no negative impact that I observed. I believe that people were forthcoming and open with me because of my position, and perhaps more so because of my reputation in the community for seeking social justice and improving services to the vulnerable. I realized that no one is entirely without biases, conscious or unconscious, and this is another reason why the story-based approach is so important in studying the subjective phenomenon. It is somewhat of a paradox that someone with absolutely no background in the subject being studied may be the least biased.

No one is purely neutral and objective. Victor Frankl was a psychiatrist and a Second World War concentration camp survivor. He wrote about his experiences and how people survived extreme oppression in the concentration camps. Frankl addressed positionality in his seminal work *Man's Search for Meaning*, in which he states:

> To attempt a methodological presentation of the subject is very difficult, as psychology requires certain scientific detachment. But does a man who makes his observations while he himself is a prisoner possess the necessary detachment? Such detachment is granted to the outsider, but he is too far removed to make any statements of real value. Only the man inside knows. His judgments may not be objective; his evaluations may be out of proportion. This is inevitable. An attempt must be made to avoid any personal bias (Frankl, 1959, p. 24).

A researcher with no background whatsoever in the phenomenon being studied might be able to claim a more neutral position; however, that person might also miss the nuances of specific components of the subject under examination. At the same time, it is essential that a researcher acknowledge potential biases and ensure that they do not influence interpretation of the data. The point here is to recognize and remain aware of positionality in the conduct of interviews, analysis of the data, and the conclusions drawn from that data. I believe I was well situated to conduct this research, and cognizant of my own potential biases in analysing and reporting the results.

My background and graduate education provided me with some awareness of feminist, Indigenous, and social issues as well as power dynamics around interviews. The interview process has been a significant part of my work throughout my policing career. My intention was to be sensitive to potential biases and dynamics and account for them in my interactions with subjects, and I believe this was achieved. I advised study participants that my goals in the research are to raise awareness and make recommendations, and to include and share the voice of a broad range of people. Most of the participants expressed appreciation for this approach. This was also evidenced by subjects' unanimously positive response when I asked them if they would like to be advised of the publications, including this book, that would result from the study.

The research outlined in this book explores the complex topic of the sex industry, sexual exploitation, and human sex trafficking in

Manitoba. The framework attempts to follow a logical flow, with this chapter outlining the scope and focus of the study; chapter 2 describing the context in Canada and worldwide; and chapters 3 through 9 featuring the themes that emerged from the interview data as well as specific challenges, opportunities, and recommendations identified. In chapter 10, I sum up key findings and the recommendations that flow from them, as well as areas that require future research. The stories are compelling and I have striven to reproduce them intact, as they provide so much insight and emotion that it would be a shame to reduce them to smaller, less impactful fragments. A primary goal of this book is to include and amplify the voices of people on this important topic, and the most powerful way to do this is to highlight their stories.

2 Canada's Sex Industry

KAITLIN: I was twelve years old when I did my first hit of crack, and I was hooked. And by the time I was thirteen, I was already out on the street. It was probably mostly to do with gangs and drug dealers. I believe now that I'm older that I was lured by this older crowd of girls because I was young, and there was more money. I was lured into this. I remember I was hanging out with this girl, and next thing I knew I was in this house in the West End. And this guy was, "Here, want some crack?" And I said, "No." They kind of tricked me into it. I thought it was like weed, or whatever they told me it was, and I did it. And after I was hooked. By the second night, I remember the guy telling me, "Well, you owe me so much money, and if you don't get it, I'm going to kill you." So I had to go out and work. He said I owed him about two grand, but I don't remember smoking that much. I think I only smoked a couple of pieces because I was really scared and I didn't know what to do.

And I thought this girl, she was my best friend, she was doing it, too. I thought she was my friend. And I thought she cared about me and I told her I wanted to go home. I didn't want be here anymore. And she just said, "Well, you can't go anywhere. You have to stay here or else they'll hurt you." So I stayed. Stupid me, I stayed. From that I think, after, I was going home once a month just to say hi to my mom. And she was still doing crack. But I would just go home and get clothes or whatever and then leave.

By the time I was fourteen, I was pretty much homeless and living at a crack shack and on the street. That's all I lived for is crack. You know, sleep two days, I'd sleep at a john's place for a night, someone that I trusted. I'd go spend a night there and he'd take care of me, feed me, shower, buy me clothes. Then I'd say, "Okay, I'm going." I'd be gone for a couple of days, and same thing over and over right up until I was seventeen when I was pregnant with my oldest. I went home pregnant.

Kaitlin's story was similar to others that I heard while conducting this research. It is a common Canadian experience, and this chapter delves into it further. I outline the international context and situate Canada within it, then look more deeply at the Canadian and Manitoba's regional situation and what people like Kaitlin have endured.

The United Nations *Global Report on Trafficking in Persons* (UNODC 2014) states that sexual exploitation and trafficking affect people in "virtually every country in every region of the world" (p. 1). The same report indicates that while increasing numbers of people are being trafficked for forced labour, sexual exploitation remains the primary reason. Worldwide profits from sexual exploitation are estimated at over $99 billion (USD) per year (Nelson, 2014, UNODC, 2014). Buttigieg (2014) points out that the Palermo Convention brought together 147 member states to acknowledge the seriousness of sexual exploitation and human trafficking and the need to collaborate at the international level to eradicate it. Yet the global nature of trafficking and people's increasing mobility makes it a difficult and complex crime to investigate. Buttigieg (2014) wrote about the challenges that numerous countries have in devising strategies to identify, legislate against, prosecute, or prevent human trafficking.

Cullen-DuPont (2009) describes sex trafficking as so widespread that it affects some national economies, for example accounting for up to 14 per cent of Southeast Asia's gross national product. The sex industry is a massive and growing international enterprise (Mizus et al., 2003; Schauer & Wheaten, 2006; Wheaton et al., 2010). Cullen-DuPont (2009) found that approximately eight hundred thousand people are taken across national borders each year for trafficking in the sex industry, and of those 80 per cent are female and 50 per cent are children. In addition, Mizus et al. (2003) estimated that of the eighteen thousand people trafficked into the United States each year, 96 per cent were female and almost half were children.

Schauer and Wheaten (2006) and Venkatraman (2003) have both argued that sex trafficking in the United States is more of a domestic issue that often does not involve international smuggling of people. Research has repeatedly and consistently confirmed that most sexual exploitation occurs in local contexts (Estes & Wiener, 2001; Venkatraman, 2003), although it is difficult to detect or measure (Cullen-DuPont, 2009). Canadian survivors I interviewed repeatedly described how they were recruited and trafficked locally within Manitoba, never leaving the province. In rarer cases they were moved across Canada and sometimes briefly into the United States and then returned to Manitoba. None of the participants I interviewed spoke of people being taken off the continent; however, it is likely that this does occur.

Despite significant efforts worldwide to curb sexual exploitation and human trafficking, the problem in most regions of the world is continually evolving and getting worse (CWF, 2014; Nelson, 2014; UNODC, 2014). Social media platforms are now globalizing and collapsing the universe to the point that conventional paradigms of space and time are becoming obsolete. People are now so closely connected through social media that groups with a common purpose, such as organized criminals and the police, have the capacity to communicate and operate worldwide in real time. Our only constraint is often our inability to harness and fully utilize burgeoning technological advances.

Traffickers selling people in the sex industry now have social media platforms to advertise discretely and more broadly than could ever have been imagined decades ago. In my online undercover operator training in the ICE Unit, I went online once, posing as a thirteen-year-old girl seeking to sell sex; within minutes I had middle-aged men in five different countries negotiating with me for sex. This was done in the deep web, where it is even more difficult to investigate; but it was also ten years ago. Just imagine where things are today. My first book, *Canadian Policing in the 21st Century: A Frontline Officer on Challenges and Changes* (Chrismas, 2013), outlined the changes I had seen in policing over the past three decades of my career. One of those changes was the evolution from manual typewriters that we used to write reports in 1989, when I started recruit class, to the introduction of computers in the early 1990s, to a globalized universe now. If this much change happened over the past three decades, what is going to happen in the next thirty years?

To understand the importance of further research and better methods of exploring globalization, one need only turn on the daily news. The threat of international terrorism and globally organized crime is looming, imminent, and continually changing. Anyone who uses email receives fraudulent requests daily from all corners of the globe, and I know from my policing experience that these organized groups are difficult to investigate because they move virtually and freely around the world. Human exploitation is now also facilitated more through the internet, and this growing platform demands further research (CISC, 2008; CWF, 2014; Richardson, 2015).

Globalization not only extends the reach of criminals around the world, but also extends responsibility. Law enforcement agencies all over the world now have responsibilities for global safety that spread beyond their local jurisdictions. One brief example I can offer is an investigation we conducted in the ICE Unit several years ago. A small police unit in Wiesbaden, Germany, that actively investigates internet child pornography sent a package to Winnipeg with DVDs containing evidence of transactions involving an undercover police officer in Wiesbaden trading images of child pornography over the internet with an unknown male using his Manitoba Telephone System internet account. We obtained a search warrant for the subscriber information, which turned out to be in Winnipeg, then obtained a search warrant for the subscriber's house, and the resulting seizure was among the largest made in Canada at that time. We confiscated several hundred thousand images of child sexual abuse along with evidence that the male we arrested had gathered information about two dozen Winnipeg women he was stalking; they were customers and fellow employees at his place of work. He had images of the women, fantasies he had written about them, and maps to their homes. In this case a covert police officer in an office in Germany gave us evidence that resulted in protecting dozens of women who did not know they were being stalked by a predator. This is just one small example of how globalization is changing the nature of crime and its investigation.

Another continuing change is the evolving public discourse around basic human rights and social disparity, which extends to growing concerns over sexual exploitation and human trafficking. In Manitoba, for instance, there is an increasing sense of the acute need for answers and more effective strategies to combat sexual exploitation. The public discourse around missing and murdered Indigenous women and children (Welch, 2014), the over ten thousand children in the care of Manitoba's child protection agencies (Puxley, 2014), and children who are continuing to be exploited and hurt is lending a sense of urgency to calls for change. It is imperative that government and non-government service agencies find more effective ways to respond (J. Smith, 2014a, 2014b). These issues have been at the top of the agenda for many police agencies as well as leaders in the broad spectrum of partnering agencies for over two decades. For example, at the 5 December 2014 meeting of the Winnipeg Police Board (the civilian oversight board of the WPS), then Police Chief Devon Clunis was directed to make the protection of Indigenous women and girls a priority for the city's police service (Friesen, 2014).

Many people are working diligently within their respective communities as well as in government and non-government organizations to curb child victimization, yet the tragic murder of fifteen-year-old Tina Fontaine, who was in the care of child protective services – a chronic runaway who may have been sexually exploited – serves as a stark reminder that there is much more work to be done (CBC, 2014a). Tina Fontaine's murder was no anomaly; the circumstances are similar, in some ways, to previous Manitoba homicide cases, including seventeen-year-old Cherisse Houle and eighteen-year-old Hillary Angel Wilson, who were both murdered and left in different locations outside Winnipeg's city limits in the summer of 2009 (Paperny, 2009). Similar dynamics seem to be at play across Canada in relation to missing and murdered cases that span the country.

What is even more disturbing than young people being murdered while a vast array of service agencies and dedicated people watch, almost helplessly – knowing that certain children are bound to turn up dead – is the common knowledge that the clear majority of victims are not ultimately murdered. Many are exploited, abused, beaten, neglected, and suffer in silence amid a sea of fragmented agencies and programs that may or may not ever touch or empower them in their troubled lives. Some elements in the system work well together while others work in isolation, and some work against each other, sometimes due to opposing outlooks on how issues should be addressed and sometimes due to competition over limited funding dollars. This book identifies areas where we could improve, for instance by making existing agencies work better together and by adding needed resources to fill the gaps.

Many challenges are involved in developing strategies to address sexual exploitation and human trafficking. The environment is continually changing, as are the perpetrators' tactics. Law enforcement and the broad spectrum of other services and agencies must be flexible and responsive to meet those changing demands. For example, changes in Canadian laws over recent years caused trickle-down effects, and police and partner agencies were required to develop new approaches. Internet-based sexual exploitation also requires entirely different tools and approaches to identify victims, intervene with survivors, and prosecute or otherwise deter offenders.

One challenge encountered by law enforcement is the flexible nature of criminal activity; organized crime adapts quickly to changing pressures from law enforcement. Parrot and Cummings (2008) wrote that "sexual slavery and human trafficking are highly lucrative and secretive businesses; the likelihood of perpetrators being caught is very small; the conditions that make women vulnerable are constantly being created; and the cultural assumptions that minimize women's worth persist" (p. 99). These cultural assumptions, such as viewing women as perpetrators or willing participants, have started to change, and are addressed throughout this book – starting with the language we use to describe those exploited in the sex industry.

The "4P" approach of the United Nations' 2010 global action plan (in Buttigieg, 2014) included the following four pillars: (1) prevention of trafficking, (2) protection of and assistance to victims of trafficking, (3) prosecuting crimes of trafficking, and (4) strengthening of partnerships against human trafficking. In 2000, the Canadian federal government ratified the United Nations "Protocol to Prevent, Suppress and Punish Trafficking in Persons, Especially Women and Children," and later adopted the internationally accepted "4P" approach (United Nations, 2000; see also Buttigieg, 2014).

Canada still does not have a comprehensive national strategy, but it is being worked on. Diane Redsky describes the need for national coordination that was identified through her study (CWF, 2014):

DIANE REDSKY: The national task force has now become an advisory committee to a national coordination centre. We raised the first year of funding from the private sector, and we hired an executive director just in late December. So we hope by April or the fall to launch our national coordination centre that will coordinate much of what's happening across the country on the issue of sexual exploitation and sex trafficking.

Ms. Redsky continues to be a Manitoba leader in advocacy around combating the sex industry. Manitoba has a plan to prevent sexual exploitation that is framed within Tracia's Trust and that guides groups including the Sexually Exploited Youth Coalition (MB Family Services & Housing, 2008). However, there is much debate even within Manitoba, never mind nationally, about how to proceed.

Ms. Redsky and Joy Smith, founder of the Joy Smith Foundation, explained that Canada is in a time of change around addressing the sex industry problem; the coordination of a national strategy is only now starting to take shape. The plan guiding national-level strategies appears to be sound, covering the multiple broad pillars; however, time will tell how it rolls out. The laws have also changed on the federal level, and are being worked on to improve cross-jurisdictional communication.

Sex trafficking for the purposes of sexual exploitation is a global concern and is considered by many to be a modern-day form of slavery (Bales, 2004). The research I conducted for this book sheds light on the dispute between those who view prostitution as a legitimate profession of choice and those who hold that prostitution necessarily involves exploitation and victimization. O'Brien, Hayes, and Carpenter (2013) point out that contemporary activists, scholars, and policymakers broadly define sex trafficking as slavery. Lee (2011) comments that despite the debate over what constitutes slavery, the issue comes down to the degree of coercion, evidence of abuse, and measures taken to prevent the escape of people selling their bodies.

John Lowman (2000), a criminologist who has extensively researched sex industry issues, describes the sex industry in the Canadian context as characteristically involving "survival sex" that includes impoverished women selling sex as they struggle to eat and get a roof over their heads (also see Cool, 2004). The argument that most women in the sex industry are exploited has been growing in popularity, especially over the past decade as awareness of victims' perspectives has grown. It has influenced changes in Canadian law and perspectives on the best approaches for the eradication of the exploitation of girls and young women.

In her book *Walking Prey: How America's Youth Are Vulnerable to Sex Slavery*, Holly Austin Smith (2014) further highlights the degree of coercion and manipulation mentioned by Lee (2011). She describes in detail, from first-hand experience, being trafficked in the sex industry: how young girls are targeted, manipulated, and coerced, often with little chance of escaping the power and control of pimps and traffickers. The reality of victims' unwillingness to testify against their pimps, due to manipulation, makes intervention in this form of slavery very difficult.

The sex industry commonly involves the forcible conscription and manipulation of vulnerable individuals into relationships in which people profit from their exploitation. The United Nations "Protocol to Prevent, Suppress, and Punish Trafficking in Persons" (United Nations, 2000; see also UNESCO, 2014) defines slavery as

> the recruitment, transportation, transfer, harbouring or receipt of persons, by means of threat or use of force or other forms of coercion, of abduction, of fraud, of deception, of the abuse of power or of a position of vulnerability or of the giving or receiving of payments or benefits to achieve the consent of a person having control over another person for the purpose of exploitation.

This UN definition fits with what we see happening to youth in the sex industry in Manitoba. Venkatraman (2003) also argues that modern-day trafficking is slavery because it is an "assault on fundamental human dignity" (p. 2). Debt bondage is the most common form of modern-day slavery in the sex industry (Bales, 2004).

Parrot and Cummings (2008) point out that prostitution in and of itself does not constitute slavery unless certain conditions exist, such as "debt bondage and involuntary sexual servitude." Sex trafficking, according to Lee (2011), involves strip clubs, bars, massage services, internet-based pornography, forced marriages, and mail-order bride schemes. Most of these scenarios, she writes, include debt bondage, wherein women or their families have incurred some form of debt and then are made to "work it off" through sexual services. This use of indebtedness as a manipulative tool by pimps and traffickers is a very common theme in the interviews I conducted. Most survivors described how indebtedness for clothing, food, shelter, street drugs, and protection was used quickly by traffickers, sometimes within two days of being introduced to a new victim, for oppressive manipulation of young girls.

Drescher (2009) notes that the British Slavery Abolition Act of 1833 abolished slavery throughout the British Empire, making the purchase or ownership of slaves illegal within its confines. In practice, slavery continues, in the form of coercion and exploitation of women and girls in Canada, but "since slavery is no longer a legally recognized institution, enslaved people are often hidden from sight or closely monitored to prevent disclosure of their situation" (Cullen-DuPont, 2009, p. 7). Having worked in law enforcement, I have seen first-hand how difficult it is to detect and infiltrate the sex industry with law enforcement tools, and this point was reinforced by the respondents I interviewed for this book. While working with sexually exploited youth, I observed the way predators use debt bondage, psychological manipulation, social isolation, and threats of violence to force young girls into prostitution. The police officers I interviewed for this book also confirmed how difficult it is to enforce the laws. Street-level activity is relatively easy to enforce and prosecute; however, arresting people who are exploited does not solve the problem. The real challenges are in prosecuting traffickers. There are no complainants, the victims often won't report, and much of the activity is now hidden in the internet.

Ham and Gerard (2014) interviewed fifty-five sex industry workers who work mainly indoors in Melbourne, Australia, and learned that they are strategically invisible, despite the need to be somewhat visible in order to gain clients. This planned invisibility is similar in most places, including Nepal, where Anuradha Koirala has dedicated her life to rescuing young girls from brothels (Wrede & Stiftung, 2013). When I met this brave woman, I asked her the naive question, "Shouldn't it be the government doing all that you do?" She just smiled. It is simple: she does it because they don't. Strategic invisibility creates challenges for law enforcement to detect, infiltrate, and prosecute or to intervene and assist youth in exiting the sex industry. My participants expressed this point consistently, and it is described in later, empirical chapters of this book.

The design and enforcement of laws to prevent and control sexual exploitation have been a challenge worldwide. For example, a recent analysis of human trafficking trends in 150 different countries concluded that legalizing prostitution tends to increase human trafficking (Cho et al., 2013). Legalization may push aspects of the sex industry further underground, denying protections and resources that might be afforded to "legalized" sex industry survivors. Based on my over thirty-five years of law enforcement experience, I strongly suspect that full legalization would further marginalize those who are deemed to be "illegal," making them more vulnerable to exploitation by predators and more distanced from the reach of people wishing to assist them. For instance, if legalized prostitution requires sex industry workers to have medical check-ups, what happens to those who do not have the requisite medical certificates? They may still perform sex for money, but without the protections that the "legal" ones have. Lack of certification may also make them more vulnerable to predatory traffickers.

Some women do say that they went voluntarily to work in brothels and massage parlours. However, the degree of their voluntariness is debatable; it's frequently argued that in many cases they are manipulated or coerced and have little chance for escape, or have limited alternative means of earning money to survive (Farley, 2003). Certainly, many youth and young women are forced into prostitution as a means of survival. A child cannot give informed consent to embark on a life in the sex industry, as she or he would be oblivious to all of the anguish that it entails. And according to the definitions of basic human rights and human dignity given in the 1948 United Nations Universal Declaration of Human Rights, young women involved in the sex industry are in fact enchained in modern-day slavery.

The survivors and practitioners I interviewed almost universally characterized the sex industry as slavery. While most did not use that word, what they described fits the working definitions that I previously outlined. The following account by Kaitlin, who was trafficked in the sex industry for many years, graphically describes the type of degrading and oppressive experience that is typical of the survivors I interviewed; her story says it all.

KAITLIN: Usually with the gang members, they – you know, they scare you up. And I remember I had one biker tell me that "You know what? I'm gonna fuckin' have you locked in the basement. And no one's gonna know you're down there. Guys are gonna be coming from all over just to fuck you. And they're gonna be paying me, not you. They'll do whatever they want to you. Shit on you. Piss on you. Make you eat their shit." And I remember I was crying I was so scared, "I'll do whatever you want. They'll do whatever they want, but they'll pay me not you."

And then I was just, "Okay, I'll give you your money." It really scared me. I paid, doing what I had to do. And I just gave them all the money. Then it was just like, "Here, chill, relax, have a beer." I remember, too, thinking once I don't owe any of these guys any money I am outta here. It was how they tricked me. They said, "You don't have to worry about food. You don't have to worry about clothes." Like a pimp. But they didn't come out and say, "I'm gonna pimp you out." They basically sug-ar-coated it. I remember that there was a couple of girls sitting there with a bunch of gold and jewellery. And they had a bunch of crack. And they were saying, "We never go out on the street." And little did I know these guys were pimping them out like escorts or something like that. And they made more money, I guess. It was degrading.

By all measures, this account by Kaitlin depicts slavery and torture. While voluntary sex-selling does occur, involuntariness due to physi-cal threats, fear, and manipulation was a consistent element of the sto-ries of all of the survivors I interviewed. What Kaitlin endured clearly meets the definitions of slavery laid out by the United Nations "Proto-col to Prevent, Suppress, and Punish Trafficking in Persons" (United Nations, 2000; also see UNESCO, 2014).

Most sex industry survivors are from impoverished backgrounds and many are living with multiple traumas, often associated with their Indigenous heritage (Lauwers, 2012). Survivors often become involved in the sex industry as a result of their vulnerability to gangs and pred-ators (Comack et al., 2009; Totten, 2009). Some feminists have argued that women should be free to choose prostitution as a legitimate pro-fession, while others argue that any time a woman sells her body for money she is being exploited (Lozano, 2010; Meyers, 2014). Regardless of the perspective taken, research has revealed the degree of oppres-sion and victimization that does occur against people in this vulnera-ble group (Farley, 2003). We can debate whether a small percentage of women who say they should have the right to be a professional pros-titute are exercising free will or not. However, the sixty-one experts I interviewed, with one thousand years of collective experience, are without exception adamant that no child freely chooses to participate in the sex industry. Many children are targeted, and youth wind up in it due to lack of educational and employment opportunities that would afford them other choices.

While selling sex is often referred to as "work," this is a distaste-ful characterization for many as it implies willingness and a legitimate business transaction rather than, as most see it, the exploitation of one human being by another. One of my research participants, Kelsie, is a sex trafficking survivor who described the importance of language around the issue as follows:

KELSIE: So, some of our women don't even use "sex trade" because that indicates a choice, and we never had choices. And then, on the flip side, some of our women say, "Yes, we have no choices but we still have the agency to make choices, despite our choicelessness." So, we want to empower our women to not feel like they're choiceless even though they are in many aspects. But they still have agency. They still have resiliency. They still have validity to survive despite those choiceless options. So, that's why we talk about "sex work." Because it is work for them. Even if it's a choice or no choice, they still see it as work – work that they didn't necessarily choose or that they necessarily like.

Kelsie draws the important distinction between "work" and exploitation, while also highlighting that people need a sense of agency and control even while they are "choiceless." While she mentions the term "sex trade," her intent aligns with that of the majority of my respondents, who stressed that it is not a trade, that women participating in selling sex generally do not have a choice in the matter.

Most of my participants also described youth involvement in the sex industry not as a free choice but as a choice made under duress. WPS superintendent Liz Pilcher, who has over twenty-five years in policing and has worked for a large part of her career in sex crimes and counter-exploitation-related work, elaborated on this issue of coercion:

LIZ PILCHER: I really believe that we have a lot of victims out there who don't choose to live this life. I think there is a misnomer that it's something that, you know, is luxurious that this is the life that people want. But most of them are drug addicted and, you know, dealing with drugs and gangs. It's not a good lifestyle. I think it's important to deal with the youth before they enter the sex trade. And I think that has to do with the education system, our whole child and family services system. There has to be something – programming, resources – better to help these kids out because I don't think they're choosing to do that. And included in that is the violence. I mean I think sometimes we forget about the violence, the coercion, you know, the threats to family and harm. Those are all things that really mentally take away from a person's humanity.

Hennes Doltze has run the "John School" at Salvation Army Winnipeg for several years. (This is a one-day program that men who have been charged with criminal communication for the purpose of prostitution can attend and have the charges stayed, after proof of completion of the program.) Mr. Doltze underlines that only a small number of people feel they are or were participating freely in the sex industry.

HENNES DOLTZE: Often [prostitution] is happening through some sort of force by another person or coercion or even life circumstances that people get in. So, for the most part people who are involved in prostitution are being sexually exploited. However, I would say there is a small number of people that are involved by their own choice where they feel this is something that they like to do, that this is their choice. They fully understand the consequences – they choose to be in it. I would personally say, given my background, it's a small number. But it does happen that people choose to be in it.

It is important to point out, as Mr. Doltze does, that there are a small number of people working in the sex industry who view it as a right and a free choice that women (and men) should be able to make. However, it is also important to note that this view seems to be held by a relatively small segment of the community involved in the sex industry.

The business of sex trafficking and exploitation is alive and well in Canada. The Criminal Intelligence Service of Canada (CISC) has estimated that the average annual profit from each female trafficked in Canada is $280,800, with profits of up to $1,000 per day from each trafficked woman (CISC, 2008). The RCMP reports that a pimp in Canada can earn $168,000 to $336,000 per year from a single girl (Grant, 2016a). It is easy to see the attraction for organized crime, as traffickers face much lower risks of both prosecution and danger in the streets in the sex industry than in other criminal enterprises, such as drug trafficking.

The RCMP "Human Trafficking in Canada Fact Sheet" (RCMP, 2014) points out that trafficking doesn't necessarily mean being taken across borders; it means being socially isolated and used for the purpose of sexual exploitation. Over 90 per cent of Canadian trafficking victims are originally from Canada. The US Department of State (2014) estimates that about 800 people are trafficked into Canada and 1,500–2,200 people are brought from other countries through Canada into the United States each year.

The defining factor in trafficking is not travel; it is coercion and control (RCMP, 2014). Manitoba's sexually exploited youth are normally from within the province. They are physically and socially isolated, coerced, controlled, and manipulated by people known to them, often by their own family members and legal guardians (CWF, 2014). As mentioned above, all of the survivors I interviewed for this research were from Manitoba and were trafficked in Manitoba, although some were moved to other provinces by their traffickers for short periods. Many young people move from rural areas in Manitoba to larger centres such as Winnipeg and Thompson, often relocating out of necessity to attend high school, college, or university, which are not available in their home community. Traffickers know this and exploit vulnerable youth who are in transit from their home communities.

The financial costs of sexual exploitation and trafficking to Canadians, and the risks to people involved in the sex industry, are substantial. A recent study of sexual exploitation and human trafficking by the Canadian Women's Foundation (CWF, 2014) found that 70 per cent of two hundred victims studied used hospital services at least once for assaults, rapes, and other injuries resulting from their participation in the sex industry. Other medical costs related to the sex industry can include emergency room visits ($212–$820 per visit), ambulance trips ($690–$785 each), and hospital stays ($720–$1,115 per day). One quarter of women reported participating in the high-risk activity of not using condoms regularly. The average lifetime treatment for HIV/AIDS costs $181,129 and treatment for hepatitis C costs $29,526.16. Other significant sex industry–related costs that are more difficult to quantify include legal counsel, complex national or international criminal investigations, social assistance and other services, intergenerational impacts, lost income, and foregone education (CWF, 2014). Other human costs, which are considerable, include the physical and psychological suffering that survivors endure.

Some significant events have driven issues around the sex industry more into the Canadian public discourse in recent years. The Pickton mass murder case in British Columbia was a wake-up call for Canada (Oppal, 2012). The start of Canada's Missing and Murdered Indigenous Women and Girls Inquiry in September 2016 also provided a great catalyst for change in the narrative around this issue.

Missing and Murdered Indigenous Women and Girls (MMIWG) has become a social movement in Canada based in the growing public discourse over the marginalization and violent oppression of Indigenous women and girls. The Native Women's Association of Canada (NWAC) coined the phrase "missing and murdered Indigenous women" in a funded study carried out over several years, in reference to Indigenous women and girls who are missing and/or have been murdered across Canada over recent decades (NWAC, 2010). As of 2009 NWAC was reporting 520 cases of missing or murdered Indigenous women and girls, of whom 67 per cent were identified as "having died as a result of homicide or negligence" (NWAC, 2010). In 2016 NWAC reported more than 1,000 missing or murdered Indigenous women in Canada. NWAC has played an important role in raising awareness and feeding the public discourse around the marginalization of Indigenous people in Canada.

The MMIWG movement has raised awareness of situations including the victims of the serial killer Robert Pickton in British Columbia (Oppal, 2012) and the Highway of Tears, a seven-hundred-kilometre stretch of Highway 16 in the interior of British Columbia, along which it is believed that between 1989 and 2006 nine women were murdered, or missing and believed murdered (http://www.highwayoftears.ca). I once attended a seminar in which the coordinators described how the Highway of Tears threads through impoverished neighbourhoods that are inhabited by Indigenous people across Canada. (In chapter 4, I focus on Indigenous perspectives.)

Manitoba is a fitting place to examine sexual exploitation. For one, it is the home of a troubled past that was revealed by the Aboriginal Justice Inquiry that was sparked by the death of J.J. Harper during a scuffle with Winnipeg Police officers in 1988 (Hamilton & Sinclair, 1991). The inquiry exposed historic racism and tension between government agencies and First Nations and Métis people. Manitoba has a long-standing problem with exploitation, punctuated by the tragic murders of several youths including Cherisse Houle, Hillary Wilson, and Tina Fontaine (CBC, 2014a; Paperny, 2009). The province, situated in the centre of Canada, has the highest number of children in care per capita in Canada (Puxley, 2014). It is also the seat of much activism around the national Missing and Murdered Indigenous Women movement (RCMP, 2013; Welch, 2014). Both children in care and the Missing and Murdered movement are closely connected with the sexual exploitation issue.

In 2002, Manitoba's provincial government established a multidisciplinary team to develop and implement a strategy to address the sexual exploitation of children and youth. The Multi-Jurisdictional Implementation Team (MIT) comprises numerous organizations involved in serving sexually exploited youth. Several initiatives involving prevention, intervention, legislation, coordination, and research/evaluation were implemented between 2002 and 2008. In 2008 Tracia's Trust (Manitoba Family Services & Housing, 2008) was established as phase two of Manitoba's sexual exploitation strategy.

Rebecca Cook was Manitoba's child exploitation program coordinator at the time I interviewed her for this study. She outlines how Manitoba is unique in Canada with regard to its response to sexual exploitation.

REBECCA COOK: So, in Manitoba we are the only province right now that has a provincial strategy to address exploitation. It was mandated by the

Healthy Child Committee of cabinet in 2002, actually also a push from
the community at the time saying there is lots of children and youth
being exploited on the streets and we need to do something about it.

Ms. Cook stated that Manitoba has had some original solutions, yet it is
also unique in its ongoing challenges. She also emphasized the importance of the language employed in addressing the issue, including not
identifying high-risk youth as "prostitutes" or criminals.

Because of leaders like Gord Mackintosh and Jane Runner, Diane
Redsky, Dianna Bussey, and others, Manitoba has been a national leader
in developing approaches to intervene in victimization through sexual
exploitation and human trafficking, and should naturally be a national
leader in evaluating lessons learned and in moving forward. Former
attorney general (and also former CFS minister) Gord Mackintosh outlined how the formal counter-exploitation strategy started in Manitoba.

GORD MACKINTOSH: By December 2008, Tracia's Trust really all came
together from a lot of that experience from the Sexually Exploited
Youth Coalition, people that were on the front lines and leaders and
so many NGOs that came to us and said, "Here are the pieces that we
have to focus on: we have to have more beds, we have to have some
better coordination of all the work on the street by all the agencies,
which led to StreetReach. We had to do better in terms of some civil
laws to deal with this one. And so that's where it went to and now it's a
ten-million-dollar-a-year investment and growing.

So, that's how I came to it. It was like, it wasn't a light switch, you know,
that went on and all of a sudden, I could see the way – It was really like
I say, the product of so many people bringing their insights to bear,
inherent with all the conflicts.

Mr. Mackintosh emphasizes, as did my other research contributors, that
Manitoba is a leader in Canada with respect to funding and strategizing to reduce sexual exploitation, yet there is room for improvement.

Tracia's Trust was named after Tracia Owen, a fourteen-year-old girl
who committed suicide while in care of Child and Family Services.
It was a defining event in Manitoba's counter-exploitation strategy.
Judge John Guy presided over Tracia's inquest (Guy, 2008). His report
stressed the need for greater cooperation between all agencies involved
in child welfare in Manitoba. He called for round tables to create a comprehensive provincial strategy to counter sexual exploitation. Then
Family Services and Housing minister Gord Mackintosh hosted a two-
day summit in 2008, based on Judge Guy's recommendations, attended

by 65 people at the northern Manitoba summit and 130 at the southern Manitoba conference.

Police and justice officials, community groups, educators, Indigenous groups, Elders, and other stakeholders discussed strategies to support sexually exploited children and how to help prevent other children and youth from being exploited. The Front Line Voices summit workshops produced four main recommendation themes: (1) legislation and law enforcement, (2) continuum of services, (3) raising awareness, and (4) child, youth, family and community empowerment. The subsequent report outlined that in Manitoba most sexually exploited children and youth are Indigenous females, although there is a growing awareness of the exploitation of boys and transgendered youth. It also reported that a large proportion of exploited youth are wards of the child welfare system, having experienced childhood sexual/physical abuse, and many have been homeless at some point and exchanged sex for the necessities of life, including food and shelter. That report listed the underlying factors that contribute to children's vulnerability to sexual exploitation as including poverty, racism, colonization and the legacy of residential school experiences, social and cultural isolation, marginalization, peer pressure, past abuse or trauma, sex-based discrimination, mental health or developmental disorders, system gaps or inaccessible services, and other social and financial inequalities (Manitoba Family Services & Housing, 2008).

A prosecutor was assigned to focus on sexual exploitation–related charges. Some existing sections in Manitoba's Child and Family Services Act (updated in 2020) were seen as potential tools for addressing exploitation. These included failing to report a child in need of protection (section 18) and interference with a child in care (section 52). At the time I was the coordinator of the WPS Missing Persons Unit; I and my team took the lead seeking legal tools, and started enforcing CFS Act's section 52 "harbouring" provisions. The act allows for a mandated social worker to serve a warning letter on any person who harbours or allows a runaway to hide in their home, thus interfering with their lawful placement in a foster care home or another facility.

No prosecutions had ever been pursued under this legislation; however, social workers and our police detectives saw its value. Working with the Justice Department, we clarified the elements of the offence and requirements for prosecuting cases. The process was prolonged, and so we decided to take the initiative and lay charges to expedite the use of the act for protecting at-risk youth.

Some experienced social workers were thrilled at the police interest and actual use of the harbouring legislation. Much positive press ensued. Social work and police partners appreciated this collaboration and viewed the use of the harbouring legislation as groundbreaking. However, it met some resistance in the Justice Department and sentences on conviction were small, despite the maximum penalty having been raised to fifty thousand dollars in fines and up to two years in prison (Giroday, 2009). The enforcement of anti-harbouring legislation was a useful tool for bringing runaways to safety, yet ultimately one of the smaller implements on the tool belts of people working in the counter-exploitation field.

From 2006 to the present, the WPS Missing Persons Unit implemented several strategies, including teaming police investigators with social workers to intervene with high-risk youth who were being groomed and exploited in the sex industry. We realized that marginalization was at the root of this growing social problem. Vulnerable girls were being identified and preyed upon, and many were in the care of child protection services.

The following are some initiatives that began after 2006 and have continued to this day: (1) continually returning runaway youth home to safety, always seeking to build trust with them; (2) partnering with social workers and participating in care plans for high-risk youth; (3) seeking to use and change laws, such as CFS section 52, harbouring, for use in protecting children; (4) establishing unique new media partnerships to provide stories on intervention innovations as well as on daily urgent public appeals for help; and (5) challenging the systems of service providers on issues such as the lack of secure facilities that could prevent high-risk youth from running away and becoming vulnerable to predators.

By 2008 WPS Missing Persons Unit members realized that more data were needed to make arguments for change in the child welfare system and policies concerning police and social worker responses to high-risk exploited youth. Anecdotally, it was clear to everyone involved that children in foster homes, group homes, and CFS facilities were being preyed upon. In January 2009 we audited all missing person investigations in Winnipeg for the three-month period of October to December 2008. We found that of the 1,275 investigations examined (425 per month), about 70 per cent were children running away from CFS placements.

This finding sent shock waves through government and the Department of Child and Family Services (later the Department of Families). However, senior bureaucrats and social workers were happy that we had finally confirmed the reality everyone already understood, that children in care made up the bulk of children at risk. Many were repeat chronic runaways, some with over one hundred police contacts (runaway and other crime reports) and as many child welfare contacts attached to their names. This chronic runaway behaviour led to dangerous complacency in the system. Police and social workers get tired of repeatedly returning runaway youth to group homes only to see them reported missing again hours later. The situation becomes perceived as a nuisance, yet ironically those children are often at highest risk (Hedges, 2002). We now know that when youth are out on the run, they are often being groomed for the sex industry (Dedel, 2006; Lanning, 2001).

One place where the vulnerability of runaway youth to sexual exploitation was first observed and prioritized is Dallas, Texas. The Dallas Police Department is renowned for its leading-edge strategies in countering sex trafficking. It based its strategy on tracking runaway reports and sending detectives to meet and build relationships with chronic runaways, eventually gaining their trust and receiving their disclosures about who was exploiting them. This information would then be used to build cases and prosecute traffickers. In 2009, I travelled to Dallas with Jennifer Richardson, my counterpart in social work, to learn from the Dallas police, and we later had Dallas detectives come to Canada to teach our multidisciplinary teams how to intervene with high-risk youth.

Missing persons are a difficult challenge for contemporary Canadian policing. Investigations are complex, labour intensive, and politically sensitive (Hedges, 2002). Serial homicides and public inquiries across Canada over the past decade have highlighted the need for deeper sensitivity to vulnerable people, in particular women and children, who are often reported as missing and are at risk of sexual exploitation (DeRiviere, 2005; Klaine, 1999; Outshoorn, 2004; Stittle, 2007). The tragic deaths of several Winnipeg youth mentioned above created deep concern in government and other service agencies and throughout our communities over the need for greater focus and collaboration between agencies that are mandated to protect vulnerable people, including high-risk youth (Guy, 2008).

Some of the current contention in Manitoba has been over how to get more proactive, preventing at-risk youth from becoming victimized and exploited. This involves a debate about how we work with the high numbers of children who are in care. Some argue for approaches that leave the child in his or her familial home and remove the problem adult rather than the child (Ostroff, 2015). The Northern Misipawistik Cree Nation is trying this new approach in certain circumstances (Ostroff, 2015).

Manitoba's Child Advocate, Darlene MacDonald, examined the deaths of 166 Manitoba children (under eighteen years old) between

April 2013 and March 2014. She reported that improvements are required in three different areas to address children's needs in Manitoba: (1) better access to mental health services, (2) protection from sexual exploitation, and (3) better protection of children's rights ("Manitoba's Children's Advocate," 2014). Research to date has created a clear picture of the ways that troubled youth get recruited and involved in sexual exploitation; however, the literature on effective interventions is lacking (Berckamns et al., 2012; Richardson, 2015).

In Manitoba, we have faced significant problems with cases involving missing persons. The WPS was experiencing intense difficulties with such cases, tying up massive amounts of uniform patrol unit resources, a problem it still faces in 2020. Generally, any missing person event that presents risk factors, such as gang involvement, risk of exploitation, substance abuse, or risk of suicide, results in a uniform crew continuing to look for the missing youth for many hours, sometimes handing off the investigation to the incoming shifts to continue around the clock for days. Vulnerable people, such as young children and the elderly, are also given high priority and searched for continuously, often with massive resources, until they are found.

In 2008–9, sexually exploited youth were added to the list, which is continuously being updated, for higher-priority investigation due to their vulnerability. In my role as a WPS duty officer overseeing police operations, I can say that these cases were given high priority. In 2009–10 the WPS Missing Person Unit was responsible for over five thousand short-term, emergent investigations per year, and was carrying over one hundred unsolved long-term missing person "cold cases." The number of short-term, emergent daily investigations had climbed to over seven thousand by 2017 and remains about the same today. Every case is urgent to loved ones reporting a person missing, yet the police have the difficult task of prioritizing cases with limited resources.

Runaway youth have been a significant challenge for police agencies across Canada because they present as low-risk cases, yet there is growing awareness that these youth are being preyed upon by sexual predators, pedophiles, gangs, traffickers, and organized crime, and are in fact at highest risk of harm. Girls exploited in the sex industry in Winnipeg are often "trafficked" in the sense that they are socially isolated and marginalized, forced to perform sex acts in exchange for basic human needs – the bare necessities of shelter from Winnipeg's often frigid temperatures, of food, or to feed addictions to street drugs (Giroday, 2010). Those who worked in government and non-government agencies and the community in 2016–18 say that sexual exploitation, economic disparity, and all its related problems are as bad as they ever were. The police have come to understand that they are only a small part of the larger spectrum of resources required to address these issues. In the following chapters I present the opinions and insights of those who have lived with this oppression, those who grapple daily with these vexing problems, and the associated findings and recommendations that flow from them.

3 Vulnerability and Protection from Sex Industry Predators

ASHLEY: I think the critical moment when I entered the sex trade was when I was fifteen. Like I had been bullied in school, I was vulnerable, I felt a need to belong and feel accepted. I had been going to community centres and spending time with friends. A couple of the girls and myself met some guys there and they introduced us to crack, and we wanted more and then that was the point where I was on the streets.

Ashley describes the vulnerability that predators exploit; they watch for girls who are having difficulty and want to belong, and they pounce on them. My respondents held strong ideas about children's vulnerability and how traffickers capitalize on it. Virtually all of the individuals I interviewed for this book maintained that no child makes a conscious choice to enter the sex industry unless she or he is under duress and being manipulated and has no other choice. Several of the interviewees mentioned that a child's vulnerability is tied to her/his basic human need for love, and that predators understand and take advantage of that need. My interviews, consistent with the existing literature, show connections between childhood sexual abuse and a high likelihood of vulnerability to later involvement in the sex industry. This is significant, because identification of predictors of later involvement in the sex industry also presents possible opportunities for early intervention.

Another strong connection was identified between sexual exploitation and children in care of child protective services. While this is a known phenomenon, my research unearthed insights into the child welfare system and potential opportunities for improvement. Parts of this chapter provide details of how people are preyed upon and groomed and what makes them vulnerable to being exploited. Another part is dedicated to prevention, and participants' advocacy of early intervention to prevent exploitation rather than deal with it once it occurs. This chapter alone is probably broad enough in scope for a book, but is only intended to identify vulnerability issues highlighted by study participants. It is not meant to be exhaustive or conclusive, but rather to set the stage for later discussions about interventions and responses, and what we as a society can do to reduce sexual exploitation.

This research contributes insights regarding the existing system of resources and agencies related to youth vulnerability in Manitoba. Most of my interview participants could not identify one critical issue or turning point wherein youth enter the sex industry, instead stressing that young people become vulnerable for varied reasons, including loss of resilience, dysfunctional family ties and supports, and mental health issues. When a youth, for whatever reason, loses his/her sense of place and connection with a family, it seems s/he will desperately seek it elsewhere, and this is where the gangs and exploiters step in. The key, it seems, is in identifying vulnerable youth and getting them appropriate resources early on, before they are trafficked.

In many cases, children are on a clear track to being exploited if someone does not intervene. For example, Kaitlin, a survivor, talked about growing up in a house where prostitution and drug abuse were normal.

KAITLIN: I was twelve. I hung around with girls who were doing it, an older crowd of girls. They struggled with addiction, but I can say, honestly, I kind of think I grew up around it. My mother was a prostitute. And I remember growing up in a house with a bunch of prostitutes. So I kind of think that has something to do with it. My mother was an IV user so I grew up around that. And I think that's why it was so easy to go into addiction.

Kaitlin had little chance to do something different, with a drug-addicted prostitute as a mother and role model.

Previous research has revealed that women involved in sexual exploitation tend to experience alarming levels of physical violence and abuse. Farley (2003), for example, found that most women and youth involved in sexual exploitation are trapped in violent exploitive relationships, experiencing and fearing violence, resulting in mental health, trauma, and substance abuse problems. Her study of 854 survivors in nine countries revealed that violence is a common experience in the sex industry. Women and youth reported being routinely subjected to various forms of oppression and violence, including sexual harassment, verbal abuse, stalking, rape, battering, and torture (Farley et al., 2003).

In Canada, Farley (2003) interviewed one hundred women involved in the sex industry in Vancouver's Downtown East Side, a historically central prostitution area. She found that over 91 per cent of her sample had been assaulted repeatedly during acts of prostitution. The assaults included stabbings, beatings, concussions, and broken jaws, ribs, collarbones, fingers, spines, and skulls. Fifty per cent of the women had experienced serious head injuries from assaults with baseball bats or crowbars or from having their heads slammed against walls or against car dashboards. Of the women she interviewed, 67 per cent had been raped five times or more and 74 per cent were diagnosed with post-traumatic stress disorder (PTSD).

The psychological effects of being exploited have even deeper impacts than those associated with physical violence (Yuen et al., 2014). There is a growing body of literature reporting the high incidence of psychopathologies such as anxiety, PTSD, depression, and other psychological problems among people involved in prostitution (Rössler et al., 2010; Yuen et al., 2014). For example, Lau et al. (2010) studied the sex industry in Hong Kong and found that 53.9 per cent of sex workers were notably depressed. Wong et al. (2008) found that female sex workers experienced a significantly diminished quality of life in almost every measure.

Many female sex industry survivors struggle with negative self-views and emotionally tormenting guilt and shame (Holroyd et al., 2008; Vanwesenbeeck, 2005; Wong et al., 2008). Jennifer Richardson stresses that being trafficked is different from other kinds of abuse; people often see it as the survivor's fault, viewing survivors more as complicit perpetrators than as victims (CWF, 2014).

Sex industry survivors are exposed to the stress of negative social stigmas and often live in constant fear of their activities being discovered by family or friends (Wong et al., 2011). Some women perceive the reasons leading to their entering the sex industry to be out of their control (Sanders, 2004). The media's normalizing or downplaying of the sex industry's impact on women can only exacerbate the emotional effects for survivors. This may contribute, as some researchers have found, to severe substance abuse and dangerous risk-taking behaviours such as inconsistent condom use, increasing women's chances of contracting sexually transmitted infections and HIV AIDS (Hong et al, 2007; Lau et al., 2010).

Many children inherit a legacy that places them on the track towards exploitation. Indigenous children, for instance, often live with the trauma that is passed on from their parents and grandparents. It is easy to understand the concept of "the transgenerational transmission of trauma," identified by Volkan (1997). This phenomenon is illustrated broadly in Canadian Indigenous populations wherein many are suffering from the lingering impacts of Canada's aggressive assimilation programs that sought to extinguish their traditional culture and integrate them into Western settler society (Younging, 2009). A good number from impoverished backgrounds seem fated to wind up being exploited. Helping people to break these trajectories, build resilience, and achieve better lives will require an understanding of structural or invisible violence and ways to empower people to overcome it.

Many people involved in selling sex are victims of childhood abuse. Constable Anna Janzen of the WPS says, "I have found in my fifteen plus years of policing, I have yet to come across anybody that is involved in the sex trade that has not been a victim of either child abuse or sexual exploitation at a very young age. So, it's just a huge problem." Constable Janzen also emphasizes the importance of practitioners being non-judgmental when dealing with survivors. She describes how survivors have their childhoods stolen from them:

ANNA JANZEN: I truly think each is on a case-by-case situation and the dynamics of the family or what's happening in the child's home. I've spoken with sex trade workers that – one girl, in particular. I clearly remember the conversation. She said to me, like, she doesn't ever remember being a child. Like, her earliest memory ever was her mother's boyfriend coming into her room at age four and abusing her. Like, she doesn't ever remember playing on a swing set or going to the park. She just remembers like always being abused. She didn't even know she was being abused back then. She had no concept of that, and that stems from a very early age.

Constable Janzen points out the opportunity to intervene, possibly in schools, to educate young people about the perils of predators in the sex industry, and to use risk factors as indicators for intervention to assist young people caught up in the sex industry.

Constable Rejeanne Caron of WPS provided one survivor's story that illustrates how vulnerable children are victims of the circumstances into which they are born, and are often neglected or abused by the ones they rely on to care for them.

REJEANNE CARON: I've always viewed them as victims of circumstance of life that put them in that position. For example, when I worked in the prostitution diversion camp, I had a young girl who had hepatitis A, B, and C, was a sex trade worker, was addicted to drugs, and managed to get herself out of it. And she explained her story. [When] she was a thirteen-year-old girl, dad had criminal associations to a major gang in

Winnipeg. And dad – this young girl who expected dad to take care of her – exploited her and basically had all his friends have sex with her. So, it was a gang rape. So, you hear stories like that. Why are we criminalizing these girls? And I think the approach now is the view that girls should not be victimized. And we, as a society, and we as a police service, and all those collaborative efforts are to help girls get out of those situations. The days of criminalizing prostitution – I feel that shouldn't be. And I know the [Winnipeg Police Service] is moving in a direction that we are not criminalizing them, and obviously throughout Canada as well.

The fact that one's own parents could allow this to happen to one is difficult to comprehend, yet it is important to acknowledge if we are to make enduring and sustainable change. The stories are gut-wrenching and hard to hear, but it is this type of honesty that might result in real change.

Previous research has found correlations between childhood sexual abuse and later sexual exploitation (Kaestle, 2012; Klatt et al., 2014; Lalor & McElvaney, 2010; Lavoie et al., 2010). For example, Klatt et al. (2014) studied records of 175 youth receiving treatment for sexual exploitation in Leicester, United Kingdom. They reported that childhood sexual abuse correlates highly with high-risk sexual activity and trading for sex. General physical abuse has also been associated with later sexual exploitation (Greene et al., 1999; Roe-Sepowitz et al., 2011). McIntyre (2012) interviewed forty-one females and nine males involved in prostitution in Alberta, Canada, and found that 82 per cent experienced sexual abuse prior to entering the sex industry. The average age of entry into the sex industry in Canada was fourteen years old (p. 64).

Historically, numerous other factors have also been found to correlate with later sex industry involvement, including family dysfunction, educational difficulties, poverty, drug and alcohol abuse, involvement with child protective services, friends or family members involved in trading sex, running away from home, homelessness, school delinquency, and sexual activity (McIntyre, 2012). Research has also found that sexual exploitation, sexual harassment, and sexual violence are often correlated with homelessness among women (Huey & Berndt, 2008; Huey & Quirouette, 2010). None of these factors on their own raises flags for youth vulnerability to exploitation, but taken together they hold much more meaning. Early childhood abuse and lack of opportunities seem to indicate a higher likelihood of later participation in survival sex.

My findings are consistent with those of the Canadian Women's Foundation study, which reported that factors correlated with youth vulnerability to sexual exploitation include (1) being female, (2) being poor, (3) having a history of violence or neglect, (4) having a history of child sexual abuse, and (5) having a low level of education (CWF, 2014, p. 27). My findings partially parallel those of McIntyre (2012), with respect to young recruitment age and the tortured backgrounds of survivors. My findings also agree with previous research that correlates run-away behaviour with children who are vulnerable to targeting by predators and being recruited by them into the sex industry (Brock, 1998; Lowman, 1987).

These findings indicate possibilities for constructive intervention measures to prevent children from later becoming involved in the sex industry. For example, as several of my research participants point out, there is a need to train teachers, social workers, and police to identify signs of early sexual abuse and then act appropriately to prevent later exploitation of young by family members, predators, and pimps.

A significant theme that arose during my research was the need youth have to feel loved and to belong, and how that increases their vulnerability to exploitation. Sex traffickers are very aware of these human needs and dynamics and how to take advantage of them. In plain English, we all need love, particularly teenagers, who are finding their way in the world and feeling a strong need to belong. It is clear, according to participants in this research, that teenage girls need a sense of belonging and predators are adept at identifying youth who lack that in their lives. Ashley, one of the survivors I interviewed, spoke of how she was vulnerable and looking for somewhere to belong when she was targeted and introduced to crack cocaine by some "guys" who were either traffickers or passed her on to traffickers once she was hooked on crack. Another survivor, Elizabeth, had a similar story. She had been trafficked in the sex industry for many years and now works helping other women to escape the sex industry. She describes the importance of family dynamics, as Anna Janzen and others had, and specifically mentions the role of a father.

ELIZABETH: If I could say one thing that would have prevented me [from entering the sex industry], it would have been father love, you know. That having the love and support of a father that is present. You know my dad provided financially, but he wasn't there emotionally, so that – I hear it over and over again. And when women are transitioning, it's – they get hooked up with johns that are safer than the regulars. So, they will start their transition out that way, and it's convoluted.

Elizabeth pinpoints the need that predators cunningly fulfil for young girls, providing them with attention and being emotionally present.

Jane Runner, executive director of TERF (Transition, Education and Resources for Females), also highlights our human need for love and belonging and how it makes us vulnerable. Beyond that, she assigns a high priority to the need for hope.

JANE RUNNER: We need to interact non-judgmentally. Love conquers all. I think every woman or man that's out there selling themselves does not feel very good about themselves, and for them to be put down further is the worst [thing] we can do. I think basically for me right now working in the field I'm working is – you can come across myself or even Dianna [Bussey, from the Salvation Army] – it's just meeting girls where they're at and being there and just encouraging them, believing in them when they're unable to believe in themselves. We can't do it for them, but we sure encourage [them] to do it. Give them hope.

Ms. Runner emphasizes that the sense of being loved is critical for youth. She also touches upon a point mentioned earlier, the importance of practitioners being non-judgmental. Based on the comments that my sixty-one participants made with respect to vulnerability, my sense is that love means that youth need to sense that someone cares about them if they are to be resilient.

RCMP Deputy Commissioner Kevin Brosseau, speaking from his years of experience working with various components of the sex industry, similarly underlines the significance of love in the lives of young people and the need for a child's positive attachment with family.

KEVIN BROSSEAU: I can tell you of a couple other situations where young women who for real, perhaps started as teenage rebellion, got themselves connected with older guys – who out of a misplaced loyalty and/or feelings of love or relationship ended up on the street having to work.

Deputy Commissioner Brosseau describes how predators fill a void for vulnerable young women: the women are first made to feel like they belong via gifts and attention, and then they are suddenly declared to be indebted and made to sell sex to pay off their debts.

Claudia Ponce-Joly, former Manitoba director of child welfare, speaks of how every child wants to feel significant and valued in our society.

CLAUDIA PONCE-JOLY: There are many thousands of children who are lost and unattached and do not know there is help. And these children are vulnerable to being sexually exploited. I believe that making each child feel that they count and that they're valued and that they deserve respect, dignity, and a place in our community makes a difference. It may sound like a soft approach, but in my view, it's not. If children and youth don't receive that type of constant and consistent communication from people in their lives, that's when their risk level will increase and somebody else will have ulterior motives that will take place in that child's life because that child is being pulled into sexual exploitation. The messages, the actions, and involvement of those around the child need to be stronger, much stronger than from those who may harm your child.

Ms. Ponce-Joly's emphasis on the number of children who feel unattached aligns with previous participants' comments about the significance of family dynamics and having a home with a support structure and role models.

Most of my research participants highlighted that one of the main underlying factors resulting in people's exploitation in the sex industry is the lack of other employment opportunities. A search of the sixty-one transcripts of participant's interviews found ninety-seven occurrences of the word "poverty." Poverty was identified as a root cause underlying young people's lack of opportunities. This is the type of oppression that represents "structural" violence as defined by Galtung (1996), who describes structural violence, or invisible violence, as poverty and lack of educational and employment opportunities. The oppression of women and children in the sex industry also takes the form of direct physical and psychological assaults perpetrated by pimps, traffickers, and johns. This oppression often starts long before entering the sex industry, as most women involved in the sex industry were previously abused as children. Reimer et al. (2015) also write that people's vulnerability and victimization are tied, at least in part, to the structural violence of marginalization that flows from poverty and economic disparity.

One survivor of fifteen years of exploitation in the sex industry, Marie, now assists people striving to escape that industry. She considers poverty and lack of proper housing to be key factors contributing to young people's vulnerability to sexual predators.

MARIE: Some people want to legalize [the sex industry]. Some people want to create safe houses. Some people think that the perp should be more accountable. I really think that if people were given equal opportunity in the world, if people had self-esteem and motivation to get upgrading and to go to school and bigger EIA [employment income assistance] benefits, or working well on EIA, you know. Because people who live on social assistance are living more than 50 per cent under the LICO [low income cut-off] guideline, which is obscenely low. So, I feel if people had maybe a guaranteed income to maintain their home, it would help them to maintain their home, it would help them to feed their kids so they're stressed less.

Marie's point is echoed by former grand chief Ron Evans, a leader in Manitoba's counter-sexual-exploitation planning, who regards poverty and lack of opportunities as the fundamental cause of young women and children's vulnerability to exploitation by sexual predators. Chief Evans specifically points to poor housing as the main issue that leads to all manner of social ills, including the exploitation of youth in the sex industry.

RON EVANS: I've seen the challenges. I've seen governments. I've seen how things were. There's been progress, but I've seen where there isn't. If there was true progress, the numbers would have declined, you know, from the number of people in jails, the number of murdered and missing women, the number of, you know, how people that are impacted by the health care system.

And so, governments over the years have made every effort to say, "Okay, education is the key. Education is the key so that you can get yourself out of poverty." Or "education is the key so that you can, you know, make a contribution to your community, to society." Or they'll throw money at economic development so that you can have jobs, you know, and begin to make your life better. Or they'll throw money at social programs. They'll throw money to the front-line workers. But nobody is dealing with the root cause. The root cause is, as you have probably read in the paper now last week, where Manitoba needs $1.9 billion for housing. In my community alone we have 8,000 people and we have a birth rate of 200 a year, and so in the last eight years we have not been able to build a house for that 1,600. We've grown by 1,600. So, where do people live when there is no housing? We've not been able to build a house. But we've been able to build other infrastructure like an entertainment centre, and we're going to build a baseball field. We've got other economic initiatives because we've partnered with others so our community grows in that regard.

So, then we talk about the number of inmates. You know, the jails are bursting at the seams. The health care system, the health care cost and future [costs] rise because of the illnesses – whether it's illness caused by mould in the home or there's just not enough services to meet the needs.

Chief Evans's account provides an example of the hidden, structural violence described by Galtung (1996) and Reimer et al. (2015).

Marie's story highlights poverty, lack of opportunity, and exposure to the sex industry, in conjunction with having been sexually abused as a child by her father, as factors in later being "put into" the sex industry.

MARIE: Well, I didn't really make a decision, when I was put into the sex it just seemed right at the moment because there was no other way to support myself. I wasn't old enough for welfare so that was my only means of obtaining clothing and stuff.

The survival sex that Marie talked about is a theme that threads throughout this book, illustrating the direct relationship between poverty and lack of opportunities that have a higher likelihood of making children vulnerable, especially when coupled with traumatic childhood abuse.

Many from impoverished backgrounds seem fated to wind up being exploited. Helping people to break these trajectories, build resilience, and achieve better lives will require an understanding of structural or invisible violence and ways to empower people to overcome it. Vulnerability and victimization are tied, at least in part, to the structural violence of impoverishment (Reimer et al., 2015). That violence occurs when societal institutions are arranged in such a way that people are systematically discriminated against, and have fewer economic and educational opportunities than others. This disparity is apparent in Canada, as many Indigenous people live in poor conditions on reserves and impoverished city cores, in stark contrast with the relatively high living standards enjoyed by most people across mainstream Canada.

Galtung (1996) contends that peace extends far beyond the mere end of active warfare (negative peace) to social justice (positive peace), which is only possible in the absence of structural violence. Positive peace should be a social justice goal in modern Global North society. In any examination of structural violence and exploited youth, it is crucial to consider the dynamics and structures via which vulnerability is correlated with sexual exploitation and the structural violence of impoverishment.

In one case in which structural violence was addressed to improve public safety, two Boston emergency room doctors named Prothrow-Stith and Spivak (2004) presented a paradigm shift with respect to severe ongoing violence against African American males in and around Boston in the late 1980s and early 1990s. By declaring street violence to be a medical health crisis, they engaged multiple systems in cross-sectorial violence intervention and prevention strategies, eventually reducing violence against African American males substantially.

This medical-science-based cause-and-effect paradigm has not often been applied to crime and public safety issues, but my research into sex trafficking and exploitation connects in some ways with the Boston case. For example, women are viewed as survivors of the impoverished social milieus they were born into, just as violence-afflicted gang members in the Boston area became viewed as victims of their life circumstances rather than only as criminals. And, as Prothrow-Stith and Spivak (2004) maintain, children are not to blame for the circumstances they are born into in life, and therefore they should not be punished for them.

In a similar vein, Muftic and Finn (2013) present human trafficking as a "heinous crime and a public health issue" (p. 1860), describing the health implications as severe, annually affecting hundreds of thousands in the United States (also see Siskin & Sun Wyler, 2010; Winterdyk & Reichel, 2010). Muftic and Finn (2013) point out that despite increasing public awareness of human trafficking as a growing global issue, there is still relatively little primary research published on it. Zimmerman et al. (2011) also noted from a health perspective that "health is a subject that has been largely neglected in anti-trafficking work" (p. 237).

Impoverishment and lack of opportunities seem to correlate with being victimized, whether the victimized are African American gang members in Boston or young women in the sex industry in Winnipeg. Therefore, economic disparity is an important element to understand in analysing who is vulnerable to exploitation. Sixty-seven per cent of Canada's wealth is held by a small number of elites and "the poorest fifth of Canadians own no share at all" (Broadbent, 2014). The aphorism "the rich get richer" seems true historically, and it reverberates today with our everyday observations that wealth gaps in the world are ever widening (Rugaber, 2014); the tragic outcome is that disadvantaged people become further oppressed. As mentioned above, people tend to blame sex industry survivors for their plight, seeing their involvement as a matter of free will (Bishop, 1994); what we sometimes overlook is that people do not have a choice over the conditions they are born into.

Burton (1997) argues that beyond financial material needs, social institutions and structures can suppress one's identity, personal status, and security, and can become a source of conflict at all social levels from the interpersonal to the international. Foucault (2010) describes power as diffuse, reinforced, and perpetuated through societal structures and social reproduction. It seems clear that there is psychological oppression involved in trafficking, and that financial control is part of the overall manipulation that occurs when someone is trafficked.

The structural violence of impoverishment is difficult to overcome. It is like the vivid memories I have of being stuck while playing in the mud when I was a child. The harder I pulled, the more my feet would be sucked down, until I could not escape without help. While we all know of individuals from disadvantaged environments who later became successful, they are rare exceptions; the fate of most people is to live and die as members of the socio-economic classes they were born into, for "social reproduction processes" tend to keep people locked in their place in the social economic order (Macleod, 1995). Following people in one urban neighbourhood longitudinally over several decades from childhood on, Macleod (1995) found that social structures create a destiny for each of us that is difficult to escape. The same dynamics seem to be at play with respect to sex industry survivors. Impoverishment and the related lack of opportunities are clearly linked to resort to survival sex.

Cullen-DuPont (2009) described how traffickers recruit people who are desperate to escape lives of poverty by luring them with lies, such as the promise of legitimate work. In some cases, parents sell their children for what they thought was manual labour, in the hope of a better life for them. Tragically, legitimate work often transmutes into torture and servitude in the sex industry (Cullen-DuPont, 2009).

Canada's Indigenous people are, as Chief Evans eloquently pointed out, more socially and economically disadvantaged than mainstream settler society, suffering more impoverishment and lack of opportunities for education and jobs (Ham, 2014; Younging, 2009). However, poverty affects people of all groups. As Rosemarie Gjerek of Klinic Community Health stated, "poverty is the root of all evil," and alleviating it would likely have an impact on a broad spectrum of social problems, including exploitation in the sex industry.

Darryl Ramkissoon is a WPS staff sergeant who has worked in counter-exploitation for over fifteen years and believes, with Chief Evans that poverty is a key factor in making children vulnerable to exploitation.

DARRYL RAMKISSOON: Based on my experience, poverty makes them more prone to be exploited. We have a huge problem with child poverty, and it makes them vulnerable. Eliminating that would help prevent exploitation. Just based on my own experience with these youths and kids, poverty in this city is huge. The demographics – because we have a higher percentage of Indigenous people who are prone to a lower social-economic lifestyle – they're more prone to being exploited. These are people that are usually targeted because of their vulnerability. And what we're noticing, these kids, because of their situation they turn to drugs. They turn to people who realize they're vulnerable and exploit them.

Kelly Holmes, executive director of Resource Assistance for Youth (RAY), a non-profit organization that works with youth in Winnipeg, also noted that poverty was a cause of vulnerability. She adds that the combination of youth homelessness and poverty constitutes the greatest risk and challenge to at-risk youth.

KELLY HOLMES: I think 24/7 opportunities and safe spaces can help them exit. If they know that they have somewhere to go. I think that, you know, more services, even if they are daytime services, that they are steeped in harm reduction and the understanding of what we're dealing with. I think less systemic barriers. Like minimum wage should be increased, and the EIA rate should be increased because it's really hard to make a hundred dollars in a night in the sex trade, and then not being able to make that after four days of work at Tim Horton's. It doesn't make any good financial sense. And you don't have to be a genius to figure that out. I mean, we've had kids here that, you know, "Why would I want to work at McDonald's when I have to work five hours, when all I have to do is run down the street to unload this pot, and I'm making fifty dollars?" We're setting up kids to go towards crime because it's more lucrative. So, we have to look at that. So, equitable jobs – we have look at EIA increases. Minimum wage. I mean, the other piece to that is wait times for treatment, counselling services, and supported transitions from off the street into mainstream society. All of the kids that I've come across in the last fourteen years all have skills. And they may be using it for the powers of evil, but they're still skills. If we can take those skills and turn it into mainstream economy skills, we've won.

Of all the participants in the research for this book, Ms. Holmes most clearly articulated the missed opportunities to assist young people to develop skills for making a living outside of the sex industry.

Friederike Von Aweden is a nurse who works with women involved in the sex industry, through anti-trafficking programs, Klinic Community Health, and New Directions and its program TERF. Like Ms. Holmes, Ms. Von Aweden identified housing and poverty as critical risk factors for children and women.

FRIEDERIKE VON AWEDEN: What could be done to prevent it [sexual exploitation] is to end child poverty, to end unplanned pregnancies, too. We can't change history but we could change inequalities. Those are things that are long term. They're very upstream. But I think, really, by the time we see youth, there's usually something – even though we don't know the women by the time they enter the TERF program – there is usually something very obvious why they are so vulnerable, such as a learning disability. Housing is huge. I would say 60 to 70 per cent of women at TERF have problems with housing and that issue is the springboard for re-engaging in behaviours because it's so difficult to cope with living with someone who exploits you or being offered drugs or trauma, anything like that. I'm not convinced that money is what will make a difference. I think it's childcare, not separating women from their children. Putting a lot of support into places like the mothering project that provides very unstructured support that's not, you know – we often have programs that you only qualify [for] if you meet these criteria, right? But if we have very flexible open programs that help women where they want to go – Education is huge. I think we undercapitalize on [it].

What Ms. Von Aweden said is worth repeating: "housing is huge," and she estimates that up to 70 per cent of the survivors she works with have housing troubles.

Rosemarie Gjerek of Klinic also emphasizes the role that service providers can play in helping people who are struggling to escape the sex industry where the barriers are compounded by poverty and lack of hope for the future. She maintains that people enter the sex industry because they see no other options for them to survive and to succeed in life.

ROSEMARIE GJEREK: I think poverty is the root of all evil. It's people making money off of other people. If you have a choice, if you have options, if you have that, then, you know, if I need to have a place to sleep, if I need food, I need to take care of my kids … Minimum wage is not going to necessarily make that happen. I think things like, just again, helping families be those environments that help kids develop. To have trauma-informed care providers and counsellors and recognizing those cycles that can continue because of that pain that we can carry. I think it's absolutely looking at … resources to really support people in their journey out. And so, hearing from women who talk about the fifth, sixth, and seventh time they tried to get out was just how difficult it is. We need to understand this better and provide resources in a different way. Not in a way that's comfortable for us, but in a way that reflects the needs of the individual.

Ms. Gjerek notes, as did the other participants, that poverty is linked to the lack of opportunities that young people encounter in their communities. She also stressed that services need to be provided in a way that is useful for survivors. This might mean, as she points out, that service providers need to be client centred in providing services in a way that is convenient for recipients rather than for service providers.

Jane Runner of TERF also talked about the importance of youth having access to a safe place to live, and how the fundamental element in improving their lives is money.

JANE RUNNER: Drug trafficking and all that kind of activity comes out of oppression and people struggling and people needing to find a way to get money. So, if there was money to really focus in on poverty and helping build strong communities, and, certainly for Indigenous communities, have a good chunk of that, to get them back to land that's going to work for them. And where they have opportunities for economic growth, you know, for their kids to be educated. We really do have to deal with that kind of poverty.

And not all sex trade and that stems from that [poverty and oppression] because, again, there's a lot of, you know, middle-class, different types of families that get involved. I don't know. It's never going to stop. You know, that's such a big question. But as long as we keep educating and people understand and people stop judging and stop racism, and those "-isms," right? As a country, we just really need to keep at it. Maybe with our new prime minister [Justin Trudeau] we'll get a little further ahead.

Similarly to Jane Runner's point, another survivor, Grace, stated that what is needed is "equal opportunities for women to not have to use their vagina to support their families."

Ndinawe's child and youth care program, run in coordination with Winnipeg's Red River Community College (RRCC), is a job preparedness program that my respondents described as effectively helping sex industry survivors prepare for job placements. Ndinawe's program basically surrounds people with resources so they can successfully complete the child care certificate program at RRCC. One wonders: why couldn't this be done with other programs? MLA Andrew Swan, another who believes we need to provide better job creation to give people improved opportunities, responded to this question:

ANDREW SWAN: In many cases, if women who are being sexually exploited have kids, what do they know how to do? Well, we wouldn't agree with all their parenting choices, but they know how to look after kids. If you were to tell somebody that we would help them get to a place where they could go and be a childcare worker: "You're not going to make a ton of money. It's going to be thirteen, fourteen dollars an hour. But how much money are you making if you're out on the street? And you've got to give money to your pimp and you're using drugs. Your take-home pay is not going to be much different from that, if at all." That's one example. You think, "Well, if somebody hasn't had a lot of formal education, they've suffered all these traumas, they have all these issues, what can they do?" I mean, frankly, most of them do a decent job looking after their own kids. Maybe we find a way to help them look after other people's kids in a field where we always need more workers, where there is a fairly short and basic way to train people up. That's just, that's one example of something maybe people can do. But you talk to some experiential people who've gone on to do all kinds of things, they would say, "Well, why are you just limiting people to being childcare workers?" I'm not. I think we've got to be practical though, and if we're trying to turn people around and get them back doing something positive, we want to be able to give them a clear path to do that.

Here Mr. Swan touches on a theme that Kelly Holmes initially brought up, that society is not recognizing and expanding on the skills and talents sex industry survivors might have. Not everyone wants to become a childcare worker. We can assign some responsibility for lack of employment options to government policy and programs: Levasseur et al. (2016) found that governments in Canada tend to provide gender-biased support for skilled trade education and development, continuing to favour men for several trades. The 2017 Canadian federal budget, for example, did not prioritize the creation of a broader range of career options for women. As well, Cattapan et al. (2017) analysed that federal budget and found that it fails to address the unpaid work that falls mostly on women, as well as the structural social conditions that continue to exclude the female half of Canada's population from many occupations.

Jay Rodgers, Deputy Minister of Manitoba's Department of Families, was at the time I interviewed him the executive director of Marymound, which provides services for exploited youth. Like others, he highlights how poverty contributes to reduced opportunities for young people and to their exploitation in the sex industry.

JAY RODGERS: From my perspective, the best thing that could happen in Canada wouldn't necessarily be specific to this issue [sexual exploitation] but would just be something that would address a lot of the issues that we end up seeing, and I think there's two things. I've always believed in things like guaranteed annual income because so many of the problems that we see here are related to families not being able to have enough resources to care for themselves. I'm a big believer that there are very few really bad parents. They're just parents who don't have the skills or resources to care for their kids. So, if we were able to have greater redistribution of the wealth that this country has, there's lots of research to show that families, if they have access to resources, are healthier, there is better outcomes for their kids.

The early childhood investment mentioned by Mr. Rodgers is a theme that came up repeatedly in the interviews I conducted; ideally, it would set children up to be resilient, less vulnerable to exploitation, and successful in their career choices.

This research contributes to our understanding that poverty and lack of opportunities are a root cause of people selling themselves in the sex industry for survival. My participants referred to "survival sex" as performing sex acts in exchange for the basic necessities of food and shelter. Shelter in particular can literally mean survival in northern climates such as Winnipeg, where cold winter conditions can badly injure or kill an improperly dressed person within minutes. Inadequate or no housing can lead women and girls to adopt the easiest available path to survival: performing sex acts for money. Therefore, it often takes multiple attempts for women to escape, if they make it out at all. While the complexity of poverty reduction economics is beyond the scope of this book, the fundamental idea of reducing poverty and providing other opportunities for young people to earn a living and obtain safe housing seems to be at the root of any solution to the problem. Some have pushed for a minimum guaranteed income for all Canadians, which might alleviate some social problems related to poverty ("Guaranteed $20K," 2014).

My research participants consistently reported a direct correlation between being placed in the care of CFS and later exploitation in the sex industry. Kerri Irvin-Ross, CFS minister at the time of this research and a trained social worker who worked in social services before entering politics, concurs:

KERRI IRVIN-ROSS: Well, I think the turning point for some youth that I am familiar with was the day that they were apprehended and removed from their family. And they might have been a year old. And then moved from foster home to foster home. That's kind of the context that I will answer this question in. That's kind of the turning point. I believe the sense or the lack of belonging and identity and how that manifests itself in individuals and children and youth around mental health and addictions. And no coping skills because they haven't had that unconditional support and love and stability because of multiple moves in the foster care system. I think that we have to do a way better job of preventing kids from coming into care. And that when they come into care, we need to be able to provide them with more stable opportunities.

As Ms. Irvin-Ross pointed out, coming into care at a very young age often removes the opportunity for children to have a supportive family network that is so important in their resistance to exploitation. As such, entry into care is often a critical juncture in youth's becoming vulnerable to predators and getting coaxed into the sex industry.

Marie, a survivor of sex trafficking who now works in an NGO assisting others to leave the sex industry, draws a more direct connection between being in CFS care and being vulnerable to sex trafficking and exploitation.

MARIE: Seventy-six percent of all females in CFS care end up being prostituted or exploited after they enter the system. Why? Because they are being taken from their home and placed in a stranger's home and being treated as such. There's no sense of belonging there. CFS should be putting resources in the home, and not the support worker that comes in once a week. If the parent has issues with addiction, then remove the parent, keep the kids in the home and add a support worker instead of removing the kids and putting them in a locked facility or a group home, which is just a pre-institution to a bigger one like jail.

Marie states that young girls are rendered vulnerable when they are placed in CFS care because removing family structure and supports can exacerbate their problems. She describes, as did several participants, how children with issues are often placed into a situation where people who fully understand their vulnerability prey on them, and stresses that resources should be put into the home rather than removing the child from it.

Grace, another survivor, addresses placement within CFS, suggesting that the causes of youth's underlying issues are often not understood by the people around them.

GRACE: Yeah, I really honestly feel that Child and Family Services needs to be a little bit more fucking mindful of where they place children, right? Like, no, first of all no one ever asked why I was misbehaving.

No one ever said, "Why are you so angry?" Maybe you should ask the kids that are having a fucking temper tantrum. Like, I wasn't acting out because I wanted to be a rude kid. I was traumatized with being raped at the age of eleven. I don't know. I just feel like if my child right now at the age of twelve or eleven started smoking pot and drinking alcohol in excess, I would think, what is wrong? That is not a normal behavioural development for children, and no one ever asked, what was wrong?

Survivors like Grace and Marie point out essential gaps in the system, such as the need for more training for staff and social workers to ensure they recognize the indicators of sexual exploitation and have the tools to intervene appropriately.

Chelsea Jarosiewicz is the manager of the Girls Crisis Stabilization Unit (CSU) at Marymound, and formerly a placement social worker with CFS. She holds similar views, among them that the child's removal from the home and placement in a facility can create new problems: young people wind up in crisis and are vulnerable because, among other factors, they lack a sense of belonging.

CHELSEA JAROSIEWICZ: The youth that I worked with have been anywhere from – the youngest I can remember was eleven, up to seventeen. So, I'm trying to think of the young ones. For me, from my knowledge, what's mostly gotten them into it has been that lack of belonging, peer pressure, problems at home, unhappy with the system and CFS and their placement, and frequently getting involved in gangs, and to me that's sort of the turning point, unfortunately. It happens a lot in CFS, which is really sad to think. A lot of our kids get put into a place and don't see their family, lack of a sense of belonging, and you know they need to be with somebody. They easily get preyed on at that point, the most vulnerable. I think what needs to change, needs to happen within the field of social work [is] looking at our apprehensions. Can we focus more on prevention of that? Family. Keeping families together. Can we put resources in to ensure kids can stay at home with their families? What I see a lot is that kids get taken away from their homes. And they just don't understand why and they run away to go back to their homes. And at that point they get really lost. So, I think prevention is key in keeping families together and even educating young girls and young families from a young age.

Ms. Jarosiewicz strongly suggests, as does Marie, that it is more effective to place resources into the home to improve the family support system than to remove children from the home and their kinship network. She added that keeping a child in the home environment might reduce the runaway behaviour that leads to increased risk of exploitation by sexual predators.

Constable Andrea Scott is a member of the WPS Missing Persons Unit, working with exploited and high-risk youth with a high incidence of runaway behaviour. She illustrates the increased dangers of the runaway behaviour that often follows a child's removal from the home and placement in foster care or group homes.

ANDREA SCOTT: I think once you start getting bounced around in CFS – and I'm going to say CFS because that's the majority of the people that we deal with – some do go missing from home. But the majority we have are from group homes, from shelters, used to be from the hotels. Once they start being more inclined to be on the street, they get more involved in addictions, and the people that they hang out with. And I think once they really get into CFS and into different homes, multiple different homes with kind of no stability and no sense of home, that's a really big turning point, I think.

Constable Scott makes the important point that placements often lead to other placements and even more instability, resulting in higher-risk behaviours such as drug and alcohol abuse for youth.

WPS constable Trevor Bragnalo, an RCMP officer for several years in Thompson, Manitoba, doing counter-exploitation work, highlights challenges in the CFS system, which has few resources for runaway and exploited youth and so constantly turns to the police to look for missing children.

TREVOR BRAGNALO: When I called Winnipeg Police, they're like, "Oh, yeah? We have 110 missing kids tonight?" I'm, like, "How's that even possible?" Like, that's crazy. Then I thought, "Wait a second, Winnipeg's a city of 800,000, right? But do you have police officers looking for every single kid every single second?" You can't. It's not logistically possible to do it, you know? But then why are these kids running away? Like, because they hate their group homes. So yeah, that needs to be rectified ... Sometimes these girls, when they are taken into the CFS system, if there's something that could be done to educate them. Say, "Look, like Winnipeg isn't Pukatawagan. Winnipeg is a dangerous city, and there's people here that are going to pretend to be your friend. They're going to befriend you –."

Constable Bragnalo discussed the high demands placed on the police when they are continually asked to look for runaway youth from group homes and CFS facilities. He sees this situation as rooted in a lack of resources in the CFS system for high-risk youth in care; for lack of other options, group homes and foster parents call the police.

Kelly Dennison, a WPS inspector with many years of experience working with exploited women and youth, describes the significant strain placed on the police by child welfare systems.

KELLY DENNISON: One thing that comes out loud and clear to me is the relationship with Child and Family Services and missing persons and sexually exploited youth. I think there's a direct relationship between those youths that are constantly missing and reported to a police service as missing and those youths that are involved in being sexually exploited. And to look at them as two different things, I think is a mistake, because it's the same issue. We've got girls right now, Bob, I can tell you – and you know. You've seen the queue [the backlog of pending police service calls]. You've got five missing persons calls. Four of them are for habitual runaway kids. And those habitual runaway kids are all at very high risk of being exploited. Four out of five. So, there's a direct correlation, a direct relationship, I believe, between missing and sexually exploited youth in our city.

Inspector Dennison highlights, as did many of my interviewees, the high correlation between runaway behaviour and the child's vulnerability to exploitation.

Liz Pilcher (WPS superintendent) adds that there is a lack of accountability in the child welfare system, among the people who are charged with the care of vulnerable youth.

LIZ PILCHER: I think that attending school is huge for these kids. A lot of them, once they get into care, aren't attending school. There's really nothing done to cause them to go to school. There's talk that we do have truancy officers, but I'm really not sure what they do. So the educational system, I think, can play into this, and it's again that collaborative effort among a number of systems to really start getting engaged when these kids are young because that's when they're going to start delving into drugs and alcohol.

Part of the reason youth become vulnerable in CFS care, according to Superintendent Pilcher, is the lack of oversight of school attendance. She emphasized that youth are more vulnerable when they are younger and that children as young as eleven years old are being preyed on in the sex industry. Her observation of the need for more accountability among agencies points to the need for all of the stakeholders to be part of the solution. This is consistent with the findings of Prothrow-Stith and Spivak (2004) in Boston, where they found great success by engaging multiple sectors in working together to combat violence among young African American men.

Mandy Fraser, who works with sex industry survivors in the Dream Catcher program at Klinic Community Health, describes the cycles of substance abuse and selling sex, and some of the dynamics of why it happens and how it starts.

MANDY FRASER: So when you learn that at a young age it becomes the easy way to live, you know. And no judgment there whatsoever. I can totally appreciate that. So, I think getting introduced to drugs and then being addicted to drugs and then needing to support it and get fast money. It also can be part of the culture of street life or of gang involvement where it's just normal to buy and sell hard drugs and sex trade is just there as an option. And then it's a cycle. So, you're going out and blowing these strange men. And then you can't do that sober. And you need to get high to get that out of your head, the smells, the tastes, all the memories, and let alone the violence that you know. You know what, I'm going to turn that around – the violence that men are inflicting on these women. And those women are trying to survive. That doesn't just go away. It's a cycle of numbing and coping, and just trying to avoid the reality of what you've been through.

Ms. Fraser underscores that traffickers do not necessarily pluck girls off the street. The girls are made vulnerable by the absence of support structures at home, physical and substance abuse, and lack of resilience. These human needs and the resultant vulnerability to predators were described earlier (see also Comack et al. 2009; Totten, 2009). Here is how Kaitlin, a survivor, recounts her experience in the sex industry.

KAITLIN: The very first guy I remember – we were standing on Higgins. And I remember I was asking [another girl], "How do I stand?" She told me, "Stick your head forward and your leg, and hold your hip." And I remember I was doing that. And all of a sudden this guy came driving by. I know he was Italian. He was this old Italian guy. And he told us to jump in. And she jumped in the front, and I jumped in the back. He goes, "How old is she?" And she was looking at him, and, I don't know, she was playing him, rubbing his leg. And she was like, "Why? What do you like?" He said, "How young is she?" And she told him I was twelve. And he looked at me and said, "Is she bald?" She said, "Yea." And he said, "Okay, yeah, I'll take her." Like I was a piece of lunch meat or something. He asked her, "How much do you want?" She said, "Just give me $80." So, he gave her $80. But she said, "I'm coming with you guys." 'Cause I guess he thought she was gonna get out of the car. I was wondering – I wondered if they knew each other? Like if he'd done this with her before, like with another younger girl? So, I remember we went to the Holiday Inn on McPhillips. It used to be there. And we went there. And he gave me $240, and he told me, "Don't tell her." He said, "Here, keep this to yourself." And I remember like, you know, what happened in the hotel. And she was sitting outside in the hallway. And then after, he just dropped us off. I remember that it was gross. And I remember I didn't like the way it made me feel after. And I remember that we ended up getting high and drinking. And that was the first guy, the very first john.

In Kaitlin's case the traffickers recognized and took advantage of a vulnerable child, knowing she had no familial support and would be susceptible to substance abuse. They got her addicted to crack cocaine, which can happen rapidly, after only a few uses. They made her feel like she belonged, promised her money, and made her feel ashamed of her behaviour so she would not want her family to know, ensuring she quickly became entrenched in the sex industry subculture. This is a very common path, one repeatedly described by survivors I interviewed. These stories are significant because embedded in them are the turning points where intervention and prevention might have occurred. They also shed light on the structural oppression that might have been reduced to make the victims more resistant and less vulnerable to exploitation.

Some youth are recruited and groomed right out of group homes. Grace, another survivor, describes how critical it is for social workers to be trained and aware of indicators of sexual exploitation:

GRACE: OK, so I was raped at age of eleven. And it caused me to be really erratic, and I started drinking a lot. My mom was unable to cope with that and so placed me in the care of CFS under a VPA [voluntary placement agreement] in hopes that I would change focus and go back to being how I was prior to that rape that I experienced. I was really young. I didn't know what to do. I had nobody to talk to about it. Rape wasn't really something that was even in my mind to understand or comprehend. And my mom didn't have the supports. And I didn't have any knowledge about where to go and how to get help. It was just very shaming and dirty. So, I was placed into a short-term group home. And I was angry. And it didn't matter who tried to help me and support me, I was mad. And it just kind of spiralled out of control. I was living in a group home just up on Margaret and Salter over by Kildonan Park. And there was another youth there who AWOL'ed, so unplanned absences. It started off as very harmless. Like we were hanging out downtown, drinking Stone Cold two-litre beers, right? At this point I'm twelve, and then there was this about-sixteen-year-old youth. I can't even recall her name, but I remember what she looks like. We were standing on the corner of Ellice and Spence right by the university. There is a restaurant right there on the corner. And she was like, "I'll be right back, guys." And she hopped in a car, and then came back with eighty dollars. I was like, "How do you do that?" And she said, "Oh, you just go with them and have sex." And so I thought at that point, "I've already been promiscuous and abusing substances so I didn't have any care." So, I jumped in the next car that came. And then it just kind of escalated for years until I was really badly beaten by a young adolescent female who was pregnant. So, I guess, from the age of twelve to fifteen, I was exploited in street work.

Grace voices a theme raised by many of the survivors I interviewed, that no one understood what she was going through and therefore no one intervened effectively to help her. If people around her had understood Grace's situation and if effective resources were accessed, she could have been helped without placing her in a group home, where she became more vulnerable to exploitation.

Patricia Haberman, the manager of Rose Hall, a group home run by Marymound for high-risk teenage girls, describes themes similar to those Grace discusses, but from the social worker's point of view.

PATRICIA HABERMAN: This is just from my experience and what I've seen. And I'll just give you an example. That young lady I was talking about being entrenched, we're attempting to have discussions with her to kind of change her thinking because right now she's glorifying it. You know, "Look at these nice boots I got. And I got my nails done at this fancy salon." And, "Look at all my fancy makeup and my new bras and panties," and whatever. Coming home and bragging to staff and to the girls. She actually calls me "mom" in the group home, so "Mom, come and see all my new stuff." We're very sensitive and gentle around it, and we have our own sort of guidelines around that. Like we know where this stuff is coming from, and she's not listening to any of it.

This is awesome that she's getting all these new things – that's what's in her mind. So, we're trying to help her to switch that mentality – that what you're doing is hurting you, inside and out. Just from that instance, I think that's the turning point, and having the supports in place for someone.

Ms. Haberman articulates the difficulties of dealing with children who are entrenched because they are being groomed and led to believe the sex industry provides a glamorous life with many rewards.

Similarly, Constable Liz Kaulk, who is with the RCMP Exploited Persons Pro-active Strategy (EPPS) team, attached with Project Devote, Manitoba's Missing and Murdered Task Force, highlights that family dynamics are important and there are opportunities to intervene to prevent trafficking of young girls.

LIZ KAULK: Like the girls I've spoken to on the street level in Winnipeg do say – when I asked them when they began working in the sex trade – when they were youth at thirteen years old, fourteen years old some of them. Some of them have been there for ten years or more and it's kind of shocking, what has happened. Why can't something be done in that time or any time in the continuum? But it starts young, and they see no way out of it. It starts with families. And you see a lot of the niche or pros screens [the RCMP records/reporting system] come up with domestic violence in their youth. You'd go to that home for domestic violence. And then you go to that home for a runaway youth. You go to that home for all the criminal activity. And then, of course, addictions are huge. And that is a huge issue from youth. It starts way back when they're young as well, and just continues on the whole way. So, it's complicated for a lot of people. But it certainly starts young.

WPS sergeant Cam MacKid asserts that resources should be devoted to incorporating more collaborative and multidisciplinary approaches to protect children. He articulates some of the challenges of working with multiple agencies with different organizational cultures and perspectives, in tandem with limited resources.

CAM MACKID: There's no barriers within our service, whatsoever. We've got phenomenal support from our street-level guys, through our unit and right to the executive. Whatever we want to try – if we think it's going to help – we've got support in our organization. Absolutely no barriers. Within other organizations – I mentioned a little bit, there, with our partnership with child protection – there are different cultures.

A lot of it comes back to liability. There might be a seventeen-year-old girl on Backpage [a commonly used social media platform] for child protection. That's a child. She's under eighteen. That's a child needing protection. That's an emergency for them. For us, if we've engaged with that same woman fifteen to twenty times and she's basically told us to fuck off every time, at some point that can't be a priority for us because we do have other priorities. And our priorities don't match with other agencies. That's just one example that by and large we're all after the same thing. We've got very good relationships with child protection. They always want a little bit more from us. They'd like us to sit in the car with them and drive around. Child protection would love full-time officers. It comes down to resources.

Sergeant MacKid asks an important question: who is responsible for protecting a high-risk youth? Child welfare agencies point fingers at the police and say it is a legal issue of people breaking the law. Police point back at child welfare and say these are child protection issues, not legal ones. No one is pointing fingers at the health and education systems, yet they surely have a stake in the outcome of these issues. Ultimately, it becomes a question of how we can collectively share responsibility for high-risk youth, rather than deferring risk and assigning blame. As the African proverb states, "It takes a village to raise a child."

Participants were asked if there is a critical turning point for youth when they enter the sex industry and if so, what could be done to prevent it. The stories were insightful and contribute to our knowledge about youth vulnerability to exploitation. Generally, participants stressed that there is not one specific risk factor, but that every case is different. This view was articulated by Daphne Penrose, the acting executive director of Winnipeg CFS:

DAPHNE PENROSE: So I think that there's no way to answer this question – Is there a critical event or turning point for youth? – because what I've come to learn is that every single child is unique and every single child's entry into the sex trade for them is unique. And what you would consider to be a turning point for each child is going to be very different. And it can, again, look like mom allowing uncle to have sex with her child for drugs, and the child may not even know that's the turning point for them. They may see the turning point as coming into care, but that's not the turning point. I think that every story I've heard from experiential folks has been different about what's worked for them to exit the sex trade. I think, going back to the coordinated response, is that there isn't a one-size-fits-all. There is no one answer because if one of us had the one answer there's not one of these organizations that wouldn't do it. But we don't have one answer for every child or adult that's exploited or in the sex trade. We don't have one answer, and for those folks who think they have the answer, they are becoming part of the problem.

Kelly Dennison's view is consistent with Ms. Penrose's, but he believes there is a common starting point: when a child hits rock bottom, when a child feels helpless and thinks s/he has no other options. Inspector Dennison points out that youth often have no place else to go. He makes the important point, one raised in several ways throughout the research for this book, that a young girl does not make a conscious decision to engage in the sex industry; that engagement normally results from lack of opportunities to do something else.

KELLY DENNISON: I guess from my experience going back – You know what, Bob? The critical event or turning point was nowhere else to go. That's what we saw so much. The girls that I dealt with in my career that are on the street, they never intended to be there. They didn't wake up and go, "I'm going to be a prostitute today." That never happened. They may have woken up one morning and didn't know where they were. They may be having a drug problem or an addictions issue, with no money, no way to feed that addiction, and they found themselves on the street. Whether they were exploited by an individual – which is what we see now – for drugs or alcohol or whatever. So, I think their turning point was, it was almost rock bottom. These girls had nowhere else to go, nothing else to do. Well, they need help. Exiting the sex trade, to me, I liken it to somebody who's an alcoholic, or drug addicted, or a lot of other situations they find themselves in, that they don't have the ability – once they've gotten to that point, whether they've been exploited to that point or not – to get out of that vicious circle. They need some interventions.

Cam MacKid describes children's vulnerability to sexual predators in a similar way, but also stresses that a child's rock bottom is affected by a large number of variables. He outlined the typical scenario:

CAM MACKID: I think that it's almost like the death by a thousand needles. It starts at a young age in a vast majority of cases. The parents, from a young age, they aren't doing what they should be doing. And the kids either end up in a house [where] there's abuse, there's addiction issues, there's abandonment there, either in that environment.

Or, [they are] taken from that environment or put into another environment where now you don't have that parental care there. There's still someone who's well-intended in most cases, trying to guide this child, but without that parental structure there, they're not going to get the same attention. I think the kids understand that, and it leads to running away and a lack of barriers. And I don't think there's a single defining moment where this happens, especially if you're being groomed by one of these predators that I mentioned. It happens very ·slowly. And a lot of girls, even once they're being exploited for several years, they won't even realize that it's even happening. And they'll think they've had control this whole time. So, they don't really even see the big picture.

Similarly, Constable Andrea Scott of the Missing Persons Unit highlighted the importance of family connections in keeping young people off the streets. Constable Scott stressed that these youth need attention and something to keep them busy and engaged. That view aligns with Liz Pilcher's comments about the need to have youth actively involved in school. The whole debate around what type of facilities could help, if they should be secure or open, or whether the rural-urban dichotomy makes a difference, sheds light on the complexity of the issue and the need to tackle it in a multimodal and multilevel intervention process.

Kelly Holmes (RAY) outlines how homelessness makes youths vulnerable to being exploited and trafficked by unsavoury characters, and makes the connection among sexual exploitation, poverty, and lack of opportunities.

KELLY HOLMES: Well, again, my framework from which I work is homelessness. And so, I see anything that happens on the street as dangerous. Sex trade is part of that. Gangs are another part of that. Violence is part of that. You know, drug dealing and getting involved in serious kinds of addictions or people or whatever. It's all part of that. And it's always been my understanding that we have about two years from the time they exit a place of support to hitting the street where they get into real trouble. Often in this world that we know, Bob, kids are being discharged from jail, from child welfare and jail, on the same day. They're leaving to nothing, without a plan. And so they show up to places like mine, that is only really open until ten at night. And they don't have a clue about where to begin. And so these types of kids in scenarios are all the breeding ground for future exploitation of any kind. They're that vulnerable. And it could be, "Look, I'm hungry. I will give you a blowjob for a Subway sandwich. I will do whatever. I will bargain with you because I'm that bloody desperate." And then they're marked. And they're set up to, you know, continue on and fail. So I think the other thing is to – and again, this is more societal – but youth and children born into abject poverty often are set up from the get-go. And, I mean, in this city, as you're well aware, we're talking about three generations of welfare, maybe third- generation gang members.

That many exploited youth have developmental challenges is well known among practitioners, yet the topic is under-represented in the literature on youth well-being. Most interviewees did not mention this issue, perhaps because they were not specifically asked about it. One exception is Ed Riglin, an RCMP sergeant who has dedicated much of his professional career to counter-exploitation work. He considers mental health issues/developmental challenges to be another major correlate of a child's vulnerability to exploitation, and so the health system must be involved in multidisciplinary work around the issue.

ED RIGLIN: In child abuse cases, child exploitation cases, often I'm dealing with a girl that is fifteen or sixteen years old, but is only functioning as an eight-year-old and not that wise in their concepts. Sometimes twelve years old, but only functioning as a five- or six-year-old. They are exploiting them because of that. They're exploiting these girls, knowing they have that mental deficiency. They're not stupid. These guys know what they're doing.

We need that component at the table so any time we're going to put together – say they say, "Okay, Bob, you guys are going to put together a unit and a strategy to deal with Winnipeg. You guys create a hub." If we had a hub around the table here, we would have probation services, social services. We would have the abuse investigator and abuse teams from the social network represented, the abuse units. We would have mental health services from the province and/or private, whatever. We would have them all sitting around that table and we would actually put a case on that table and look at [it] from all aspects.

Once a predator identifies a vulnerable individual, the next step is to manipulate that individual into the sex industry. The term for this in policing and social work circles, and among people who work with sexually exploited youth and women, is "grooming." Grooming occurs when a person psychologically manipulates someone in a position of less power into participating in the sex industry. The approach can be subtle and convincing, and people are often unaware that they are being manipulated until it is too late: they are already indebted to the pimp and are being exploited.

Member of Parliament Joy Smith (retired in 2016) of Manitoba has worked with sexual exploitation and trafficking survivors across Canada. She articulates the dynamics of psychological manipulation, or grooming, used by sex traffickers.

JOY SMITH: The criminal is to blame. Nobody else. And for parents to understand that their kids can make mistakes, parents can make mistakes. It's called life. But when a criminal targets your kid and makes sure they're gang-raped and makes sure they make money off them – . And how they do it is they hang out where kids hang out. And what they do is target someone who they think is vulnerable. They prefer virgins. They get a higher price. They prefer the younger the better. They prefer someone who is very vulnerable and needy. And every child fits that description at some point in their life. Why? Because they're children. So let's say a young child doesn't fit in at school for whatever reason, they would be a target, particularly if they're beautiful because beauty means a lot. But it's both a heinous and insidious crime because the perpetrators come on as friends to their potential victims and they gain their trust, and often they become their boyfriends. The young girls get gold necklaces, get nice clothes, and they get taken to parties. Gradually [the perpetrators] introduce them to a drug. Many are introduced to drugs that they don't even know how bad they are because they're told, "Oh, it's nothing. You'll just enjoy the feeling. I do it. You do it, too." And so they have a sense of belonging. The tragic thing is once they have them hooked then they start moving them. It can be from different parts of town. It can be into the country. It can be into another city. And they have routes all across the country. And these traffickers then work very hard to make a lot of money out of these girls.

Smith's description accords with Diane Redsky's account of the life cycle of grooming, which she bases on twenty years of working with women in the sex industry and the 160 survivors interviewed in her study (CWF, 2014). Ms. Redsky describes the life cycle of a sex industry career as follows:

DIANE REDSKY: This is a very general description of what we learned with the task force on the stories that we heard from women – and we met with over 160 survivors of sex trafficking and heard their stories. And so what we learned is at the very beginning, as a child, there is some form of trauma happens. And this is not in all cases, but there is a consistent theme that something happened when they were little, some kind of trauma – whether sexual, emotional, physical, spiritual – some kind of trauma. Then when they get to the age of thirteen, that made them vulnerable to exploiters or traffickers or pimps to recruit and lure them, and they do that in a variety of ways. But there's a certain point in time it moves from the honeymoon to the, you know, really reeling them in, to now you are going out. And the relationship changes to fear and shame. And so, you're thirteen. You are then considered a victim of child abuse under our current laws. Then when you turn eighteen, it is, you know, your society will often say these are now consensual prostitutes whereas they [society] don't recognize all of this abuse that happened before then. And that's a very a common story of women that are in the sex industry, that they started – thirteen is the average age.

When I first started doing this twenty years ago – working on the issue – the average age was sixteen. And so where it's younger and younger today. It's thirteen. Then they're trafficked from thirteen till about that they're twenty-three-ish, and twenty-three to twenty-five. And then they become of no value to a trafficker any more. They become of no value because they are most likely drug addicted. Or they are too old because the demand wants younger and younger girls. So they try to get girls to look younger and younger. And when they can't anymore then they become of no value.

Here, Diane Redsky describes how a young girl can be trafficked into the sex industry in as little as two days (see also CWF, 2014):

DIANE REDSKY: What we learned is that it's getting younger and younger. And the younger you get, then the more naive you are. And it's easier for them when you're younger. We heard stories of one of the girls from Winnipeg here. Hers happened over a weekend. Friday. By Sunday night she was in Calgary on the street. Like, that's how fast she went from fighting with her parents and being too embarrassed to go home because she was sexually assaulted that night to Sunday now being forced to be on the street in Calgary. So all of that can happen really fast, and to any girl. And as I said, there are other risk factors that can make them more vulnerable. And those exploiters and pimps are just good at picking out the vulnerability.

Jane Runner, executive director of TERF for over twenty years, is a leading Canadian advocate for developing resources for young women exiting the sex industry. She further describes the grooming process:

JANE RUNNER: So that turning point can be different for everybody, but it's usually at a point where they need to belong somewhere. And predators know that, right? You know, predators will look for that, and they know what to look for. They're quite well trained and educate themselves in how to look for the vulnerable people, right? So that's whether kids coming from up north to the city and just not having the right supports. It's for maybe one person who's got maybe everything – good supportive family – but something traumatic happens, and their life is just in chaos, and it can happen like that. Or we've seen situations where it takes a few months, where someone's getting groomed, someone's getting them ready, and turns them out. That's where you have the ability to maybe help stop it. So when it comes to preventing it, the more aware everybody is in a community that if they see something, you don't let it go.

Ms. Runner is suggesting there is a need for training among teachers and other professionals, which ties in with the findings of Prothrow-Stith and Spivak (2004) in Boston, who emphasized the need for practitioners to be trained to see and act on the early warning signs of youth vulnerability.

The multitude of factors discussed above lead to the question, how can we prevent sexual exploitation? A contemporary trend in research recognizes the importance of early investment in youth to prevent their later criminal involvement. Heckman et al. (2010), for example, found that every dollar spent to improve the education of children under five can potentially save up to seventeen dollars in their later usage of health, welfare, and justice dollars. This economic argument is a strong impetus for directing more money into early childhood development and education programs. Clearly there is potential for developing early warning systems, based upon known correlates such as child abuse, to identify and intervene with high-risk youth and prevent their exploitation in the sex industry. The idea of getting upstream and addressing the root causes of sex trafficking early is critical if trafficking is to be prevented. It is also an idea suggested by several contributors to this study, some of whose insights into the need to invest in prevention, in healthy families, and in creating a safer healthier start for all children are included in these pages.

Police superintendent (ret.) Bill Fogg stresses the need not only to invest in families early on – the need for well-thought-out early prevention strategies that provide resources to support healthy families – but also to ensure greater collaboration and information and resource sharing between agencies in their daily work.

BILL FOGG: I really do believe we need to invest in that front end, trying to make those healthy families and help those people all the way through. And prevention is the right way to do this. But we have a bunch of people right now who are already struggling – whether it's through addictions, or mental health problems, or gang affiliations, or involvement in the sex trade either as an exploiter or as an exploited person. But that can't come by redirecting other existing resources or existing money, because police departments, despite what people think, are basically minimally funded in the sense that there's structure and function that are set out by the courts and collective agreements and things. And we're already doing reasonably as much as we can do with what we have. So, to take on something like that takes on additional resources. And in my mind, that's one of the most important things that we could possibly do as society. We're talking about the future of this country and the ability to sustain our systems and population. And we need to get that right and we need to get it right now. And to not invest in this right now is a far greater crime than not investing in climate change or any of those other things. This is about our future and the future of our children in this country.

Shannon McCorry, a social worker/family liaison with Project Devote, also speaks of the need to identify families requiring resources and to intervene earlier.

SHANNON MCCORRY: I think there is a critical point, I think that part of what happens for children – it's just when families are struggling. I think we need to put the resources in right at the very beginning. So, when families are identifying that they're having problems and issues, we have to find a way to kind of be really support-heavy, and offering those families support. And I think sometimes what happens is there's – not necessarily in all cases – but when there is a breakdown within the family, and there's issues happening and maybe parents don't have the right resources to work with their kids to help to support them, then they're going out and becoming involved in the street gangs and all the different things that can lead down the path to sexual exploitation. So, I think that if we can catch kids when they're young and when parents are struggling and really put in resources, that could be a turning point for kids.

Rose, a senior Crown attorney with Manitoba Public Prosecutions with extensive experience in cases involving the sex industry, similarly endorses preventative measures.

ROSE: Manitoba is a front-runner, looking at it from a social services perspective. StreetReach has been effective. The difficulty, I think, though, with this area is that we're trying to fix something that is already broken. So, in my experience dealing with victims who are sexually exploited in the sex trade, typically they have escaped from somewhere else, right? So, in one of the cases that I prosecuted, the woman – my case involved her being procured at the age of eighteen, but she had been working sex trade since she was eleven years old. She started doing that because she had fled her home where she was being abused by an uncle ... So by the time people are trying to reach out to her, she'd already been exploited for a long time. Of course, once you're on the street at eleven, what happens – you get a drug addiction. And then you need things to feed that drug addiction. So, the efforts have to be at strengthening families and early intervention with children. That's to me where we really need to focus on as a society.

Rose highlights that better outcomes can be achieved through prevention-oriented resources as opposed to reactive strategies later on.

Christine Kun, a WPS sergeant who has worked with sex industry survivors for years, elaborates on the need to support families by providing resources for youth at younger ages.

CHRISTINE KUN: That's the hard part, right? Because, again, does it come down to, you know, as a police service, is it our responsibility to support families to provide them with the supports that they need in the community? That's where we say we work with agencies because we can't do it all, you know? So I think that there is a role for social agencies, but it comes down to how do you stop that? How do you teach people to be good parents? The people who have been good parents have had someone in their life – it doesn't mean their parents – but they've had someone in their life who has pointed them in the right direction, or who has placed value on them, or shown them that they can be more than what they were. And I know that, you know, based on my own experience and my own upbringing, and my own successes. So, I really think [the answer is] placing value on youth and giving them opportunities and broadening their horizons and, you know, opportunities, but supports that follow them because it's a life-long, you know, character trait. It's letting people know that that isn't normal, that that isn't okay, that you do have support, and I think it's a difficult challenge. I don't know how you start that, and I really don't know as a Police Service that it's something that we can achieve. We can strive to work with agencies in support of it, you know?

As Sergeant Kun notes, there is a challenge in determining whose role it is to support healthy families. This question is similar to one raised above, of who is responsible for child welfare. That responsibility, as I stated above, should be everyone's, rather than one particular agency's.

RCMP sergeant Ed Riglin also spoke of the need to do more prevention early on, including multisector collaboration and in-school programming involving the whole spectrum of stakeholder agencies in a multimodal and multilevel intervention process.

ED RIGLIN: Organized crime don't pick on the strong. They pick on the weak. They pick on the mentally challenged. They pick on those that are separated or falling out from their family, all those things. We have to tie these things together and go back to the thing that has to be a multi-agency, for lack of a better term, approach for them. We have to be in and educating at the school level. I think [this] is the best start because for the most part most kids have to go to school. But we need to be in there with teachers, the police, the social services, the NGOs, and putting into these children that "You're not alone. We are here. If there's a breakdown in your family, you can call us." Give them that information. All these kids, they don't have that information because you can't go into somebody's home and deliver that.

Gord Perrier is deputy chief of the WPS and has worked in several policing roles focused on counter-exploitation. He underlines the fact that offenders' behaviour also needs to be addressed by an intervention process.

GORD PERRIER: So I'm going to talk about the offender now, rather than the victim. And I, personally, like to talk about victimology a lot more, but you can't talk about victims unless you talk about offenders. I really believe that as well. So, about interrupting that [sexual exploitation], that often is about, to me, it's about a number of things. One is it's about providing security and health to individuals so they can move past if they're victimized, or [a second focus is] the person that's doing the victimizing. For instance, if the person is suffering from severe substance abuse and they're offending, they may have a sexual interest in children that they would not have acted on if they were not ... high on drugs or alcohol, where in that case their inhibitions have been lessened and now they're offending.

I'm not saying that's an excuse. I'm not discounting sexual interest in children, for instance, and not that this sexual interest in children would go away. But the event in itself may not actually happen. And that's where this gets to be a really complicated topic, if we're talking about offending and coming to it from that end [involving disinhibiting factors such as substance abuse]. Or, are we talking about people that have sexual interest in children and making that end disappear. Those are very different conversations and one may not actually even be possible. So I don't want to go that far. But in familial settings, it's about providing security. It's about providing education. It's providing substantive employment. And it might be treating those illnesses to treat the others. And then when those events occurred, now that family unit needs to heal.

Consistent with other participants' points of view, Jane Runner (executive director, TERF) emphasizes the need for awareness education and for providing resources at all levels in order to prevent the trafficking and exploitation of young people.

JANE RUNNER: We certainly need to do a lot more where the least amount of focus is on – in educating kids more, in supporting families more, so they don't get to that point of breakdown where kids are running away. That [being in school] in itself is reducing the amount of time that kids are running around the streets, getting either involved in drugs, or guys running around and luring them with money to get in their car and do whatever. So, those are the types of approaches that work where you can spend a lot of time either keeping kids in school plus keeping them active – sports, right? All those initiatives. They work, right? – if you're keeping kids busy and healthy and supporting the family.

Ms. Runner also echoed Deputy Chief Perrier's comments that offenders must be considered and offered resources.

There is an economic case to be made for prevention as well. DeRiviere (2005) studied the economic impacts of the sex industry in Manitoba and found that financial investments in preventive measures are far more effective than strategies that only respond reactively. Unfortunately, the stories of a significant number of my research participants substantiate the fact that we are still generally reactive. Prevention is a theme that threads throughout this book. Most if not all of the participants I interviewed noted that we need to intervene earlier and invest more resources upstream to prevent children from finding themselves in a position where they are vulnerable to exploitation. This finding supports previous research that indicates the need for early childhood development and upstream prevention (e.g., Heckman et al., 2010).

Below, I list the nine significant findings that emerged from my analysis of interviews conducted with experts, practitioners, and survivors concerning how young children become vulnerable to, and are trafficked and exploited in, the sex industry.

First, no child aspires to grow up and join the sex industry. A child becomes a sex seller usually as a last resort when other options are not available, and when a lack of basic human needs creates the need for survival at any cost. For example, one survivor, Ashley stated: "No child says when I grow up I want to be a prostitute." Most of the participants who now work as practitioners in various agencies assisting those involved in the sex industry saw survivors as victims rather than as criminals.

Second, children are being targeted at younger ages. The age of recruitment in the sex industry in Canada has dropped over the past ten years from sixteen to thirteen years of age. This has important implications for future intervention and prevention strategies that must include building resilience and support for families of youth at younger ages.

Third, being sexually exploited often correlates with earlier childhood abuse. My research participants emphatically stated that nearly all survivors in the sex industry were previous victims of childhood sexual assault and/or abuse. This finding supports existing literature that has described the correlation between childhood abuse and high chances of later sexual exploitation. My findings, along with those of previous research, have important implications for counter-sexual-exploitation intervention and prevention strategies that might include follow-up with child abuse victims and their families.

Fourth, children need to belong somewhere, even if it is in the sex industry. Children will seek the love they are missing in their families within the sex industry. Interviewees voiced a strong theme concerning childhood needs and how gangs and traffickers often fill the void that is created when a child perceives s/he is not getting the love and attention s/he needs at home. It is clear, from my research participants, that teenage girls need a sense of belonging and a strong male role model, and predators are often experts in identifying youth who are alienated and lack strong family connections and positive role models in their lives. This finding again has implications for potential intervention and prevention strategies, in particular around building stronger and more supportive and resilient families.

Fifth, children in care are at higher risk. Children in care of the state are at high risk of exploitation. My participants stressed that coming into the care of child protective services is perhaps the strongest warning sign of a child's vulnerability to exploitation. Some survivors even described how traffickers targeted them while they were living in a group home; sometimes they are recruited and preyed upon by the people they are living with, who are also connected with the sex industry. Survivors and practitioners that I interviewed stressed that more care must be devoted to how children are placed within group homes and foster placements.

Sixth, vulnerable youth are lost in the system. Participants described how youth are often lost in the cracks and gaps between service sectors. For instance, when youth chronically run away from foster and group home placements they are at high risk of sexual exploitation by pimps. However, it is often unclear who has responsibility for their safety. The implication is that the elements of the system are shifting liability and accountability when they could be acting collaboratively to solve the problem. This lack of ownership also overlays and corresponds with the lack of coordination and collaboration among all of the agencies that form the systemic response to sexual exploitation.

Seventh, the structural violence of poverty leads to vulnerability. Another strong theme that emerged from my participants is that poverty often leads to a lack of economic and educational opportunities, and that in turn can lead to young people becoming vulnerable to sexual exploitation by pimps and predators.

Eighth, the nexus between mental health issues and the sex industry needs further research. Several research participants emphasized that many sex industry survivors struggle with mental health challenges. This issue is under-represented in the literature and previous empirical research, and clearly is an important topic for future research, which could have a tremendous influence on collaborative agency policies and strategies to identify vulnerable at-risk youth and intervene before predators get to them.

These findings concerning mental health connect with the issue of youth "aging out" of the child welfare system, in which people, including sex industry survivors, are on the day they turn eighteen suddenly denied access to services that are only available to youth. Many youth, according to my interviewees, are developmentally delayed and cognitively challenged, operating mentally at a younger age. It is thus critical to shed light on this developmental vulnerability to stimulate further research on mental health challenges among youth in general and youth in care. Respondents also emphasize that it is important to encourage continuing services where it is beneficial for survivors to remain in particular programs.

Ninth, early childhood intervention and prevention is needed. There is a need for more early childhood investment in families and violence prevention. Participants stressed the need for commitment to invest more resources in violence prevention by supporting healthier families and in creating safer and healthier milieus for children. Most respondents stressed the need for more resources devoted to intervening in and providing support to families where violence and abuse have occurred.

This chapter reveals, through the stories of survivors, the connection between early sexual abuse and the likelihood of later sex industry trafficking of the abused child. The stories recounted by the survivors and practitioners I interviewed stressed that there are opportunities for intervention where early childhood sexual abuse has occurred. Perhaps a significant contribution of this book is to highlight that we need further research specifically into the warning signs and indicators of abused youth's vulnerability to sexual exploitation, in all its various forms, in order to intervene earlier to prevent it.

4 Violence against Canadian Indigenous Women and Girls

MARIE: Me and my friends, we all came from poor backgrounds; we all lived in the North End, my mom had severe addictions issues so a lot of the times there wasn't the basic needs at home so, when I found out my friends were doing it, just seemed to happen I guess. For me I think it was a lot easier for me because my dad was a pedophile so I already had that experience of being with older men so when I made the, well, I didn't really make a decision, when I was put into the sex it just seemed right at the moment because there is no other way to support myself. I wasn't old enough for welfare so that was my only means of obtaining clothing and stuff.

Marie's story is, tragically, not unlike the experience of many I interviewed for this book: born Indigenous, female, and in poverty, the cards are stacked against them from the start. As a member of the Poverty Reduction Council of Winnipeg, in late 2017 I participated in a blanket exercise, led by Jessica Dumas, a consultant providing awareness training on Indigenous issues in Manitoba. The exercise involved working through a script and playing the part of European settlers and Indigenous people; it is a very emotional and hands-on exercise that really drives home the impacts that colonization has had on Indigenous people. At the end, we had a round circle and I was so shaken that I cried, realizing that in many ways not much has changed. I started in policing in 1989, going to recruit class during the Aboriginal Justice Inquiry (Hamilton & Sinclair, 1991). It was a tough time, as Manitoba's justice system and police agencies were scrutinized and targeted for change to reduce racism and increase Aboriginal people's participation in justice systems. It was visceral for all of us in policing: one Winnipeg police inspector committed suicide on the evening before he was set to testify at the enquiry.

My first policing assignment was in Winnipeg's North End, which is where the city's largest Indigenous population is. Every second police call someone would be talking about their uncle "J.J.," referring to J.J. Harper, whose death during a police encounter, as well as the murder of Helen Betty Osborne, had kicked off the Aboriginal Justice Inquiry. For decades after the inquiry, and to the present day, much diversity training and cultural transformation has taken place; nowadays, at least, sexist or racist jokes and comments in the workplace would not be tolerated. What hasn't changed is the deplorable economic diversity that exists in our community. I have come full circle in my career, starting as a constable in the North End and now, in my twenty-ninth year, back to working the street, by choice, as a staff sergeant. I find myself back in those same homes I was in twenty-nine years ago, and not all that much has changed. So when we had a sharing circle to talk about the blanket exercise, I welled up; I had to say that extreme poverty, severe substance abuse, lack of opportunities, and unbelievably bad living conditions still exist. In a way, the sixties baby scoop is still going on, as Manitoba has over ten thousand children in care, the majority being Aboriginal. This is not a criticism of Child and Family Services: they have a tough job. Rather, it is a comment that we need to do something about the economic disparity that leads to so many troubled families. It may take a century to undo what it took a century to create, but in the meantime many people are suffering living conditions that, I have said many times, you cannot believe unless you see it with your own eyes. We have come a long way in Canada in reversing the impacts of colonization, but we still need a concerted effort focused on decolonization.

A growing body of literature describes the marginalization that Indigenous people have endured in Canada, including over-representation in the sex industry. Participants in my research raised significant themes around vulnerabilities that are created by the conditions on reserves and rural communities, and the dangers caused by migration of large numbers of Indigenous people into larger urban centres. I also asked each of the participants if existing programs are culturally sensitive. Their stories were diverse and contribute new knowledge on this topic.

Recent research by the government of Canada found that First Nations women and girls are four times more likely than mainstream Canadians to live in crowded conditions in homes that are in a state of ill repair (Mandel, 2016). A substantial body of research has confirmed that Indigenous communities in Canada are still suffering the impacts of colonization (Ham, 2014; Younging, 2009). A strong discourse about continuing marginalization of Indigenous people has also been long established in the literature, exposing their experience of higher crime, lower employment rates, and overall poor education completion in relation to Canada's mainstream population (Hallett et al., 2006).

Canada's residential school system was established in the early 1880s, and the last school was not closed until 1996. The residential schools and mass government adoption (seizure) of Indigenous infants in the 1960s were aggressive assimilation programs that have resulted in tragic disconnects in parenting skills for multiple generations of many families (CBC, 2008, 2011; Comack et al., 2009; Galley, 2009; McCracken & Michell, 2006). Similar systemic oppression is occurring in the United States among large African American and Hispanic populations with massive incarceration rates and broken families (Nebbitt et al., 2013).

Many of Canada's Indigenous people continue to live in marginalized conditions on reserves with inadequate drinking water and unreliable electricity sources (Lauwers, 2012). Indigenous youth suffer a higher rate of suicide and engage in more violent behaviours than any other Canadian ethnic and age group, especially on reserves, and some experts report that the problem will likely increase and possibly double in the next two decades (Paul, 2012; Totten, 2009). Lauwers (2012) attributes tragically increasing suicide rates on the reserves to a lack of emotional resilience, poor physical and social conditions, and the absence of perceived opportunities and hope among Indigenous youth.

McCracken and Michell (2006) explore the contemporary challenges of Indigenous people and find that they simultaneously face low incomes and poverty, as well as the persisting impacts of colonization and racism. Volkan (1997) outlines how traumas such as these can carry forward and affect the psyche of successive generations. A higher birth rate than any other Canadian ethnic group also exacerbates Indigenous people's future social challenges (Comack et al., 2009; Hallet et al., 2006).

Indigenous people are migrating in increasing numbers from impoverished reserves into poor neighbourhoods of Canadian cities (Norris et al., 1995). In the cities, street gangs often provide the identity and structure that children need and are not finding at home (Comack et al., 2009; Totten, 2009). As we have seen, my research participants confirmed that the same dynamic applies to the sex industry. The need for a sense of belonging and access to life's basic necessities of food, clothing, a bed to sleep in, and social interaction are often an acceptable trade-off for children who succumb to being sexually exploited.

Intervention and exit strategies for sexually exploited Indigenous girls must consider these deep-rooted transgenerational impacts, and culturally appropriate interventions.

The RCMP recently conducted research, based on case files gathered from police agencies across Canada, and concluded that between 1980 and 2012 there were 20,313 homicides across the country (about 923 per year), including 6,551 female homicide victims (32 per cent), of whom 1,017 (16 per cent) were Indigenous (RCMP, 2013, p. 9). The number of Indigenous female victims climbed from 8 per cent in 1984 to 23 per cent in 2012, while the number of non-Indigenous female victims remained constant (p. 9).

According to the RCMP study, Indigenous victims were also likely to be involved in illegal activities for financial support (18 per cent for Indigenous vs. 8 per cent for non-Indigenous); more likely to be unemployed (12 per cent for Indigenous vs. 8 per cent for non-Indigenous); more likely to be on social assistance or disability insurance (23 per cent for Indigenous vs. 9 per cent for non-Indigenous); and more likely to have substance abuse problems and to be under the influence of intoxicants at the time they were murdered (63 per cent for Indigenous vs. 20 per cent of non-Indigenous). As well, 12 per cent of Indigenous female homicide victims had known involvement in the sex industry (RCMP, 2013). This state of affairs is occurring in the context of ongoing unresolved economic and social disparity issues for Indigenous people, and a continuing movement around the related issue of missing and murdered Indigenous women (Oppal, 2012; Welch, 2014). The urgency of this issue is heightened by the tragic murders of several sexually exploited Indigenous youth in Manitoba (e.g., CBC, 2014a) and ongoing challenges Manitoba's child welfare system faces in fulfilling its mandate to protect children (Puxley, 2014).

Research by Farley et al. (2003) found that 52 per cent of women in the sex industry in Vancouver are Indigenous. The proportion is much higher in some areas, including Manitoba: Cook and Courchene (2006) found that 70 per cent of sexually exploited children and youth in Manitoba had Indigenous ancestry. This is a massive over-representation of Indigenous victims, considering they make up about 4 per cent of Canada's population (McCracken & Michell, 2006). Rabson (2013) wrote, based on the 2011 census, that First Nations people make up 10 per cent of Manitoba's population, and 60 per cent of those live on reserves. About 6.7 per cent of Manitoba's population is Métis (Rabson, 2013).

Gord Mackintosh, former MLA and attorney general of Manitoba (as well as former minister of Child and Family Services), has been a leader in creating strategies to combat sex trafficking and sexual exploitation in Manitoba. He describes the reality for many Indigenous girls, and his government's engagement with the issues:

GORD MACKINTOSH: Well, [my] initial involvement in this area was as attorney general. And before I came into government, and I was the justice critic in the 1990s, and we put together a caucus task force on violence against women to find out how we could develop stronger policies in that area. We travelled across the province. I was struck by the information we were getting. I remember, for example, up north a girl came to speak to us and we offered off-the-record opportunities, and [she] said that of the fourteen girls in her group she was the only one who hadn't been raped or molested in her community. And she said that a man in the community said, "Well, that's just the way it is, it happens to everyone, all the girls." I couldn't believe my naivety, first of all, but I was infuriated by that. And then, with that task force, I learned about the challenges that the young women on the street were facing.

This context is important in understanding the social situation and background that many Indigenous youth come from. It sheds some light on the over-representation of Indigenous girls in the sex industry, particularly in Manitoba.

Violence against Indigenous women and girls is central to the issue of sex trafficking and sexual exploitation. One survivor I interviewed, Grace, describes the jeopardy that many Indigenous children face.

GRACE: I was recruited out of child welfare. I had been adopted, and things were not going well so I was put into "care." I was sexually abused at the age of eight. I am Native and no one liked Natives where I lived in Thunder Bay. So I hid my identity. I was eleven years old when this happened, and I was first exploited at age twelve.

That Grace was abused as a child is consistent with the experiences of my study participants. The high incidence of childhood abuse correlates with the high number of Indigenous young women who end up trafficked by predators.

McCracken and Michell (2006) highlight the impacts on people of low income and poverty as well as colonization and racism. Those designing intervention and exit strategies for sexually exploited Indigenous females must consider these deep transgenerational impacts, and culturally appropriate resources and structures (see Volkan, 1997). For example, Andrew Swan (MLA and former attorney general for Manitoba) commented on the high numbers of Indigenous girls who are exploited in the sex industry that operates on the streets in his constituency in Winnipeg's downtown and west end.

ANDREW SWAN: Anecdotally the great majority of young women who you'll see on the street in this part of town are Indigenous. That matches with every study I have seen, every piece of research. There was one study out of British Columbia that said even though only 4 per cent of the population of British Columbia is Indigenous, some 60 or 70 per cent of sexually exploited individuals are Indigenous. Historically, I don't think there's been a really wide range of agencies and services that have focused on the cultural issues. Right now, I mean, some of the agencies I have the most respect for – Salvation Army, they do really good work with the prostitution diversion program, they also run the john school. Dianna Bussey is tremendous. I can't speak for how the services are viewed by Indigenous people. Sage House, a tremendous organization that's provided front-line services and a safe place. Again, I can't actually speak to how culturally appropriate they are. And I know they provide service to Indigenous people. I don't know if there's the appropriate level – I think other people would be better placed to deal with that.

Mr. Swan has done considerable work in the political arena aimed at curbing the sex industry. His observations regarding the high percentage of Indigenous women who are exploited in the sex industry are consistent with the literature as well as my research. While this is not a quantitative study of the demographics of the sex industry, it is clear from my interviews that the majority of survivors in and around Manitoba have Indigenous or Métis ancestry. Some of my interviewees see sexual exploitation as largely an Indigenous issue; however, there are also a growing number of newcomers from around the world that are also potentially being exploited by sexual predators.

My research also highlights the social challenges faced by Indigenous people who are raised in isolated rural reserves and then move to larger urban centres. This phenomenon has been explored in some previous studies (see Norris et al., 1995). My respondents bring to light some of the specific difficulties with respect to Indigenous children's vulnerability to sex trafficking and exploitation. Lack of opportunities in the rural environment seems to be a critical factor affecting later youth victimization by sex traffickers. For instance, several interviewees said many rural communities do not have high schools, and so youth frequently leave their families and community to attend high school in larger urban centres.

Indigenous youth have intersectional challenges that make them more vulnerable to exploitation than mainstream youth who travel for school. For one thing, they can feel out of place moving into a primarily white community where they are now seen and treated as a visible minority. Second, on top of inevitable homesickness, they often have less support in the city, and even encounter language barriers. Third, they may have mental health or substance abuse issues, stemming from the transgenerational trauma described above (Volkan, 1997). Fourth, traffickers often target them, knowing that many of these children are entirely vulnerable, alienated, and lost.

Sheldon Beaton of the RCMP EPPS (Exploited Persons Pro-active Strategy) team voiced concerns about the vulnerability of girls who have to relocate for school:

SHELDON BEATON: There's a big draw to the city from rural areas to come to the city. Some people will come for school and because they don't have, say, grade 10, 11, 12 in their home community. And they get in with the wrong crowd. And, again, obviously drugs and alcohol are huge. Even from the human trafficking training, people will meet that boyfriend or girlfriend, and they get them hooked on stuff – and now, "You owe me money!" And how else are they going to pay [that person], kind of thing. I find now with the invention of iPhones, everybody's got a phone and sexting. And compared when I grew up, there was none of that, you know? I don't know if I grew up in a sheltered life or not, but I grew up in a small town.

Karen Harper, community liaison with the Assembly of Manitoba Chiefs (AMC), maintains that youth who move to larger urban centres for high school, and their parents, need better awareness of the dangers that await them. In her role as community liaison, Ms. Harper is trying to correct this gap by talking to people living on reserves and in rural communities.

Kaitlin, a survivor, describes how many rural girls are vulnerable to being taken advantage of when they come into the city:

KAITLIN: You know, if someone would have come up to me when I was in high school, and would have said, "Hey, you know, what if you go on the street and smoke crack and that, and showed me a picture before and after of a girl" – I probably would have been, like, "Okay, ya you know what?" I would have probably looked at my friend and said, "You know what? You're not my friend. Fuck off." There are a lot of girls that come in from the reserve, and they're naive. They don't know how the city is. They come in, and right away they get sucked in. I've had a couple of friends who went missing and murdered all because of one girl that got them started. The one girl that got me started got them started. And all of a sudden they are gone. I'm proud to say that I've never introduced anyone, never got anyone hooked on crack.

Kaitlin's story is similar to that of other contributors to this book, including former justice minister Andrew Swan, who specifically discusses the challenge Indigenous youth face in having to relocate from their homes to urban centres for school:

ANDREW SWAN: I guess I, like you, I'm just shocked to hear consistently and regularly everybody saying that sexual exploitation often begins for kids as young as twelve or thirteen or fourteen. And is there a turning point? I don't know that there is. I think it may be more the trauma most of those kids have already suffered. The conditions they've lived in – whether it's in a big city, whether it's in a First Nation. I don't know that there's a single thing that happens.

   One of the things that I have always been concerned about is young people who leave their community to go to school because their community schooling goes to grade 8 or 9, which puts them thirteen, fourteen years old. I know there's always been the concern that that makes those kids very vulnerable.

Mr. Swan notes, as do several other participants, that family members do not always have the child's best interests in mind. Perhaps there is room to build greater awareness of this issue among parents, for community liaisons like Karen Harper (AMC) and Gabriel Simard (RCMP) to advise parents to be careful whom they send their daughters to live with while those daughters attend school in the city.

   Kelly Dennison (WPS inspector) also addresses some of the ways that trafficking differs between regions across Canada, and some of the unique dynamics existing in Manitoba:

KELLY DENNISON: Manitoba is unique in this issue because a lot of our girls that are – if you want to call trafficked into Winnipeg – they come from Thompson, northern Manitoba. They come from almost an impoverished area outside the core, the greater Winnipeg area, for example where I see that differs from a lot of the other major centres.

I've had a chance to work with Toronto. I've travelled around a bit and worked with sexual exploitation teams in the country. What they see and what we see is different. Now, the end result is the same. Somebody is being exploited. Somebody's being trafficked. That's the same. But in York regional or [the Greater Toronto Area], you're seeing a girl from Holland. And in Winnipeg, you're seeing a girl from Thompson. So the end result's the same, but we're not seeing girls trafficked from European bloc countries and from around like they would be in those major centres.

Inspector Dennison observes that it is difficult to recognize or identify the trafficking of children, even for law enforcement or social workers, when people move from rural areas to urban centres for school and end up being exploited.

Countrywide and international trafficking of young people does occur in Manitoba (Taylor, 2015). For example, Sethi has written that there is a sex trafficking route between Saskatoon, Regina, and Winnipeg: survivors reported a girl going to sleep in one city and waking up in another (see Sethi, 2007, cited in Taylor, 2015). This type of movement between Canadian cities was outlined in my participants' stories. The majority of participants stated, however, that people who are trafficked in Manitoba are usually from Manitoba.

Gilbert Fredette, a First Nations councillor from Norway House Cree Nation, said, "We take it upon ourselves to go to school and talk to the youth and say this is what child exploitation is, these are the warning signs, these are the triggers" (Taylor, 2015, p. 1). This is very similar to some of the initiatives described by my research participants. Karen Harper, Gabriel Simard, and Rebecca Cook (Manitoba's child exploitation program coordinator) all related that they travel to rural communities to raise awareness of the dangers inherent in the city for Indigenous women. The people I interviewed for this book highlighted the importance of these initiatives and stressed that we need much more of these effective intervention processes.

My participants presented a wide range of perspectives on the question of whether existing programming that seeks to address the trafficking of Indigenous youth is culturally sensitive. The observations ranged from the view that existing programming is very culturally sensitive, even overly so, to the other end of the spectrum, that it is inappropriate or sadly lacking. Below I present some representative views expressed in interviews, and some interesting ideas put forth on cultural sensitivity and programming.

Kim Trossell works with sex industry survivors at the Dream Catcher program at Klinic Community Health. She believes cultural sensitivity in her agency has come a long way in recent years, but must still improve.

KIM TROSSELL: Culturally sensitive? Considering people don't even acknowledge the fact that a lot of the sex trade, especially here in Manitoba, is a direct result of colonization and long-term effects of that. So if people can't even come to the table and agree on that, that is an issue. It's hard for them to be culturally sensitive. I mean our agency in itself made huge changes since Dream Catcher became a part of the programming here. You know, we now have a space that is considered culturally friendly, where we have smudging available for all clients, not just clients of our program but Indigenous within our agency. So there has been a huge movement within our own agency. I don't know as far as the outside world and being culturally sensitive. I don't think that that is even a reality. You know, 80 per cent of our street population in the street sex trade is of Indigenous descent. That was identified over twelve, fifteen years ago. But it's still working towards a language that is appropriate, and practising and, like, the ceremonies that we've attended. Our Elders have talked to us about the importance of bringing the teachings back to the Indigenous community that was stripped of these things, originally. So just rebuilding what was taken away, creating space for it to happen is so essential.

Because, in Ms. Trossell's experience, over 80 per cent of people in the sex industry are Indigenous, it is crucial to be more culturally sensitive in terms of understanding the emotional trauma that many carry as a result of colonial impacts (despite great strides having been made in that area). She points out that even after many years, appropriate language around cultural sensitivity has still not been defined. Perhaps this signals the difficulties involved in defining what is culturally appropriate or sensitive programming.

Similarly to Kim Trossell, Wendy Sheirich (former coordinator of Manitoba's counter-sexual-exploitation program) estimates that over 70 per cent of sex trafficking survivors in Manitoba are Indigenous, and the composition of services for people recovering from sex industry participation should be a funding priority of the provincial government.

WENDY SHEIRICH: Manitoba has instituted probably one hundred strategies and programs. Just about every sector has been pulled in. Manitoba is a leader in Canada on this issue. People come to

Manitoba to ask us because we are the experts. We've been focused on rescue and support for victims, and that is very comprehensive – helping people exit the sex trade. But there has been no approach to the demand side. We need to focus on that. That has been left to law enforcement, and that doesn't work. We know the majority of victims of sexual exploitation trafficking and prostitution are Indigenous. So there has been a lot of progress and strides in recent years in this area. I set targets when I was the sexual exploitation program manager to make 70 per cent of government-funded programs Indigenous to reflect the percentage of victims. After ten years, that was accomplished. When it's an Indigenous program offering the service, it is typically more culturally appropriate ... The main reasons people successfully leave is finding spirituality, or getting pregnant, or having a close-to-death experience, or [they] found a mentor. There is usually some concrete reason they got out.

However, Diane Redsky (Ma Mawi Wi Chi Itata Centre) finds that Indigenous organizations receive less funding than non-Indigenous organizations for the same level of services, and feels that Indigenous sex industry survivors are short-changed.

DIANE REDSKY: It depends on which organizations are delivering the service. So, I would say that Indigenous organizations need to be supported to develop the resources for Indigenous people. And we know, on the issue, particularly in Winnipeg and in Manitoba, that the majority of the sexually exploited youth and women are Indigenous. And so Indigenous organizations need to be supported to do so. Does that happen now? Not 100 per cent. I would say that we have a ways to go with that – particularly in the children-in-care sector. We actually did some research when I first got back in March to analyse the per diem rate of level fours. So there's five levels, one to five for kids. "Five" is sort of the most high risk, you know. "One" is low risk. So we have a few level-four facilities.

And so we compared that with non-Indigenous organizations. So we compared apples and apples on the per diem rate, and then we put them in order of who gets the most money and who gets the least amount of money. When that list came out, comparing apples to apples, the three bottom organizations were the Indigenous organizations. And so that is not a surprise, that on any given day a non-Indigenous organization gets forty-four dollars a day less than a non-Indigenous [one].

Against Wendy Sheirich's statement that much more provincial resources are now directed into Indigenous-focused programming, Diane Redsky pointed out several problems. For one, Indigenous girls are often placed into non-Indigenous programs, and they don't fit into them. She also notes, as we saw above, that fewer dollars are dedicated to programming for Indigenous people. She further noted the challenges for NGO funding. Research by Phillips and Levasseur (2004) and Creary and Byrne (2014), for example, found that governmental accountability requirements are so onerous for some small NGOs that they are forced out of business. Thus, bureaucratic processes are resulting in disparity of resources and barriers to assistance for vulnerable youth.

Michael Richardson of Marymound points out that culturally sensitive treatments for sex industry survivors do not usually coexist with other effective programming, so the elements are piecemeal in the system. He describes the disjointed system of resources:

MICHAEL RICHARDSON: We work from a stage-of-change perspective to help understand and help us identify where kids are, when they're ready to change, and if they're ready to change, and what we can do to help them change. Working from understanding their hierarchy of needs would also help us understand kids, help us understand why kids are drawn to the offenders. The offenders have something to offer through clothing, shelter, belonging. So having those understandings help us to create strategies in working with young people better. I think once you start working with the young people in care, in general, I think people recognize that being culturally sensitive is important. Obviously some places are more culturally appropriate than others. Where I think we all push to, we all recognize that it's important for kids to have, to identify with their culture. It's interesting, though, because no one really has the one-stop-shop kind of thing. We have some organizations that are really good and work with exploitation and are not very good to work with the cultural piece. And we have some organizations that work very well with the cultural piece but not very well with the exploitation piece.

That effective counter-exploitation work often does not occur in every organization that has effective cultural programming is seemingly due to a lack of coordination and because organizations have different mandates and priorities.

Some of my participants underlined the need for greater focus on new-comer communities and non-Indigenous people as well as the Indigenous survivors of the sex industry. Jennifer Richardson (StreetReach) describes past research as focused on easily accessible, visible subjects, whereas many in the sex industry are hidden from view. She noted that sex industry workers at the street level are easy to observe, but sex transactions through the internet and massage parlours are often much more difficult to find. It is frequently in these hidden places that newcomers and non-Indigenous people are trafficked, a two-tiered system with Indigenous girls prostituted on the streets and white girls more through the internet.

Friederike Von Aweden (Klinic nurse) mentioned that she wonders if non-Indigenous women feel supported or are getting lost in the system. She considers that programs are oriented more to sensitivity to the cultural requirements of Indigenous women, with very little accommodation to non-Indigenous women.

FRIEDERIKE VON AWEDEN: At TERF there is a large cultural component. And given that maybe 85 per cent of participants are Indigenous, there is a large component with it. I do wonder about women that come from other cultures, whether they feel equally supported in their own cultures.

Ms. Von Aweden is one of several respondents who pointed out that the growing newcomer population also need more resources focused specifically on them. Joy Smith commented that Indigenous programming is strong, and we now need a focus on supporting non-Indigenous sex industry survivors as well.

JOY SMITH: Well, I don't think they have been culturally sensitive, to be honest. And I think it is improving. I think it has to be culturally sensitive, not only to Indigenous, but to others as well. The culturally sensitive piece now I think is being addressed at the Indigenous level. But there are a lot of different ethnic groups that are trafficked throughout Manitoba and throughout Canada. And I think the culturally sensitive is particularly peculiar to the Indigenous population because that's of paramount importance to that population. Our population is so big here in the Indigenous circles, and they need to know what their roots are. They need to take pride. They need to know the wonderful work that the leaders have done. You know, there's a lot around the cultural aspect that needs to be enhanced. But I think there's a good start on it now and it's high time it happened.

Marie and Grace, two survivors, also feels that there are resources for Indigenous survivors but insufficient programming for non-Indigenous people:

MARIE: I think if we really want to address it we have to make partnerships with service agencies and housing authorities so we can create housing to take these people out of these areas where it's easy to access drugs. I can walk down Main Street and get any drug I want. So if you have people living in the developments [an impoverished area of Winnipeg], it makes it that much easier to be an addict and that much harder to leave, right? Because it's all constantly around you. I think that they're culturally sensitive in terms of Indigenous people. I think that that's changing. Smudging is allowed. And we do a lot of ceremony in terms of we have an Elder that comes to our drop-in every day. But there's not a lot of multicultural acceptance. There are not a lot of people who are trained on newcomers and how what works and how they may be exploited in the city when they first come. No one's studying that yet because they're such private people. So for Indigenous people, yeah, I think that it's culturally sensitive. For every other culture, no.

GRACE: Now some [resources] are for Indigenous, but the population is huge in Indigenous. But we could do more for other cultures. I wouldn't know how to support an African American or I wouldn't know how to support an Asian because it looks totally different. So I don't know if there's any resources available from that culturally sensitive perspective.

Both Marie and Grace said they wouldn't know how to support non-Indigenous survivors, even if they were given the chance to. This is an area for further research, especially given the growing number of immigrants to Canada each year.

Another survivor, Ashley, who is white, told me that she was badly beaten by three Indigenous girls while attending a program that was oriented towards supporting Indigenous survivors. She described that experience as follows:

ASHLEY: The practices of service agencies I find to be culturally sensitive. Ma Mawi Wi Chi Itata's Centre has some great services, I'm sure you know. First and Homes [Housing First], for sexually exploited youth and women, has some good programs, and they also have the Sexually Exploited Youth Community Coalition and the Experiential

Advisory Committee, which puts on awareness campaigns and conferences for youth-serving agencies. The Experiential Advocacy Committee is a great way to empower survivors by including them in the business-type meetings and having them actively involved with the work of organizations. I was in the [–] program when I was a youth. It was more for Indigenous girls and I was white, and I didn't really feel like I fit in, in a way. Like, my mom's Jewish and my dad's Christian, and I never really grew up in a religion. I'm a Christian now.

I was also jumped there by three of them, girls in the program. They beat me up really bad. The support worker had to take me to the hospital. I was fifteen.

This was the only program offered to Ashley by her social worker, so she really didn't have a choice, except to run away from the program placement. Other research participants similarly highlighted that clients are sometimes forced into cultural programming when they are unwilling. For example, an Indigenous girl who is raised in a Christian home might not wish to participate in traditional Indigenous healing practices, while others might benefit greatly from it.

Daphne Penrose (acting executive director of Winnipeg CFS) believes it is important to have options available for a child – that just because s/he comes from one cultural background does not mean s/he will benefit from programming that incorporates that culture. She emphasizes the importance of considering the identity, positionality, and wishes of any particular survivor:

DAPHNE PENROSE: I think that when a child comes into care or a child is exploited and intervention services are needed, I think that allowing a child to find their own way and making sure that different culturally responsive systems are present is appropriate, because just because a child is from Somalia doesn't mean that they want to connect back to their Somalian culture. Just because a child is First Nations doesn't mean they want to connect to that culture. They may eventually, and you'll want to make it available to them. But my perception of what their culture is may be very different from what their perception [of] self-identity and culture is. And I can't prescribe that and neither can anybody else, neither should anybody else. We need to allow these victims to heal, [to] reach out and have things available, culturally appropriate services available to them, without forcing it on them, because they've had enough forced on them.

CFS minister Kerri Irvin-Ross agrees with Ms. Penrose that not every Indigenous person is seeking cultural programming at the time s/he is admitted into treatment. Ms. Irvin-Ross also highlights that people need choices in the type of programs they enter, and that not all Indigenous programs are authentic or effective:

KERRI IRVIN-ROSS: Do we need more services that are culturally sensitive? Yes, I do believe that we do, and I think that the mainstream is becoming more and more aware of it. I once had someone say to me that, you know, five years ago when we started talking about "culturally sensitive," a group of people just started putting the medicine wheel or the eagle feather on their letterhead. And that was not culturally sensitive. We were looking for actions. So, I think that there are many examples. I think that we do have a lot more work to do.

Corporal Sheldon Beaton of the RCMP EPPS described one survivor's story in great detail. He pointed out that the young woman was Indigenous, yet she did not identify as Indigenous and preferred not to participate in Indigenous-focused programming.

SHELDON BEATON: I believe there's a lot of various agencies out there that have to deal with different cultures. And I've learned a lot over the three years I was down here [southern Manitoba, as opposed to the North] – different cultures and how people see it. I'm not sure what the answer is. I know I spoke to one girl once, she grew up Indigenous, but she didn't associate with it, so she said she did not like all these agencies because it was too cultural. But that's for one person, and, again, you can't just group everyone into one. What's good for one isn't good for the others, I guess. I found pretty much, I think, every agency was open to different cultures and stuff.

Corporal Beaton stresses that we should be careful not to generalize survivors into categories without careful assessment, such as asking them how they wish to identify and, as Kerri Irvin-Ross and Daphne Penrose both stressed, giving people choices.

Some participants, such as WPS sergeant Cam MacKid, suggest there is sometimes too much focus on culture and not enough on immediate action. He raises the idea that we should be careful not to overburden practitioners with cultural sensitivity training, for if people are overwhelmed with cultural training, they may feel defensive or numb to it, and it may distract them from the work of assisting women in immediate danger.

CAM MACKID: They're almost overly culturally sensitive. There's no shortage of cultural sensitivity across the board. No matter what issue we're dealing with and wherever we're speaking, it's the Indigenous concern, and there's no shortage of that. And it almost permeates through every conversation we have to the point [about Indigenous sensitivity]. Our Missing Persons Unit goes to this sexually exploited youth training, which I believe it's an entire week, and we send all our people on it. And it's not really about sexually exploited youth, it's about cultural awareness of Indigenous issues. So, yeah, if anything, I think it's gone a little bit too far. And our employees come back from that course, and there's some value to it, but we feel we totally understand the historical issues. It's been well laid out. But at some point, I think as policemen, we're more wanting to deal with the here and now and how can we help this person right now? It is certainly relevant, their background, but to have guys lecture our guys for several days about racist policemen, it doesn't help them. It makes them leave with a bad feeling. I don't think cultural awareness is an issue at all. I think we're well aware of the culture issues. And there are a lot of resources out there that are Indigenous based. Actually, the vast majority have been focused on Indigenous issues, and rightfully so, and that's the metric we're dealing with.

Most of my study participants expressed the view that we, as a society, have come a long way in the past twenty years but that we still have a lot of work to do. WPS inspector Kelly Dennison, for example, describes how cultural sensitivity has improved in policing over recent decades.

KELLY DENNISON: Our counter-exploitation team now is doing that on a daily basis and talking to these girls. Now, the jury's still out on how well that's working. I can tell you when I'm hearing stories about young girls that have been taken and have been involved in this program or that program. You can't help but applaud your officers for being involved in stuff like that. That's what it's all about. The rate at which they go back I don't know. I would love to know that better. I would love to know how we could be more successful at that. I wish I had an answer for you. I don't. I don't know how we could do it better. But it's changed. It's changed over time. But, like I said, the one thing that's never changed in my whole time was that the focus was on the well-being of the people that were involved. I guess the general public and the people that were really involved may have viewed [our work with girls in the sex trade] differently at the time because they see us as the bad guys, showing up with handcuffs and arrests for people who were being exploited. And, yeah, we did that.

Inspector Dennison agrees with Sergeant MacKid that sometimes too much emphasis is placed on the police, when there is a broad spectrum of other practitioners, such as social workers, that can address needs. Overall, Inspector Dennison highlights much positive progress over the past decade, but believes that roles and responsibilities of partnering agencies need to be better defined.

Kelly Holmes (executive director of RAY) raised an interesting idea: she proposes there be a cultural hub that all agencies could access to provide a range of services, from access to Elders to cultural training.

KELLY HOLMES: We could always improve on being culturally sensitive. There's so much to know and I feel like, I've been around for a long time, thirty-five years, and all working on the streets with marginalized communities, and I'm still learning about cultural stuff. And I think I always will learn, there's so much to know. But could we do it in a more organized way? I tend to have the reputation of getting shit done. That's sort of my claim to fame. And if I were in charge, I would have the Thunderbird House [a cultural centre in downtown Winnipeg] being used and funded more readily. So Thunderbird House becomes sort of the education hub for all of us non-Indigenous types where schools can access it, police can access it, you know, a number of the unrelated sector communities can access it. We can attend sweat lodges. We can do ceremonies. We can understand our colonial history. And it's done in more of an education setting. We can jump onto training. We can have trainers coming out to our agencies, and those kinds of things. We can just readily access anything that we need in terms of understanding Métis, Indigenous, Inuit people, and in a different way.

This is a groundbreaking proposal, that agencies and individuals wanting cultural resources, training, and advice could access it through a shared resource hub. Ms. Holmes specifically suggested that Elders could travel to different agencies providing teaching and healing circles, and that this hub could be a place to offer standardized culturally oriented services.

Gabriel Simard (RCMP corporal) builds on the idea that the Indigenous community is made up of numerous groups with different cultures and language, so "Indigenous" could mean a lot of different things to different groups.

GABRIEL SIMARD: I would make sure if I went, say, to a group, at community, say there's a group of twenty, I would ask, you know, should we do a prayer before we start? Should we do a smudge? And it all depends on the community. Because a lot of the communities, whether they're First Nation, especially First Nation, they, some are still practising Christianity, where they may take offence to smudging, whereas some communities have gone back to more traditional and do smudging ceremonies. So we'll ask – myself as well as the partners that I have attended with – whether they're AMC, even WPS. When I worked with Edith Turner from WPS, when she was in the cultural diversity unit, the Child Protection Branch, Ma Mawi, they would ask, right? And if the community was good with having a smudge, we'd start with a smudge. Interpreters, for example – when we went to Little Grand Rapids, Pauingassi – I would do my presentation, I would talk, then I would have to stop. We had an interpreter with us from South East Tribal Council who would do it in Ojibway, because our audience didn't speak a word of English. And Little Grand Rapids, there was a little more English understood. But Pauingassi, probably out of, I think there was about fifteen people, probably twelve could only speak Ojibway, and the rest were both Ojibway and English. So, yeah, and that's the big thing is making sure the person can understand. Because the thing some people forget, especially with First Nation people, they'll nod and you'll think they're understanding when, in fact, they're not [but they're nodding] because they don't want to offend you.

Cpl. Simard points out the challenges in providing culturally specific programming for young Indigenous and immigrant youth and that it is important to not make assumptions about people's identity. In a room full of people who appear Indigenous, possibly even those from the same community, people could identify themselves in a lot of different ways, depending on factors such as how they were raised, their experiences, and their education.

Leslie Spillett, executive director of Ka Ni Kanichihk, maintains that the whole paradigm of service delivery is wrong: funding that goes to large service providers to provide culturally appropriate services should instead go directly to the Indigenous community so they can control their own services in their own way. In her view, practitioners and service providers might prescribe better than they listen:

LESLIE SPILLETT: Everybody knows what's best for us. Everybody thinks that they have some kind of a solution for us, and it's based on a very dominant culture and belief of what is, of what that fix is. But really they're failing that fix ... What you see is their best attempts. So, I just think that the only way to really have an impact – and I totally believe this, researchers have shown that too – is that Indigenous people have to have control. We have to have control over our own lives, we have to have agency. We have to take all that power that's been displaced and build back our own capacities, using our own methodologies and using our own ways of understanding who we are and where we came from, and really understanding the picture of how we landed here. I think that you would have really different outcomes in the long term.

This colonial, paternal attitude, Leslie Spillett explains, could be perceived as an overbearing attempt at further assimilation, rather than meeting survivors where they are at emotionally and offering them the support that they need.

The following nine salient and significant findings emerged from analysis of interviewee's comments regarding the violent reality that Canadian Indigenous women and children live with daily, and how culturally sensitive the system of resources is to them.

First, most trafficking survivors in Manitoba are Indigenous. The majority of sex industry survivors in Manitoba are of Indigenous descent. Violence against Indigenous women and children is central in the issue of sex trafficking and exploitation in Manitoba. While previous studies reported that 70 per cent of sexually exploited children and youth in Manitoba had Indigenous ancestry (see Cook & Courchene, 2006), my respondents suggest that the percentage in that province might be even higher.

Second, Indigenous Manitobans are largely marginalized. Previous literature and my research have documented the systemic marginalization and impoverishment of Indigenous women in Canada (Ham, 2014; Mandel, 2016). While it is no surprise that Indigenous women are over-represented in Canada's sex industry, the degree of over-representation and attendant marginalization and victimization of Indigenous people should be shocking to all people. A key to eradicating sex trafficking and exploitation in the sex industry may lie in improving standards of living and reducing disparity among our most disadvantaged populations through improved income levels and better access to education and employment.

Third, the rural-to-urban pipeline must be interrupted. There is a trafficking pipeline of young girls and women from rural reserves into urban centres. A real and immediate threat to the safety of Indigenous youth in Manitoba is the perils they encounter when they move into larger urban centres, commonly for education and employment opportunities. Some practitioners are trying to raise awareness of these dangers among Indigenous youth and their families, to make them more resistant to sexual predators, but this is a growing threat in Manitoba and must be addressed. My research reveals that targeting of rural youth is a growing problem despite the efforts of many devoted professionals, and indicates a need for more resources to build awareness within rural and urban First Nations and Métis communities of safety measures when community members are required to travel or move to larger urban centres.

Fourth, cultural programming needs improvement. Cultural sensitivity to Indigenous and other cultures needs improvement. Often appropriate training does not coexist with other effective treatment resources. My research participants expressed mixed opinions about whether existing addiction, medical, educational, and other counselling programs offered to sex industry survivors are culturally sensitive. Most agreed that overall cultural appropriateness in the system at large has improved over the past decade. Some said that there is a great deal of cultural sensitivity, and some even opined that there is too much. Others described some agencies as presenting a false visage, for example by putting an image of a medicine wheel on their stationery solely to gain funding, without having any real substance to the services they provide to Indigenous people. Most study participants felt that there are pockets of good cultural programming, yet it is sporadic and not always available in the right programs. One possible solution is the creation of a cultural hub, as envisioned by Kelly Homes, whereby a full range of cultural services can be delivered, ensuring quality and inclusion of various Indigenous cultural resources.

Fifth, people need to be offered the right cultural programming. People are often forced into cultural programs based upon an agency worker's assumptions. An interesting research finding was that people are often not matched with the appropriate cultural programming as part of their survivor-oriented trauma care. Several of my participants described an "Indigenous" resource pool that could be tailored to fit individual wishes of people from different Indigenous backgrounds.

Sixth, non-Indigenous programming needs improvement. Several participants highlighted that there is a lot of programming for Indigenous people but almost nothing for people from other non-mainstream cultures, including newcomers to Manitoba from different countries. Newcomer populations are growing in Manitoba and across Canada, and inclusive, constructive programming is needed for those who succumb to the sex industry. This issue is becoming more salient as new information emerges about the growing internet-based sex industry that is migrating from the street. We need to be prepared to intervene and assist newcomers and non-Indigenous sex industry survivors.

Seventh, more systemic flexibility is needed. People need choices in their treatments, so that appropriate treatment resources are accessible to them when they are required. My participants described the current state of the system of resources in Manitoba as diverse, fragmented, and inflexible. They observed that there should be greater flexibility in the system with regard to cultural sensitivity and other programming dynamics, so that people get the services they need when they need them.

Eighth, Indigenous people need more control over their own healing. Indigenous people need more control over their participation in programs and healing. Some Indigenous practitioners and leaders felt that government agencies exercised paternalistic control via funding. Chief Ron Evans pointed out that people living in Winnipeg do not have to have the mayor co-sign for a mortgage, yet people living on his reserve are required to have the band chief and council co-sign for one. Similarly, Leslie Spillett stated that Indigenous people should have more control over how services are provided in Indigenous communities – that the funding that supports core services such as police and social services should go directly to the Indigenous community, rather than those agencies telling Indigenous people how they are to be served. Participants also suggested that survivors be involved in all levels of planning and development of survivor-oriented intervention and prevention programming.

Ninth, a cultural hub could improve coordination of diversity resources. Kelly Holmes suggested a unique social innovation: the creation of a cultural hub to service all agencies. Participants stated that sources of cultural resources are available only sporadically, with access depending on the knowledge and experience of the person looking for them. As a solution, Ms. Holmes proposed creating a cultural hub that all agencies could access to acquire thorough cultural knowledge and resources, including Elders and teachers who could be deployed to agencies as needed.

This research contributes insights into Indigenous, Métis, and Inuit perspectives and the choices that must be created for people trying to avoid or exit the sex industry. The overall consensus of most participants was that much work has been done to make programs culturally sensitive over the past two decades, yet more effort must be applied. A greater focus is needed on culturally appropriate programming for newcomer groups. Also, most interview participants reported a need for increased culturally appropriate resources to be provided for subgroups of people within the Métis, Inuit, and Indigenous communities. Indigenous, Métis, and Inuit people should be engaged in developing future services and treatments, and service agencies need to show greater flexibility so that people can access elements when they are ready for them. Finally, my research buttresses the theory that trauma is passed forward transgenerationally as young Indigenous people cope with the impacts of colonialism (see Volkan, 1997).

5 Awareness and Education around Sex Trafficking and Exploitation

ASHLEY: In my opinion prostitution is sexual exploitation and a form of violence against women. No child says when I grow up I want to be a prostitute; I want to be in the sex trade. I was a victim and, like, I didn't even identify, and this is what I think is a crucial point, I didn't identify as a victim because I didn't know what sex trafficking was. I didn't know what sexual exploitation was, I didn't know what grooming was, and [I] think maybe if I'd known about those things – and it wasn't until I heard about Joy Smith and the work that she was doing that I was able to identify that I was just one of many girls.

Ashley articulates a prominent theme that the contributors to this book repeated in many different ways: no thirteen-year-old wakes up one morning, looks in the mirror, and says, "I thought I'd like to be a teacher or a nurse, but I think I will be a prostitute." Most of my respondents stressed that education is critical in reducing sexual exploitation and sex trafficking of young Indigenous girls. A search of the over twelve hundred pages of transcript from my thirty hours of interviews for this book, reveals that the word "education" was used 154 times, "awareness" 121 times, and "training" 69 times. More significantly, the participants used strong language to emphasize the importance of education at all levels to raise awareness of the extent to which sex trafficking goes on in Manitoba, and ways of preventing it.

Participants identified four main groups that should be targeted by enhanced education campaigns about sex trafficking and sexual exploitation: (1) children, to make them aware of the dangers; (2) the purchasers of sex, to make them aware of the hurt they cause to survivors; (3) the public, to affect the discourse around sex trafficking; and (4) practitioners, as people who are in a position to recognize the signs of sex trafficking and to intervene. My research participants often focused their comments on the areas in which they are most involved. For instance, some survivors stated that they wished they had received awareness training to prevent their involvement in the sex industry, and practitioners often advised me that they need better training.

Participants strongly recommended that youth receive education about predators – to raise awareness that some people are not true friends, especially when drugs, alcohol, and promiscuity are involved. Survivors' voices on this subject are particularly powerful:

ASHLEY: I think a lot of youth who are vulnerable to being exploited – like maybe in those teenage years, when you're looking for that need to belong and to be accepted and to be a part of something – I think awareness is a huge thing. They need to be informed at every age about this issue. I think the police have come a long way in terms of viewing girls as victims. I think the law that was passed criminalizing the buyers of sex is a good one if the police are enforcing it. Like, the buyers need to be criminalized, not the girls. And the police need to do more outreach so that you could feel safe to come forward because maybe they don't know that they're not going to get in trouble, like they're going to be offered services. They should be teaching about sex trafficking in schools, like have the Joy Smith Foundation school program in all the schools.

Kaitlin, another survivor, suggests better training for teachers and parents to recognize warning signs and know how to intervene.

KAITLIN: It would have been helpful to hear about that [the dangers of the sex industry] in high school. I had a probation officer, but I was afraid to tell her anything 'cause I was afraid she would send me to jail.
    They need to talk about this stuff in schools. In my school, they never had any of that. So, when my friends were like, "Hey, let's go party and drink in the west end. Don't worry, my friends will take care of us." And I thought, "Okay." And when we went in this house there was all these guys dressed in vests and I knew something was going to happen, but I was scared.

She felt that she had no one she could talk to, and no one knew how to intervene to assist her. Awareness education, she says, could have saved her from being exploited and on the street turning tricks.

Joy Smith agrees with Kaitlin in stressing that children need early education and awareness of the dangers of sex trafficking and prostitution.

JOY SMITH: The critical event is being lured. They need education. They need to not listen to these predators that are going to make a lot of money off of them. And, you know, telling [them] about the wonderful future, and all the money and all the love they're going to have.

They need to be educated about what really happens, and that's why the [Joy Smith Foundation] has a school program that has – we're incorporating in River East School Division right now, and in River East Collegiate. And we did a presentation at one of the schools from Brandon. And what that does, it does more than talk about human trafficking right now. It starts about the history of human trafficking in Canada.

Emma, a senior Crown prosecutor, also highlights the central importance of education in preventing sex trafficking and exploitation:

EMMA: Well, we know the average age of entry is thirteen years old. There are a number of factors – poverty and marginalization is key. And education in the community is key. Education in schools would make children aware. And education for women would make them aware of programs and resources that are available. Many exploited youth have been in group home settings, not feeling supported. Again, counselling, culturally sensitive supports and resources, and a huge injection of supports. At the end of the day it's the manner of delivery of those services and the relationship with police, letting them know they are cared for and that they are important as individuals. We know from Snow Night that they are often surprised to hear about donations, that people cared enough about them to do that.

Snow Night is an annual event put on at Salvation Army in Winnipeg for people to get in off the street and escape the harsh reality of the sex industry.

Claudia Ponce-Joly agrees that education and awareness should start early, when children first become vulnerable to external influences.

CLAUDIA PONCE-JOLY: In my view, children and youth need constant and ongoing options because we're not 100 per cent clear which option will work for which child at that time. I think that some of the youth that I've worked with – and some unfortunately and tragically lost their lives through sexual exploitation – different approaches would have worked for them at different times. And I think the key is to address and work with opportunity and pull them back through options, and sometimes I would say even stronger strategies, or simply they have to occur as young as possible. When young people are starting to become vulnerable that is when the strategy should start. And it could be information and education. Just as young people are educated on safety and health, they should be educated on what kind of risks are in our communities, unfortunately, what kind of people may be attempting to have contact with them. And this should be part of education in my view, and especially for children that are vulnerable, involved in the child welfare system, or in corrections, or any other kind.

Ms. Ponce-Joly makes the point that education should start when children are in their formative years, so that the awareness process becomes natural and normal, occurring alongside health and social education. Survivors, practitioners, and political and community leaders stressed that education and awareness must be increased and provided earlier for children in schools.

People from the North and rural communities coming into the city are particularly vulnerable to sexual predators. Gabriel Simard (RCMP) spent five years travelling to First Nations communities and reserves throughout Manitoba, to educate people about the dangers that might await their children in the city as well as outlining the indicators of sex trafficking and exploitation. He notes that education and awareness are extremely important for youth in rural communities and reserves, especially when they're transplanted out of necessity to attend high school in the city.

GABRIEL SIMARD: If you have children that are moving on, make sure they're educated and understand that if a person's buying them clothes, taking them for expensive dinners, be a little leery because a normal person shouldn't be doing this, you know. And when we explain it in a sense that, "Tell your kid to be on their guard if they're getting things that an adult shouldn't be giving them, unless it's a close family member, parent, then something could be going very wrong, or could be misleading. And so for that question [the importance of raising awareness] I think, just being able to relate and having someone who's from the community explain [that] this is how it could look, it could very well happen in the communities.

Cpl. Simard notes that it is very helpful that he is from the community, as people trust him and know that he understands their culture and history.

Jennifer Richardson agrees that parents need greater awareness about how children are groomed by pimps, and what the indicators are. She emphasizes the need for more awareness training for children and greater vigilance among parents, teachers, and society at large. While a lot of awareness programs are currently in place, Richardson notes that we need to give a lot more attention to what we are teaching our children about the people they are meeting through the internet, and parents need to be aware of the signs that their kids are being approached or groomed by predators.

JENNIFER RICHARDSON: We could be doing a much better job at utilizing prevention resources or teaching younger kids, and all kids, the
kind of the dangers, or what are traffickers are doing. How are they
recruiting? If some guy starts talking to you online on Facebook and
is paying all this attention to you, that should be a cue to let an adult
know. Just those types of things that, again, we would as adults be
leery of, but children, because everyone's a friend on the Internet, and
their brains just aren't cooked enough to figure out what's coming
around the corner. You know, they just don't have that ability even
developmentally yet. So, I think we need to do a better job of teaching
kids that information in schools. Parents, of course, are leery. And
it's the last thing that a parent wants to ever think is going on with
their child, even if their child is using drugs or drinking lots, or going
missing all the time. Or all of a sudden, you know, they've got stuff and
[parents]'re saying, "Well, where'd you get that from?" "Well, oh, I got it
from my friend." Well, after they say that ten times, parents still aren't
checking in to that, and that always shocks me. So, again, I think, if
there was more information – general public information for parents
and information specific to kids out there – We have some [awareness
programs] in Manitoba, but I don't think it's enough. We need more.

The majority of participants I interviewed indicate that parents and the community need to provide greater awareness among youth in their formative and vulnerable years. This need is growing, as the environment is changing: some participants, including Jennifer Richardson, emphasize the growing threat of social media and the internet.

Many participants also talked about the need to "go after" the sex market, stressing that the overarching strategy of countering sexual exploitation and sex trafficking should involve pursuing the pimps and predators and deterring the purchasers of sex with fines, jail sentences, and other forms of dissuasive punishments. A smaller but still significant number of participants stressed the need for more education for boys and men to make them aware of the damage caused to young women who are forced to participate in the sex industry.

Hennes Doltze works directly with men who have been criminally charged with offences related to purchasing sex and are diverted from the courts to "john school" at the Salvation Army, where a program is in place to resocialize and re-educate johns. (After they attend the program, their changes are dropped.) Mr. Doltze understands the sex-purchaser side of the equation, perhaps better than any other person I interviewed. While the men participate unwillingly, often feeling shame and embarrassment about having to show up there, Mr. Doltze has found that they still have "aha" moments and say they learned a lot from the process despite their initial reluctance to participate.

HENNES DOLTZE: So, I'm a social worker here with the Salvation Army. And I work with men who have been charged for prostitution-related offences. So, I work with the offenders on that end, and I've been doing this for about two years now. The program is primarily an education and awareness program, educating men around the effects that prostitution has on the community, on the people that are being exploited, and also on the men themselves. So, that's the main focus of the program. We have a committee who is overseeing the program. And we've been running this program since 1998, I believe, so seventeen to eighteen years now. And it's been, in our point of view, a very successful program in helping to reduce the demands [for] prostitution and sexual exploitation. The program that we offer is, as I said, an educational and awareness program where we talk about the different effects of prostitution. So, we have a Crown attorney speak at our seminar. We have Winnipeg Police Services speaking of the law enforcement aspect. We have nurses who talk about health risks that are involved and the personal effects and the trauma that are created for a lot of the women, and it's predominately women. There are some men who are being sexually exploited, but in regard to the numbers I believe it's primarily it's women and transgender persons. So it's really about making people aware that this is not some – is not a victimless crime where people are just in there for no reason, but that it's actually harmful to a lot of the people involved and communities.

Mr. Doltze believes that educating offenders about the physical and psychological damage to survivors caused by purchasing sex, and about the fact that many young women sell sex for survival, is an effective deterrent, in conjunction with enforcement, to future sex-purchasing behaviour.

Mr. Doltze's impressions are mirrored by evaluation of similar programs that have run in the United States for many years. For example, Shively et al. (2008) evaluated First Offender Prostitution Programs (aka john schools) across the United States and found that they are generally effective in changing men's attitudes about the sex industry and in reducing recidivism. One effective john school model initiated in San Francisco was duplicated in twelve other states. Eligible arrestees have a choice of paying to attend a one-day class or facing prosecution. Over the past twelve years this program has generated $3.1 million after covering the cost of the programs, and the bulk of the profit goes to survivor support programs.

My research participants stressed the need for greater emphasis on reducing the demand for the sex industry. This calls for a balance of enforcement matched with treatment and education programs to reduce customers' appetite for purchasing sex. The effectiveness of these programs is illustrated in the above-mentioned programs.

McIntyre et al. (2015) also see a need for greater emphasis on curbing demand for the sex industry:

> For years, prevention efforts have looked at the supply side of the economic equation – unsuccessfully. There has been and likely always will be an endless supply of new workers entering the sex trade. However, with recent research studies providing data to better understand consumers, it would appear to make sense to explore prevention models that focus on the demand side of the equation. (pp. 5–6)

McIntyre et al. (2015) stress that men learn this behaviour at a young age, and therefore prevention strategies such as education must target boys and young men, not only to teach them about the damage caused by participating in the sex industry, but also about women's basic rights and dignity. They propose building on the "john school" model, however, by incorporating the internet as a tool: prevention programs delivered through social media to men of all ages, "to spell out the realities of the trade as well as the risks and personal impacts associated with being a consumer in an effort to reduce demand" (p. 6).

The need to devote more resources and efforts to informing and influencing the public was a significant and prevalent theme throughout most of my interviews. Dianna Bussey, justice liaison for Salvation Army in Winnipeg, underscores that public awareness is key. She suggests that more funding and resources should be invested in campaigns to raise the public conscience about children and women who are exploited.

DIANNA BUSSEY: I'm a huge advocate for the Nordic model. Prostitution is a form of violence against women predominantly, violence against people generally. And getting that out there. And I think if the public is meaningfully engaged in that, they will come to [the] realization that's going to cost money, right? A huge public awareness campaign. So, that would be the first thing, and just bringing that awareness to people. To really take a look at how it works. And for those who are caught up in it, both the buyers and the sellers, that there would be the resources and the supports in place for them to be able to exit. Then also exit into something meaningful as well. For those who are selling sex. It should not have to be an option of a way of making a living, right? And unfortunately it seems to be the case, if a woman is in dire straits, if a woman is having trouble, if a woman is in poverty that's the go-to, and [it] shouldn't be that way. And then it seems that on the flip side that there needs to be supports for men. We have a hard time when men are really looking for help, it's not easy to get that help.

Gabriel Simard (RCMP) expands on Ms. Bussey's call for more public awareness promotions, indicating that careful consideration must be given to how those campaigns are designed: it is important that the message be carefully crafted to reach the desired audiences. He observes that some rural communities do not have internet or cell phone service, and in-person presentations are often the only real option for educating people. The information campaigns he has conducted have been well received in rural communities:

GABRIEL SIMARD: I've found the work that I did was very good because you can share stories. Some things you just can't get from a piece of paper. You need someone telling you, explaining stories: this is what it could look like. I think what's beneficial in my case is I come from a First Nation community myself, which is Hollow Water, and I use the explanation that when I was eighteen years old, I moved to Winnipeg. And when I look back on things ... in 1996, '97, I was a vulnerable person because I wanted to make friends. The city was new to me. I didn't know any people. I'm a small-community person. You know, you're a little more trusting. You know, you meet someone, you think, "Okay, this person is genuine."

Cpl. Simard notes that the lack of internet and cell phone service in some rural communities should be a critical governmental consideration in providing those technologies in local communities as well as investing inadequate resources that inform public awareness.

Rebecca Cook, coordinator of the Manitoba Child Exploitation Program, also expanded on this discussion, stressing the importance of having input from survivors, as some campaigns can trigger and retraumatize them. In the following extract from her interview, Cook provides examples of ongoing campaigns, such as those designed to raise awareness about sex tourism and the increased sex industry activity around major sporting events. She also describes the politics around some of these issues, including concerns about showing disturbing aspects of society, such as the fact that the sex industry exists to service tourists.

REBECCA COOK: We have a public awareness campaigns partnership with the Canadian Centre for Child Protection, "Stop Sex with Kids" – [a] very prominent, historically prominent campaign. The word "sex" in it, you know, was groundbreaking. Even to this day we formed a Manitoba sporting event safety working group to address the potential for child sex tourism trafficking during the Grey Cup. We had approached certain airlines where you would go get your luggage, and asked them to put up a sign. At the beginning they were right for it; at the end the word "sex" – [as in] "Buying sex is not a sport" – was just so – like they wouldn't entertain it. They wanted to have this picture that when people were getting off the plane visiting Winnipeg, that it was a family community environment. So, there's still some businesses who lack that perception.

Our strategy itself is unique. It's got certain principles which makes us unique by having the voices of survivors or experiential folks right at the table right from the beginning with any initiative that gets developed, right from the colour on walls in your program to public awareness campaigns, everything, and then also engaging youth in engaging the Indigenous community.

Ms. Cook stresses that survivors need to be at the table consulting or participating in the design of public awareness programs to ensure that they are accurate and that they are not further traumatizing survivors.

Rosemarie Gjerek (Klinic) eloquently summed up the issue by underscoring that information about the deeper elements of the problem of sex trafficking and sexual exploitation needs to be made more available to the public. She contends that the root causes of poverty and children's vulnerability to sex trafficking need to be addressed, and forcefully describes trafficking and the selling of human beings as an act of war on humanity.

ROSEMARIE GJEREK: When we look at, how do we raise little girls and how do we raise little boys, when we look at a society for the most part that actually condones a certain level of sexual assault and sexual exploitation, when we look at the impact of pornography, these are not benign things. These are the way people learn about sex or how, I think, what people are looking for or needing. I think we have to start respecting women and respecting men and boys and girls and again take it on a global level. When we look at sexual violence and trafficking, these are crimes of war. These are commodities, they are commerce, so when we start to address this, there's a lot of money in this. There's a lot of money and that's the driving force here. So why people become involved is often related to poverty, is related to feeling you don't have other choices, is related to being groomed, being exploited as a child and thinking this is what you need to do to survive. So some of it is survival, you know. There's so many reasons and for us the important thing is being able to recognize it when it is happening around us, how do we intervene, not being people who purchase children, not being people who purchase women.

Claudia Ponce-Joly notes that the Truth and Reconciliation Commission and the Missing and Murdered Indigenous Women and Girls Inquiry that started in the fall of 2016 will raise public awareness around the sex industry.

CLAUDIA PONCE-JOLY: In my view, again I think money alone cannot solve this type of issue, because I think that the reason it exists, there is an aspect in human nature where people may harm each other, and if that wasn't true there wouldn't be violence and abuse in our world. But I view things that if someone were able to provide all the money in the world, that wouldn't necessarily fix the situation in terms of the sex trade and human trafficking. I believe that what's needed is far deeper and more difficult to reach and [not simply a matter of] having the funding for it; I believe that for true and lasting change, society has to change. I think that issue has to become an issue that is important to every Canadian. The issue has to become mainstream and I believe the inquiry's helping do that. But I don't believe that people necessarily outside of police and child welfare and health practitioners, I don't believe people are comfortable with the topic. And there's a bit of denial that mainstream society is working through. The more educated and aware that mainstream society is, the more that mainstream society becomes an ally, the more success there will be in combating the sex trade and human trafficking.

Ms. Ponce-Joly highlights that money alone cannot reduce exploitation; what is needed is a broader acknowledgment and understanding of the problem.

According to Christy Dzikowicz, executive director of the Canadian Centre for Child Protection, the average citizen prefers not to know about the sex industry and victimized women and children, perhaps because people do not want to acknowledge that this dark underbelly of society exists. However, Ms. Dzikowicz stresses that the average citizen has empathy for victimized children, even if s/he prefers not to hear about their plight, and there are opportunities to engage citizens in combating social injustice when these issues are forced into the light.

CHRISTY DZIKOWICZ: Once a child is in that scenario of being exploited and involved in that sort of high-risk life, it needs to be a huge collective effort by all organizations, by all healthy and well adults in our society, to say we're not going to be ok with letting a kid fall between the cracks. And I think separate from just the mandated organizations, or just the non-profit or charitable organizations or grassroots agencies – we need to rely on people in society as well. We need to continue it [our efforts] to engage all healthy and well adults to say we do have a population of kids who require our attention and care. So, we can speak to the value of public awareness and public engagement, and I don't think we can't say enough about that. It is knowing that we have the vast majority of people [who] actually really care about kids. The optimistic side that we always feel here is there are very few adults that sit on the fence going, I'm not sure whether a child is being exploited or not. People generally do [care], it's helping people understand what role they play.

My research participants voiced a fairly strong and consistent theme that there has been a great deal of denial and apathy among the general public with regard to the sexual exploitation of children. But they also believe there is huge potential to improve public awareness, a potential that is beginning to be tapped, and that service providers' awareness and acknowledgment of trafficking and exploitation within the sex industry is also continuing to develop.

Some interviewees were less optimistic, saying no one seems to care as long as the exploitation is not affecting their loved ones directly. This view is shared by Anupriya Sethi, who found in her research on trafficking that "society doesn't care about missing and murdered Indigenous women" (quoted in Taylor, 2015). She notes, "It's only recently that people have started talking about human trafficking taking place within Canada." Consistent with the stories of my research participants, Sethi points to the indifference that many members of the public exhibit towards the exploitation of children. In her view "there is a lot of ignorance and misunderstanding. It's poverty, it's cyclical, it's happening in the Indigenous community."

MLA Andrew Swan, formerly Manitoba's attorney general, agrees that people often don't care unless the exploitation is happening in their own backyard and threatens their property values and business interests.

ANDREW SWAN: Again, as we move towards marketing and getting the word out that buying sex is illegal – as well as "Here's why it's a good thing that buying sex is illegal, and here's how buying sex hurts communities" – there's still a lot more work to be done on that. There's still a segment of people who just see it as the way it is. People will tell you, "It's the world's oldest profession and nobody's ever gotten rid of it. So why are you spending all this time and money?" Some people will say, "This is just a cash grab. You're just going after these poor guys." I think one of the difficulties has been that nobody really wants to talk about it. And that was certainly my experience as justice minister, that my colleagues across the country just looked the other way when this was out there.

Wendy Sheirich, Manitoba's former counter-exploitation program coordinator, agrees with Mr. Swan that society tends to hide and does not want to discuss the sex industry. She also noted that when it is discussed we, as a society and as practitioners, tend to focus almost entirely on survivors and pay scant attention to the perpetrators, the pimps, and the purchasers of sex.

WENDY SHEIRICH: What I see happening across the board is a culture of silence in which we tend to not talk about who is purchasing sex or exploiting. We just focus on the survivors. I think the whole area of demand is glossed over. We need to talk about that. The intake forms for most of these programs do not ask a question about who was purchasing sex. We have access to hundreds of people who have been in the sex trade and no one asks them who is buying the sex. In the last few years we've started tracking them [the johns] more, through the forms we fill out. Well, I'd like to say in terms of some ideas about dealing with demand, so what I think is happening right now across the board, that I see happening with our stakeholders and just with everybody in general like the mass public, is that there is a conspiracy of silence. I'd say it is a culture of silence, in that we tend to just sort of not talk about those that are purchasing sex or participating in the sex industry or sexually exploiting or trafficking or whatever. We just sort of focus on the survivors.

Ms. Sheirich reveals that society turns a blind eye to the issue of *who* is doing the exploiting. There are "john schools," and john charges that go to court, and a great deal of advocacy and programming that occurs around sex trafficking and exploitation; however, most people are not aware of the extent of the sexual exploitation of children in Canadian society. Ms. Sheirich points out that a great deal more could be done to root out offenders, for example by designing intake processes for treatment programs that ask survivors who is trafficking them.

Daphne Penrose, acting executive director of CFS, agrees with Ms. Sheirich about lack of acknowledgment that sexual exploitation is going on, and provided an explicit description of the public denial that generally exists about the sex industry. She also highlights that society tends to turn a blind eye to the offenders, focusing instead on the victims.

DAPHNE PENROSE: The general population doesn't want to know that their neighbour might be accessing child porn or that their other neighbour might be buying sex from kids on the internet or that their other neighbour is actually having sex with his niece or his daughter. The general public doesn't want to know that. And this subject is so incredibly tough to get people to become motivated because it's so much easier to just make like it doesn't happen. It's dirty. It's the mole on everybody's back that they would rather just not look at or see, right? They don't want to acknowledge or have to take ownership over the fact that men in our community, men in our city, men in our area are looking at kids and wanting to have sex with them and buying them. And that's a tough thing for the average citizen to acknowledge.

And if folks knew the rate at which it was happening, they'd be astounded.

Acknowledgment, according to Ms. Penrose and Ms. Sheirich, as well as others I interviewed for this research, seems to be key in effectively addressing the sex industry. As mentioned, many people do not even acknowledge that a problem exists unless a friend or loved one has been trafficked. However, some believe that things are changing, among them WPS inspector Kelly Dennison, who worked for many years in counter-exploitation and currently oversees that unit.

KELLY DENNISON: Well, I think we're getting there. We're on the road to an acknowledgment of what it really is. And I've only seen that in the last couple years. The public has actually started to acknowledge that people involved in the sex trade are actually being exploited. To me that's the first step. We have to acknowledge what it really is. And it's exploitation. From that, once we acknowledge and everybody understands what it is that's actually occurring, then an emphasis has to be placed on the importance of dealing with the individuals that are involved in the sex trade and being exploited. And that may come in the form of funding. I think there's a number of social agencies out there that have a great mandate and no money, that have a great working relationship and no resources.

An important goal of this research is to affect the public discourse, as opportunities flow from first breaking the culture of silence and acknowledging that there is a problem.

Finally, my participants pointed out that more training is required for people who are in a position to make a difference. Daphne Penrose worked as a front-line social worker for twenty years and reports that she worked with children and never realizing they were being exploited. She didn't know back then to ask why girls who ran away from her group home often came back with new clothes and jewellery.

DAPHNE PENROSE: My background and knowledge in work around the sex trade actually happened before I knew I was working in that area. So, I started doing front-line protection twenty-odd years ago. And I had many young girls that would go missing for periods of time. And I did not understand that the risk indicators I was seeing were related to sexual exploitation. So, for a very long time I was working with kids who were in the sex trade or being exploited and I didn't even know it. I didn't identify it as that.

Ms. Penrose's story clearly indicates the need for more counter-exploitation training for practitioners.

Several practitioners as well as survivors I interviewed stressed how important training is for service providers because it provides them with the tools they need to work on such a complex issue. Survivors described how foster parents, group home staff, social workers, and police could have intervened to assist them if they had only recognized what was going on. Grace, a survivor, notes that resources and police and other service agency awareness have improved in the past decade but still need to be improved.

GRACE: Like education, I think, is totally key. I was exploited. So, I ended up in the streets in, say, 2000. There wasn't a lot there for us. When I was being exploited, there was the women's clinic in Graham that I went to get checked for STDs often, but I was lucky. There was a van who came driving around and gave me Twinrix vaccinations, Hep C. That's pretty much all that was available. I've seen a lot of change. Staff wouldn't know how to talk to you back then. Now, so many staff are calling it, "Oh, where'd the money come from?" and "Where were you all night?" That's huge. They are trained now to talk about it.

Lyn and Grace emphasized, as did several other survivors, that better counter-exploitation training among service agency staff could have prevented their victimization. Ashley describes how other girls who were placed with her in a counter-exploitation treatment program groomed her for further exploitation; they taught her how to make more money in the sex industry.

ASHLEY: I think my parents tried. I think they didn't understand what was going on with me. I think to them it might have looked like teenage rebellion. But it was addiction and everything I just talked about. But when my parents did find out, and one of the other girl's parents, we went to a program for youths who had been exploited. But I still don't remember anyone actually sitting down and discussing with me about exploitation. At that point, I just knew I was at a school with other girls like me at the time who were working on the streets. And so I learned how to do things and make more money there, working in a massage parlour. So, going to that program wasn't helpful for me. I ended up running away and going back to my predator and to the drugs. Like, I could see that being a good program. Like, I still know of it today, and I know it does help a lot of people. But for me at that point and that time it didn't help.

Ashley points out that training in counter-exploitation and intervention in human trafficking and the sex industry should make staff aware of the dangers of placing people with similar problems together in one space.

Another survivor, Julia, who now works with exploited and high-risk youth, also speaks of occasions on which police and social workers could have intervened and taken her away from a volatile milieu for her own protection. In some cases, they placed her in care as a runaway and just did not have the tools to help her escape from her hell. This is how she expressed her own experience of being trafficked:

JULIA: I think that a lot of people probably knew what was going on. Again, just kind of seen me as a bad kid, or delinquent kid. And probably didn't really know what to do. You know what happens now, right? Workers, they're like, "Oh, I don't know what to do with this kid," you know? "They keep running away. They keep doing this. They keep doing that." But is there a point in time where people could have grabbed me up? Yeah, tons probably. I remember having contact with lots of social workers that just let me walk away. And yeah, I walked right around the corner and, you know, the guy who was trafficking me was right there ... Tons of times police officers pulled up to me or, you know, see me coming out of a strip club, you know. I was thirteen. Did I really look like I was eighteen? Probably not (*laughs*).

It is disturbing to think that many youth could be saved if only the professionals they had contact with, as Julia says, had recognized the signs of exploitation and had taken some action.

My participants described the available training for sexually exploited youth as effective, but stressed that it should be provided more widely. Trevor Bragnalo (WPS constable) considers that the multisectoral case management groups in Thompson, Manitoba, worked well, and outlines how specialized training can help service providers by teaching them the signs of sexual exploitation to watch out for, as well as how to approach and intervene with exploited youth.

TREVOR BRAGNALO: When I was on the sexually exploited youth team [in Thompson, Manitoba], we'd essentially meet I think it was once a month or twice a month. There were police. And there was multiple, there was, like, different school liaisons. There was CFS. So, you had pretty much a room of fifteen to twenty people that'd meet twice a month and find out issues. Like, "Okay, what do you know? What do I know, as the police, what's going on?" And we took some sexually exploited youth training that was put on by CFS in Thompson. It was six days. And as a police officer I found that excellent. Now, when I'm on the front line I can identify girls who I think are being sexually exploited. I had all the training. And then when I came on assignment to Stonewall there was an incident where we had a car parked in a parking lot in Little Mountain Park and it was dark and there was a male in the car with a young female. And he's like, "This is my friend. We've known [each other] forever." Only you talk to the girl alone: "Oh no, I just met him the other day." And the way she was dressed and the way she was acting, I asked her right out, "How long you been doing tricks and trades for?" And her total demeanour changed, and she's like, "Yeah, I been doing it for a year, year and a half." And it's like, "Hmm, all right then." And I find that type of training allowed me to identify that issue, whereas if I was never in that type of six-day course I would never have even known to ask those questions or identify that.

Jay Rodgers agrees with Trevor Bragnalo that effective training exists but must be provided more widely through service organizations and schools so that teachers, social workers, and other service providers do not miss opportunities to recognize and intervene early with at-risk youth.

JAY RODGERS: I think there's got to be a better way of just informing the public and informing service providers how everybody works, because we all have the same objective but we just seem to want to fight over philosophical reasons sometimes. I think that within our organization we're trying to make sure all of our staff take the SEY [Sexually Exploited Youth] training. I think that's a good thing. I think a lot of organizations should do that. I think that there also needs to be broader education around this issue in schools and [the] health care system and other service providers. And it doesn't have to be intensive training. Welfare trainers or youth care practitioners should get basic awareness training, I think [this] would be important.

Mr. Rodgers emphasized the need for all front-line social workers to have specialized training in the area of sex trafficking and exploitation. He also mentioned that specialized counter-exploitation training should be offered in the University of Manitoba's Faculty of Social Work.

Some agencies are making concerted efforts to do as Mr. Rodgers recommends, providing counter-exploitation training for front-line staff. For example, Karen Harper (AMC) relates that the AMC is attempting to provide awareness and counter-exploitation training within northern reserves and rural communities, trying to expose people from multiple sectors to the training in hopes they will take it back to their respective organizations.

KAREN HARPER: We look specifically to our First Nations communities' strategies, approaches are only happening now in 2016. This project that we're working on, as I said, partnering with the province and bringing the awareness and education to our First Nations community and front-line support workers so that they have something concrete and tangible to develop a plan of protection for their women and girls. I hope that the effect of this will move them forward to continue to work on that, whoever the participants will be at the workshops – to take that back and that's encouragement to them to take it back and get your different areas – CFS, community justice workers, your law enforcement, a teacher education representative, your health people, your whole gambit – and have everyone work together. That's how I see this moving forward.

Ms. Harper stresses that agency workers' awareness of sex trafficking and exploitation must be multidisciplinary for a multisectorial safety net to be established among the broad spectrum of service providers.

The last word on the need for more counter-exploitation training goes to Jane Runner (executive director, TERF), who has been in this struggle for more than twenty years. According to her, it is easy for practitioners to miss the indicators of a child who is being exploited, and specialized training should continue for people who might recognize the signs of trafficking and sexual exploitation and intervene appropriately.

JANE RUNNER: But it's just being able, you know, so if you're an educator, you're in a school and one of your kids, all of a sudden behaviours change, there's a difference, they seem more shy or withdrawn or something, right? You know that's when people have got to step in and start exploring, you know: "Okay, what's going on for that kid?" And that's where we miss the boat because schools are so busy. But that's where they see a lot of kids, right, or in day cares, you know, drop-in centres, wherever. That's where you have the ability to maybe help stop it. So when it comes to preventing it, the more aware everybody is, right? In a community, that if they see something, you don't let it go, right? So it's education and being able to understand and see it for what's probably going on, cause a lot of people miss it, right?

Ms. Runner observes that schools are key to accessing and intervening with youth who are vulnerable to exploitation, already being groomed for the sex industry, or being exploited by pimps and sexual predators. Teachers and school staff have access to and are with children for much of each day, so they should receive specialized counter-exploitation training to be able to watch for signs of exploitation.

The following eight findings are based on the interview data concerning awareness and counter-exploitation education for children, johns, the public, practitioners, and those with access to children who have opportunities to intervene.

First, greater awareness is required for all involved. More education on the dangers of sexual exploitation is required for younger children. Survivors, practitioners, and political and community leaders I interviewed stressed that education and awareness about the dangers of predators and sexual exploitation must be stepped up for children in schools, as well as more widely in the community. This recommendation connects with other research participants' observations that (1) children are being trafficked at increasingly younger ages, and (2) those who have the most exposure to young people – parents and teachers – need more training in recognizing the signs of sex trafficking and exploitation and intervening effectively.

Second, consider the efficacy of public awareness campaigns. A strong theme identified by interviewees was the need for greater public awareness about the extent and dangers of sex trafficking and exploitation, through any and all available means. Some effective past marketing campaigns were mentioned, such as "Stop Sex with Kids." Respondents stressed that information about survivor-oriented trauma and addictions programs and resources should be included in this public messaging. However, the efficacy of such programs is difficult to measure. It is possible that people feel they are more effective than they really are (Ayers et al., 2016; Czarnecki et al., 2010).

Other research has suggested that public awareness campaigns in the modern day must focus on social media to be effective (Valentini & Kruckeberg, 2012). French et al. (2014) considered the effectiveness of media campaigns aimed at reducing high-risk sexual behaviour among men, concluding that "the limitations of mass media in imparting skills in effecting behaviour change should be recognized, and campaigns supplemented by additional components may be better-suited to achieving these goals" (p. 17). More research is needed on the efficacy of mass media campaigns aimed at deterring sex trafficking and exploitation behaviour.

Third, survivors must be included in strategizing and planning. Participants underlined that survivors should be involved at all levels of strategizing, planning, and programming. Rebecca Cook made the important point that survivors need to be at the table consulting and participating in the design of public awareness programs to ensure the messaging does not further traumatize survivors. In such programs, she has found that, beyond depictions of violence in the sex industry in films and posters, even small details such as colour schemes can inadvertently trigger and traumatize survivors.

Fourth, service providers need training to work with sex industry survivors. Some survivors told gripping stories about how they could have been saved from trafficking and exploitation if someone in their care circle had recognized the signs and known how to intervene.

Interviewees underscored the training should be made much more available and to many more service providers across multiple sectors, including social work, policing, the medical field, education, government, and NGO sectors.

Fifth, the system needs more doctors and specialists. More counter-exploitation training is needed for professional service providers such as doctors, other medical personnel, and psychologists, and survivors need better access to those services. Some practitioners say that even when they recognized a youth was being trafficked, they didn't know whom to call or what resources are available. This could be improved mainly through better communication, and by some flexibility on the part of specialized addictions and trauma counsellors and medical practitioners. This type of training should also extend to advocates such as housing and welfare officers, so that they all understand the intersectional challenges sex industry survivors face, and realize that they need to address everyday things like making appointments differently. This point ties in with another finding from this research, that sex industry survivors often have unique challenges in performing routine tasks such as simply arriving for a set appointment with a service provider.

Creation of a better communication pipeline could raise awareness among service providers about what resources exist and are available to them. More flexibility in the system might make services available on the days of the week and times of day when they are most needed by survivors. Current service agencies are open during banker's hours, from nine to five, but some interviewees report that more survivors on the streets would access them if they were open later at night. Interviewees also advised me that sundry good resources become less available to survivors because of the agencies' reduced hours of operation. Some of these services that are effective should be expanded with increased funding from the government.

Sixth, johns need to be made aware of the harms they cause. Participants highlighted that men need to be made more aware of the physical and psychological damage they cause to survivors when they purchase sex. They were unanimous on the general strategy of prosecuting and deterring johns, pimps, and traffickers and on viewing sex sellers as victims in the industry. However, respondents reported mixed views on how punishment and deterrence should be accomplished. Some felt stiffer punishments are in order as a deterrent, others that educating johns is more effective. Limited research on the market drivers of the sex industry (the johns) has found that they generally are aware that they are causing some harm to survivors by purchasing sex (see

McIntyre, 2012). However, more research is required to determine what balance of punishment and education is most effective as a deterrent to johns and pimps.

Seventh, education must be delivered in such a way that people can receive it. Great care must be taken to understand the target audience and how messages about protecting children from sex trafficking can effectively be delivered to it. Some rural communities and reserves that are in greatest need of a public awareness campaign about sex trafficking and exploitation have no internet or cell phone service. Therefore, billboards in Winnipeg and social media–based campaigns might miss much of the target audience. Here again, research is required on the efficacy of public awareness campaigns and their means of delivery.

Eighth, people in contact with high-risk youth need more training. Counter-exploitation training should be available for parents, educators, and caregivers who might have exposure to vulnerable youth. A substantial number of my participants stressed that children are groomed and trafficked right under the nose of caring parents and teachers who fail to recognize the signs that a child is being groomed or is already being trafficked and exploited. Jennifer Richardson (StreetReach) reported that she has found that many parents are naive about their children's involvement and exploitation in the sex industry. Participants spoke of an obligation for parents, other caregivers, teachers, and school staff to be trained in counter-exploitation. This training could include how to recognize the signs that a child is possibly being abused and exploited, how to intervene, and what resources and service providers are available in the community; and it should focus on caregivers of children of all ages because children of increasingly younger ages are being targeted for sexual exploitation.

Education was perhaps the most significant theme that arose from the interviews, and is the simplest intervention strategy to reduce the sexual exploitation of young people. Children need to be educated about the dangers of sexual exploitation, and this is a challenge and responsibility shared by society at large. In particular, teachers, parents, social workers, police, and all who have contact with children need to be educated about the early signs of exploitation, how to prevent sex trafficking and exploitation, and how to intervene effectively when it does happen. That message must effectively reach all corners of society, from the clients to the survivors to the multidisciplinary practitioners who work with survivors and offenders in the sex industry.

The issue is compounded by a continually changing environment in which burgeoning internet and social media platforms exponentially increase connectivity among young people and can make them vulnerable to predators trolling the internet. The only way to truly meet these challenges is to provide additional and improved training that reaches more practitioners and also evolves with ever-changing demands. While much work has been done in this area, the consensus is that we as a society need to expand our investments and efforts in the area of education and training – to raise people's awareness about sex trafficking and exploitation and to train those who are in a position to take action. This research hopefully will contribute to an expanded understanding of how to effectively address that need.

6 Canadian Laws and Sexual Exploitation

CHRISTIE: Over the years, and historically, any laws that were put in place never really did much to change it. Right? It always moved it around, as I recall. I think we are doing better now, though, like, historically it hasn't done much, the new laws that Canada brought in place, they're not gonna do anything, trafficking hasn't done anything. Like all those laws haven't really done anything. I think the best that we've done is use our Manitoba legislation to try and get at it. I think that has worked better than anything else I've seen. I was trafficked in the eighties, or I was pimped, same thing, right? So, yeah, sometimes people get too hung up on all that stuff. Let's just focus in on somebody hurting somebody else, and let's just have laws that are simple, that help you to charge people who are hurting somebody else – whether young or old, whatever.

Christie gets at the essence of what the laws should do: protect people. Laws serve multiple purposes. They can provide a framework that law enforcement and supporting agencies can work from. They can define the intent and priority that society wishes to assign certain issues, through their language, focus, and weight. Laws can affect the way resources are developed and deployed in various agencies. For example, laws directly affect the way police, child welfare, and health organizations as well as governments prioritize their budgets and resources. In addition, laws can provide a framework for public discourse, which is critical to building momentum for change. Of course, it is important to point out that laws naturally become outdated and irrelevant, as public issues are constantly changing. It is also important to remember a point made by Martin Luther King, that everything Hitler did during the Holocaust was legal. My participants had much to say about the effectiveness and impact of the laws on sex trafficking and sexual exploitation, but before

I present their views, I will provide a brief overview of the legal history of sex trafficking and exploitation and the state of Canada's laws today.

The 1979 United Nations Convention on the Elimination of All Forms of Discrimination against Women urged countries around the world to adopt measures and create laws against trafficking, sexual exploitation, and prostitution of women (United Nations, 1979). Canada signed the convention in 1980. In 2005, Canada adopted the United Nations Protocol to Prevent, Suppress and Punish Trafficking in Persons, Especially Women and Children (United Nations, 2000. Signing these declarations signalled that the Canadian government intended to act; however, substantial changes did not come until much later.

Canadian laws historically treated prostitution more as a nuisance than as oppression and violence against women. Vagrancy and bawdy house laws enacted in 1892 were clearly intended to maintain order and keep prostitution from being a public nuisance. Solicitation laws enacted in 1972 and the communication laws legislated in 1985 were designed to discourage prostitution by keeping it out of public view. In the latter, section 213 of the Criminal Code of Canada prohibited communicating for the purpose of prostitution in any place open to public view, indicating that the intent of that law was to keep the activity hidden from public sight, and from being a public nuisance, not for the safety of people performing the sex acts (H. Smith, 2014).

A significant change came as a result of the relatively recent Supreme Court of Canada Bedford decision that resulted from an appeal by three women who were charged with prostitution-related offences (Canada vs. Bedford, 2013). Their appeal argued that the existing laws were unconstitutional in that they impeded their ability to safely earn a living through selling sex for money. Lawyers argued on behalf of the three women that the laws against communicating for the purpose of prostitution prevented them from lawfully talking with customers to determine if they were safe to perform sex acts with them for money. The Supreme Court agreed with that position, stating that the existing laws prevented them from safely engaging in prostitution and ruling that several prostitution-related offences as they stood in the Criminal Code of Canada – sections 210, "bawdy house"; 212(1)(j), "living off the avails of prostitution"; and 213(1)(c), "communication for the purpose of prostitution" – were unconstitutional and were to be struck down. The existing laws were to remain in effect for one year, until December 2014, allowing government time to create new laws and strategies to go along with them. The court decision also explained that the laws were struck down because they treated prostitution as a nuisance, rather than as the serious victimization of women and children that it is.

The Bedford decision thrust Canada into a critical debate over how we should approach the sex industry in terms of law as well as strategically. Three basic approaches were under debate during 2013–14. One approach was to prohibit prostitution altogether (the abolitionist approach) for both seller and buyer. This approach criminalizes women and children who participate in the sex industry. Many argue that it further victimizes sexually exploited people, imposing criminal records that exacerbate their already formidable social challenges. (For instance, it is harder to find work with a criminal record.)

The second broad approach was complete legalization, making neither purchasing nor providing sex for money illegal. But in some places where prostitution has been legalized, such as Germany, Australia, and the Netherlands, the exploitation and trafficking of girls and young women has been found to have increased (Kelly et al., 2009; H. Smith, 2014). This may in part be because legalization brings licensing and bureaucratic oversight, and what happens to prostitutes who do not meet the legal requirements? They may be further marginalized and more vulnerable because of being deemed "illegal" (H. Smith, 2014). My sense, from a policing perspective, is that the ones who do not meet government licensing requirements would become invisible, and as such subject to any degradation from which traffickers can profit.

There is support for this view. Gunilla Ekberg, a widely published Swedish Canadian lawyer and advocate for victims of sex trafficking, speaking at a June 2016 forum on sex trafficking and sexual exploitation at Global College, University of Winnipeg, explained how legalized prostitution in Amsterdam has failed. Ms. Ekberg said that the famed legalized prostitution district of Amsterdam was recently substantially closed because it was learned that most of the women working there were being trafficked against their will by organized crime. In addition, a study of human trafficking trends in 150 different countries in 2012 concluded that legalizing prostitution generally correlates with increased human trafficking (Cho et al., 2013).

A third broad approach is limited legalization, which recognizes sex sellers as victims of exploitation. This third approach favours anti-prostitution laws targeting traffickers, pimps, and johns, arresting and sentencing the purchasers of sex and not the victims. This is known as the "Nordic model" because it was first employed in Norway and Sweden with some reported success (J. Smith, 2014b). The Nordic model, enacted in 1999, has three major aspects: (1) a national public education campaign, raising awareness about the harms of sexual exploitation; (2) programs with enhanced support for people exiting the sex industry; and (3) stringent laws attacking the market (traffickers and johns) and not the prostitutes (J. Smith, 2014b). Prostitution in Sweden reportedly dropped by 30 to 50 per cent between 1999 and 2004 (Eckberg, 2004). Several other countries, including Iceland in 2009, Israel in 2012, and France in 2013, subsequently adopted the Nordic model. In April 2014, the European Parliament endorsed it and the Council of Europe recommended that other countries, including Canada, adopt approaches that .make purchasing of sex illegal, with less focus on the sellers (J. Smith, 2014b).

The United Nations has also endorsed the Nordic approach, and in October 2014 Northern Ireland passed a bill criminalizing the purchasing of sex (J. Smith, 2014b). The Swedish Committee of Inquiry was established in 2008 to evaluate the impacts of the Nordic model since 1999, and subsequently reported that prostitution, sexual exploitation, and human trafficking had decreased. In July 2014, the Norwegian government released a similar report evaluating the ban's impact on the purchasing of sexual services, stating that in addition to reduced demand for sexual services, no increased violence against street prostitutes had been observed (J. Smith, 2014b).

In December 2014, Canada's new laws around sexual exploitation came into effect when Bill C-36 (2014), the Protection of Communities and Exploited Persons Act received royal assent. It is a version of the Nordic model, targeting the market, making purchasing or profiting from the sale of sex from a person illegal, and providing immunity from prosecution to the sellers of sex. In a technical paper analysing the decision, the Department of Justice states, "Bill C-36 reflects a significant paradigm shift away from the treatment of prostitution as 'nuisance,' as found by the Supreme Court of Canada in Bedford, towards treatment of prostitution as a form of sexual exploitation that disproportionately and negatively impacts women and girls" (Bill C36, 2014, p. 3). The Department of Justice report on the Supreme Court Bedford decision (2014) provides the conclusions of the court, based on the evidence presented during the appeal. It highlights that most affected victims in Canada are women and children from marginalized groups, many of whom are Indigenous (Bill C-36, 2014). Certainly, my research in Manitoba found that Indigenous women are disproportionately involved in the sex industry. The numbers may be different in other regions of Canada.

There is no unanimity on any of these decisions. Immediately following the implementation of the Protection of Communities and Exploited Persons Act, some alleged that legalizing the selling and criminalizing the purchasing of sex pushes the industry further underground, making regulation even more difficult and placing survivors in greater danger (Levy & Jakobsson, 2013). On 6 December 2014 several agencies, including the John Howard Society and the Canadian AIDS Society, called for repeal of the new laws and full decriminalization of sex work in Canada. In a joint statement they wrote, "Bill C-36 views all sex workers as victims of violence rather than understanding that it is criminalization, isolation and denial of rights and freedoms that breed violence and exploitation against sex workers" ("Sex workers' groups," 2014).

Prosecuting trafficking offences is problematic. Kaye, Winterdyk, and Quarterman (2014) wrote about the problems associated with the prosecution of human trafficking offences in Canada, due to misunderstanding about how the laws can be used. Despite new legislation introduced in 2005, only a handful of cases have been prosecuted (Kaye et al., 2014; Perrin, 2010). Kaye, Winterdyk, and Quarterman (2014) attribute the limited use of anti-human trafficking legislation to vagueness in definitions contained within it. They consider it important to develop approaches that include more than just enforcement: "While the criminal justice system remains an important aspect of any response model, the present research points to the need to move beyond a strict criminal justice framework when responding to the trafficking of human beings" (p. 36). They suggest moving beyond criminal law, prosecutions, and courts to engage the entire community around the issue.

There is also a question whether international and national laws reach the ground in all localities across the country. Perhaps the strongest statement on the relevance of international laws on sex trafficking and exploitation in Manitoba is that they were rarely mentioned by any of my study participants, even after participants were prompted with questions about the effect of laws on the sex industry. WPS constable Anna Janzen's comments were representative of participants' perception and experiences of trafficking:

ANNA JANZEN: Well, what I think about prostitution – we all know that that's the oldest profession in the world – and prostitution from a policing, legal standpoint is a communication of a sex act for money or goods of some sort. When I think of prostitution, I usually think of it as being an adult person doing this, and that there's some sort of consent, and that it is illegal in the sense of the communication aspect. Sexual exploitation is to me the sexual abuse, and the exposure of sexuality, illegal sexuality to children and youth, sex acts, or a child performing a sex act on somebody whether they know it is a sex act or not, on an adult person or even a teenager or another child in exchange for food or money or gifts or just necessities of, like, shelter.

And human trafficking, I think of more – even though I believe it's a more global issue – when I think of human trafficking, I think of people being sold across international borders for labour or for sexual purposes, and it's illegal. Like the person selling them, there's some sense of fear involved. But it's not just – I know that it's not just globally and across international borders. I know human trafficking occurs here in our city and from city to city and even house to house in the city.

Constable Janzen recognizes that trafficking can occur within the city or even involve moving people from house to house within the same neighbourhood. This is an important point, as many social workers and police officers do not recognize trafficking when they see it.

Sex trafficking is indeed an international problem, and some international legislation and mandates, such as the United Nations Protocol to Prevent, Suppress and Punish Trafficking in Persons (United Nations, 2000; see also UNESCO, 2014), are intended to address the problem internationally. However, the challenge in enforcing these protocols and treaties seems jurisdictional and is restricted by local police officers' knowledge and experience, and their ability to apply them on the ground. Given that my research participants rarely mentioned these international laws, there is probably room for a lot more public awareness of and practitioner training concerning international laws and how they might be applied.

Study participants were asked to describe the effect of national laws on sex trafficking and the exploitation of young people. They were overwhelmingly in favour of not charging and prosecuting people selling sex; rather, they advocated prosecuting sex purchasers and traffickers. Former MP Joy Smith spoke of her role in changing Canadian laws:

JOY SMITH: Well, I made Canadian history by passing two laws. Bill C-268 – mandatory minimums for traffickers of children aged eighteen and under – it's embedded in the Criminal Code now. And police have to be trained that it's a tool for them. It's there – a lot of them don't know about it. Also, judges have to be trained. And Crowns and litigators, attorneys have to be trained on that issue. Also, the second bill was Bill C-310, which reaches the long arm of Canadian law into other countries when Canadian citizens or permanent residents of Canada go abroad and exploit or traffic persons. We can now, if we find them, bring them back to Canada to be tried in Canada. So, those were two very important laws. I wrote the original National Action Plan to Combat Human Trafficking. It was called "Connecting the Dots." And I presented that to the government, and now they've formalized the National Action Plan, which "Connecting the Dots" was the blue-print for.

Ms. Smith discussed Canadian federal laws as they were enacted; how-ever, how those laws are enforced is also important.

The biggest change in enforcement, and one consistently raised and viewed as positive by people I interviewed, is the shift in Canada over the past decade from treating people selling sex in the sex industry as criminals to viewing them as victims of exploitation. Marie, a survivor, summed up that position succinctly:

MARIE: A fourteen-year-old with an older man is still child abuse ...
There should be stiffer punishment for perpetrators.

Gord Perrier (deputy chief of the WPS) asserts that trafficking laws might not always be the best legal tool for use against trafficking; many existing laws in the Criminal Code of Canada could be applied in hu-man trafficking situations.

GORD PERRIER: I'm going to plug Joy Smith's human trafficking law that you know got examined by Parliament and their groups and NGOs and Senate. That was really good because there's nuances within the laws that enable police to do things particular to the of-fence, like they took their ID, or they took their shoes, or they took their clothes. So, it's those actions that are elements of the offence that are encapsulated in the law. And if that is done in a consistent ba-sis then that's really what should occur when it comes to laws. I think Canada has comprehensive laws to deal with all these things. Some of them may be imperfect. Prostitution's probably one of them. But procuring and kidnapping, forcible confinement, sexual assault, sexual exploitation, and all the myriad of sexual offences that go along with that, I think, are comprehensive, and I don't think that there's any big gaping holes there.

Deputy Chief Perrier raises the interesting point that maybe law en-forcement could, in some cases, use conventional laws in combating trafficking, rather than building cases around trafficking laws that do not always fit every scenario well. For example, as DC Perrier points out, perhaps kidnapping or sexual assault charges would be easier to prosecute in some cases.

Regardless of the laws applied, the attitude in policing has shifted, with the police across Canada now generally viewing sex industry survivors as victims rather than as perpetrators. Darryl Ramkissoon (WPS staff sergeant) also concisely described the shift in police enforcement practices to target pimps and johns rather than survivors.

DARRYL RAMKISSOON: Before, we used to arrest girls and bring them to agencies, and it was kind of hit and miss if they got resources. Now we're working with these agencies trying to full-circle help these girls. We now work more collaboratively than ten years ago. Time will tell. Winnipeg is one of the few places left that still has street-level prostitution. The only other ones are Edmonton, Saskatoon, Regina, but Winnipeg has the largest. Hopefully people like you doing studies like this will show if it is working.

Staff Sergeant Ramkissoon also pointed out that not all agencies are of the same mind, indicating the need for flexibility in the legislation so that police agencies in different jurisdictions can respond according to specific local challenges. In his view we need laws that allow police the intervention tools, such as the ability to detain, required to protect vulnerable women.

Gene Bowers, a WPS inspector with over fifteen years of experience working around the sex industry, was a principal architect of the current WPS counter-exploitation model. Inspector Bowers builds on Staff Sergeant Ramkissoon's point about the need for laws as a tool for police to use to help people in trouble. He described the old method of arresting people in order to force them into programs as the best tool available at the time, yet not an effective way of preventing the sexual exploitation of young women. Jailing was historically used as a last resort that allowed police to get survivors off the street for their own benefit, at least for a few days.

GENE BOWERS: There were over a thousand women we arrested in the last decade. And although arresting them, it did save some of their lives because they weren't on the street. They were able to get off the street. Being in jail is a bad place to stay, but a place of safety for them. A lot of the girls that I ran into – and I hate the word they use, "girls" – but women involved in the sex trade, often they would be on the streets for two weeks without eating, sleeping, just all the basics that people take for granted. And jail was one place maybe they could sort of get that needed break, food, nourishment, rest, kind of thing. So, in that respect, I think it saves lives, but it really never got down to a lot of the issues that brought them there to begin with.

How tragic when the best the system can offer is jailing victims in order to protect them. Inspector Bowers characterized the old police interventions as adversarial and as pushing the sex industry from the city's core into less central different neighbourhoods. This didn't solve the issue or make things safer for survivors, so he participated in changing the policing approach in Winnipeg: sexually exploited young women were no longer arrested, but instead encouraged to seek help from the police rather than avoiding them.

Andrew Swan (MLA) outlined the challenges faced in moving from legal/procedural change – prosecuting johns and pimps rather than young survivors – to attitudinal and societal change:

ANDREW SWAN: Well, we got new criminal code provisions in Canada, which for the first time in our country's history have made it illegal to buy sex, full stop. And, again, this has been the evolution from sweeping it under the carpet, right? As long as you're not communicating for the purposes of prostitution, you're okay. Now we're on the outset, I think, to being able to change attitudes. And what these new laws will do is open the door to more focus on the demand side. And if you deal with the demand side of changing johns' behaviour, changing the way all of us perceive prostitution and sexual exploitation, that is the only long-term way that we're ever actually going to get it to decrease.

A large proportion of my participants agreed that legal enforcement should focus on deterring purchasers of sex. For instance, Emma, a senior prosecutor with Manitoba Prosecutions, called for more enforcement to be enacted against pimps and johns. She also stressed that it takes resources and effort to prosecute offenders.

EMMA: In the early days, it was common to charge the prostitutes. Over the years we recognized it is more beneficial to have the people supported. In recent years there is recognition that across society those strategies still need a significant injection of resources. We still need more focus on prosecuting the perpetrators. Victims are often scripted, oppressed, influenced by family members, so they are under pressure for basic survival.

Although Emma and other prosecutors and police I interviewed said it is clearly preferable not to arrest young women for selling sex, since they are victims of exploitation and not criminals, some in this justice group stated that the power of arrest is sometimes the only tool available to assist people by getting them away from their pimps. For example, Lynn, a WPS constable, does not agree with the new laws. She voices the position of some in policing that enforcement is the answer to changing sex-selling behaviour.

LYNN: I think that it's hard because you have to walk the line of being a police officer and treating them as victims and sort of understanding what they're going through. But we also have to uphold the law. I think it's a difficult position for police to be in, but I mean we have to follow the laws that are currently laid out to us.

Others in law enforcement advised me that they view enforcement as the only tool available to force sex sellers into treatment programs. Derek Carlson (WPS counter-exploitation detective) described arresting survivors to get them into programs as the better of two evils: it gets them away from pimps and gives them a chance to get out of the sex industry.

DEREK CARLSON: The laws prevent us from keeping the girls off the street ... It's unfortunate we can't intervene with the law in place, to pull them back and use their discretion, saying this is your time out, you're being arrested, and put them in remand so they can detox and maybe get some resources in there to help them. Or address the problems that were left for months, because we don't have the legal authority to yank them in and force them. So, I think that's a crucial step that was taken away from us. So, without that system in place we're just kind of there to make sure they're not being pimped, exploited, forced into the trade. And it's really hard because the year and a half I was out doing that I hadn't had any person step forward and say, yeah, you know, I'm being human-trafficked, I'm being exploited, pimped out.

Constable Carlson touches on the difficulty in investigating these crimes. Unlike other crimes, pimping has no clear victim to provide evidence of a crime because survivors, for a variety of reasons, rarely come forward, so the police must attempt to investigate without victim statement evidence.

Shannon McCorry (Project Devote) believes the focus in the laws on purchasers rather than victims is generally good, yet she is ambivalent about the inability of the police to arrest survivors.

SHANNON MCCORRY: I thought about this because I have mixed feelings on the laws that are changed around prostitution and around that sort of thing because, I think, that previous to the laws changing and that, we had a program through the Salvation Army – it was called the prostitution diversion program, which I'm sure you're aware of. And one of the things that happened is when a woman was charged, part of sometimes what she could do to have those charges stayed was to participate in this camp. I think for some of these women, being forced to kind of go to this camp is – lots of people think is not necessarily fair – but it gave them three days to be off the street, even three days to be fed, three days where they could focus and kind of they knew they had to stay there so they could focus, they could be safe and a variety of different things. And I think now that those laws have changed and there is nothing kind of cooking. There's no hope to get them to attend now because there's the way that the laws work. So, I'm going kind of torn about that because I think that I'm not actually sure what the right answer is.

For comparison, Ms. McCorry discusses the usefulness of having intervention tools to force people with severe addiction problems into detox programs. She also argued that a more effective approach is to offer survivors better programming with a coordinated intervention strategy.

Some participants argue that the laws still need adjusting in order to more effectively prosecute perpetrators rather than survivors. For instance, Diane Redsky of Ma Mawi Wi Chi Itata Centre suggests the laws should be adjusted to increase empowerment of young survivors. She explains that the current laws require a woman to state that she is afraid of her trafficker before the police can intervene on her behalf. This element of the offence is very difficult to prove if women are deliberately manipulated into believing that their trafficker/pimp loves them and often try to protect their abusers. She stresses that police and prosecutors must work around the need for cooperative witness evidence, and the laws should be adjusted to rely less on victims to provide witness testimony at criminal trials for trafficking. In addition, Ms. Redsky maintains that many police agencies and officers do not know how to apply or are not applying the new laws to protect young women being exploited by pimps (Toronto Police Service made 345 trafficking arrests while in other regions of the country there have been very few), and that some changes are needed to enforce trafficking legislation that strictly holds the perpetrators accountable.

DIANE REDSKY: We have some issues with the human trafficking legislation that are really critical. One, the biggest problems with the human trafficking legislation, besides the training of police on how to use it, is that it requires a woman to be in fear of her safety. And that is – so traffickers already know that – so they just went, "I won't make her scared, I will manipulate her into thinking I love her instead." So these women are in love with their traffickers. So they're not scared and they're not coming forward and there's no incentive for them to come to participate in a justice system that [they get] nothing out of.

So we need to make some changes to the human trafficking legislation so that it's easier for law enforcement to apply that law. You know, a lot of "Be here. Be here and tell your story" over and over again. So we need to make some changes to the human trafficking legislation so that it's easier for law enforcement to apply that law. That is my understanding – the number one barrier for police officers is that "I don't have a cooperative witness, so ... it's going to go nowhere. No Crown is going to pick that up." And so, what we should be doing, and what I'm actually working on with the counter-sexual-exploitation unit here, are two things. One is, we're bringing in Matthew Taylor, who was one of the authors of the human trafficking legislation, and the other woman is Nicole – Nicole something [Barrett] – and she is the author of the Bill C-36 legislation. And so those two have actually offered to come to Winnipeg to train law enforcement on applying the law and what they're learning so far, you know, about the law. And the other thing that we could do here for law enforcement is hook them up with other law enforcement agencies who are having success. Like Toronto's at 345 arrests just in the last year. And human trafficking, they're going for – well they're charging for all of it, but human trafficking and prostitution-related offences. But within one year they got, like, 345 arrests that are going through. Peel region has the most convictions of sex trafficking.

And so, some of it is a capacity issue that if we could create a better training system between law enforcement and Crown attorneys as well, and judges, eventually then you're knowing how to apply it. And law enforcement has been, in those jurisdictions in Peel and Toronto, have been really good at navigating around that fear/safety. They've figured out some way to not have a cooperative witness. And so those are some best practices I think we can take a look at.

Jennifer Richardson (StreetReach) suggests the laws could be adjusted to better facilitate resources from multiple sectors working together. For instance, she suggests that child welfare agencies should be mandated with investigating sex trafficking and exploitation, rather than the police.

JENNIFER RICHARDSON: I would change the laws, for sure. I would make child welfare be responsible to also investigate offenders – and in every province, because in some provinces they don't have the ability within the legal framework right now to do that. So, I would change that. I would give police more power to investigate in different ways, and not just, you know, be largely relying on the victim to come forward. Because lots of times everyone knows what's going on but they can't get that traumatized person to say what's going on. Or they might say, it but they won't say it to the police, right? They'll say it to their [social] worker. So there again, you know, well, "Okay, if you don't say it to the police, we can't, you know [do anything]. So, I would change the laws with respect to that. I would make sure there was an all-encompassing strategy. I know people are against secure resources, and I'm not saying I support secure resources, I wish we didn't have a need for secure resources. But, to me, when kids are not choosing to be exploited and we have these offenders who are accessing them readily in the community, and every time they walk out the door of a non-secure facility's caregiving – inside they're being taken care of but the minute they walk out that door those offenders can access those kids immediately, and they do. And they're drawing them out of those resources lots of times. Then we have a problem, right.

As both Ms. Richardson and Ms. Redsky point out, police and prosecutorial dependence on victims coming forward as witnesses is a fundamental challenge in sex trafficking cases, one in which victims are often complicit: they are entrenched in the sex industry culture and are either afraid of or unwilling to talk to authorities. Ms. Richardson also describes the continuum of services that are needed for supporting sex trafficking prosecutions.

Relatedly, Claudia Ponce-Joly contends that the laws and their enforcement are a critical piece of the justice system, yet they do not operate in isolation from the constellation of other intervention systems, including social work, health care, and Indigenous healing circles. Ms. Ponce-Joly discusses the need for multisectoral partnerships that must come together in a coordinated plan to protect women on the streets.

CLAUDIA PONCE-JOLY: I believe the laws and law enforcement do have one of the greatest roles in this. But some would say is a battle against sexual exploiters and traffickers and child abusers. Law enforcement can, well, first of all, child welfare community organizations need the partnership of law enforcement, and vice versa. Now, law enforcement will provide deterrence and the courts will provide prosecution. I don't believe that services to victims alone will solve the issue. There has to be a deterrence factor in our society. People do need to know that if you abuse a child through sexual exploitation that the police will be involved and will follow the laws and there may be a cause and effect that involves charges or investigation or a court proceeding. I believe that this is improving much, especially if everyone becomes more and more educated on how to deal with this issue and how to work with people involved in the sex trade.

Ms. Ponce-Joly raises a theme that became prevalent during my research: that the police and prosecutors play important roles, as do social workers and community-based organizations, in ensuring the safety of these young women, and that partnerships between all of these elements are key in a viable anti-trafficking strategy.

My research participants generally agreed with the new direction that Canadian criminal law has taken to the sex industry in prosecuting organized criminals and purchasers as a deterrent. However, some question the deterrent effect, and ask whether it is more effective to educate johns on how their activities affect the women providing sex. The value and impact of humiliating offenders through media exposure and forced attendance at diversion programs is an area for further research; most of my interviewees, however, were less interested in what the laws are and more in how the laws are enforced and police resources are used to tackle the sex industry. The biggest change that respondents consistently highlighted as positive is the shift in Canada over the past decade from treating people selling sex as criminals to treating them as victims.

Other participants such as Derek Carlson (WPS) stressed the need for harsher penalties for and greater deterrence of sex purchasers, as well as a need to do much more in the area of prevention.

DEREK CARLSON: If we could really set an example with sentencing, I think that could change a lot of future problems. The sexual abuse of kids – if we as a society say that's unacceptable for family to be raping their daughters and getting them to be mentally unstable, getting them into drugs, getting them into the sex trade, if we kind of just threw a book at them, as society, I'm sure that could prevent [the abuse]. So change the laws, that's probably the biggest one, and then throw the book at anyone involved and that kind of sentencing.

Rosemarie Gjerek talks about the need for the police to prosecute traffickers of juveniles using pre-existing charges, such as sexual assault and forcible confinement, which have been in Canada's Criminal Code for a long time. She acknowledges that there have been very few prosecutions for the offence of trafficking juveniles, but that a low conviction rate doesn't mean trafficking offences are not occurring.

ROSEMARIE GJEREK: It's not as simple as just, "Give us this information and we'll catch them." We know how, even from the legal perspective, the onus of responsibility is on proving trafficking. I was at a conference in Ontario and listening to some research profs present on trafficking. And their thesis is that we are putting too much attention on trafficking because ... if they looked at court cases the number of cases brought to trial and actual number of convictions is very, very low, which I thought was insane. It's like saying we know sexual assaults happen, we know the number of assaults that actually get reported, the ones that get to court, to trial. The ones that get to court and result in a conviction are a very small proportion. So then do we say that sexual assault doesn't happen?

Some police officers I interviewed reported major reservations about losing the ability to apprehend and bring sex industry survivors to safety, even against their will when they are in the grip of social influences and drug addictions that impair their ability to care for themselves. They expressed concern that have they lost the legal authority to force survivors into effective health, detox, and counselling programs. Some social workers voiced the same concerns, yet also said that the law should not be used as a tool to further oppress sex trafficking victims by forcing them into programs. But some survivors indicated that they were saved from death when the police took them off of the streets. This is a tough challenge for law enforcement officials that will need further research and continued resolve by justice agencies.

As mentioned above, most contributors agreed with the changes in the Criminal Code, that is, prosecuting pimps and johns as a deterrent to the exploitation of young people. However, some questioned the deterrent effect of targeting and harshly punishing predators, suggesting it is far more effective to educate them about the impacts of their activities on the women who are providing sex. Perhaps the most effective approach would be, as Rosemarie Gjerek of Klinic points out, to teach boys in their formative years how to respect women.

There are differing opinions among police officers, even among those who specialize in counter-exploitation, about the most effective approach to address sex trafficking and exploitation of young people.

Some in law enforcement argue that the police need the power to arrest sex sellers in order to provide needed supports and resources through the justice system – to assist them to exit the sex industry. One detective from the Peel Regional Police Service (PRPS) boasted (personal communication, 4 March 2014) that the PRPS hasn't charged a sex seller in seven years, while other police officers across the country say they need laws that empower them to arrest survivors in order to force them into diversion programs. This has been done in multiple regions across Canada, including Winnipeg, for about the past ten years: survivors are charged with offences and then the charges are dropped once they participate in survivor-oriented diversion programs.

Others stress that the laws should not be used to coerce women to obtain help that they do not want. For example, Senator Vernon White suggested (personal communication, 4 March 2014) that if the police are saying they need to be able to arrest sex sellers to help them, then perhaps provincial legislation should be designed to allow police to get survivors the assistance they need, by force if necessary, without exacerbating their problems by saddling them with criminal records. Perhaps people being trafficked and exploited in the sex industry could be apprehended for their own safety, much like the situation where people with mental health issues are apprehended under the provincial Mental Health Act (2016).

Ashley, a survivor of sex trafficking, stressed that the police need to do more outreach to build trust with sex industry survivors so they feel confident they aren't going to be arrested or acquire other troubles as a result of approaching the police for help.

ASHLEY: I think the police have come a long way in terms of viewing girls as victims. I think the law that was passed criminalizing the buyers of sex is a good one if the police are enforcing it. Like, the buyers need to be criminalized, not the girls. And the police need to do more outreach so that you could feel safe to come forward because maybe [the girls] don't know that they're not going to get in trouble, like they're going to be offered services. They should be teaching about sex trafficking in schools, like have the Joy Smith Foundation school program in all the schools.

Several other participants also said that survivors often do not reach out to the police for help for fear they will get in trouble.

Andrea Scott (WPS constable) suggested that regardless of the laws, the police must refocus their efforts on supporting victims of sex trafficking any way they can:

ANDREA SCOTT: I think the biggest change is – and I don't know a ton about it – but just the ability now to not arrest the females, because we're revictimizing them, and I agree with that to a certain extent. But I also think if we had the opportunity to still arrest them, we remove them from the situation and get them somewhere safe, even if it is in jail, where they can sober up, get off the drugs and clean up, and have an environment that's safe, that potentially they would speak to us. So, I think that it hasn't helped us as police officers, that law. But I mean we have to deal with that law so we have to put more focus on the johns, which I think that's kind of one of the biggest effects I've seen in the last year.

Constable Scott said that more proactive interactive approaches are required to help survivors, especially since legal revisions removed the police's ability to arrest and bring survivors to safety.

Wendy Sheirich (former coordinator of Manitoba's counter-exploitation program) and Daphne Penrose (acting executive director of Winnipeg CFS) both underline the need for enhanced collaboration between all agencies, including the police. Ms. Sheirich believes the police approach has changed dramatically in recent years:

WENDY SHEIRICH: Police are major players. Back in the early nineties we did not have many partners – so, many complaints against the police and RCMP, although some [officers] were more sensitive. Now there has been a huge change, more collaboration and mutual understanding now. The whole mindset has changed dramatically. The police are doing a great job now, working collaboratively, and they are adopting the Bedford decision, understanding women in the sex trade are victims. I think the police are doing a great job now and just need to continue doing what we're doing and working in a collaborative kind of way.

Daphne Penrose supports Ms. Sheirich's position that the police are major players and should be included in coordinating an integrative sex trafficking intervention system:

DAPHNE PENROSE: I think the police should be participating in the coordination of services at every level. And I think that the laws that are present need to be enforced for offenders and people who purchase sex from children. The police have a big job to do – just like CFS and just like our NGOs have a big job to do – to sit back and listen to figure out how to build our responses and to continuously improve our responses, because whatever it is you develop in the front-end to be coordinated, it's only going to work if there's a desire to continuously improve the resources that you provide.

Ms. Penrose stressed that the police, social work, health care, educational institutions, and NGOs need to be better coordinated in their efforts to get young women off the streets and hold perpetrators accountable. At the same time, they need to listen more to survivors' stories to understand how best to assist them.

Lynn (WPS constable) described how the police now focus on bridge building by listening to multiple community voices to establish relationships with sex trafficking survivors. WPS now has a counter-exploitation team that she believes is more effective in liaising and building bridges with the community.

LYNN: I don't agree with the new laws. I think that they are difficult because sometimes the only way to help somebody, I mean to keep them safe, even for a night, is to arrest them. I talked to girls before that have said, "I just got tired of being arrested so that's what caused me to leave the sex trade," because they want to move on with their life but they keeping getting breached and stuff like that. I think that it's hard because you have to walk the line of being a police officer and treating them as victims and sort of understanding what they're going through. But we also have to uphold the law. I think it's a difficult position for police to be in, but I mean we have to follow the laws that are currently laid out to us. Over the last few years a lot of things have changed and I think we've changed for the better. Like us specifically, we have the team that does a lot more of the, like, liaising with the girls and sort of that bridgework. And I think we need more of that for sure. But the problem is that you're not going to find a lot of police officers that want to do that. That's not so much policing, but that's what we need in our service.

Andrew Swan (MLA and former attorney feneral) was well placed to comment further on the province's response to the sex industry and the new laws. He reflects on police resource deployment, trust building, and support rather than prosecution of survivors. He also mentions the frustration that he has heard from police officers over losing their ability to apprehend survivors for their own safety.

ANDREW SWAN: My personal view is that the police have struggled this first year because the young women and men who are out there know that they are not committing a criminal act unless they are in one of the exclusions of being too close to a school or whatever it may be. So I think the police are struggling with that a little bit because it has always been easier when you're doing a sweep to wind up getting the people off the street. They're much easier to find. They're much easier to catch. And if you're under pressure to be seen to be doing something, that's a great way to get your numbers up, to be able to report to the community that you've been active. But it actually isn't the most helpful way. I believe the City of Winnipeg Police Service is on the right track. I know that there's some struggle right now to decide how to best deal with this. One of the issues that we knew was going to be a challenge was the connection between what the police are doing and what the agencies are doing. One of the concerns that's been expressed is that it's now harder to get someone who's being exploited to go to the prostitution diversion program. It used to be held over their head like a sort of Damocles' sword: "You're going to be charged unless you want to go into the program." Salvation Army says, "Nope. They are still getting people coming."

The theme of police intelligence gathering and use came up several times during my research. My interviewees viewed as wise the current practice of counter-exploitation detectives making regular contact with people selling sex, because eventually detectives may gain the trust that allows those people to come forward with evidence against traffickers, pimps, and johns. Others stressed that the police need to gather the right information, which they sometimes are not doing, and share it so that the right arm knows what the left is doing.

Rejeanne Caron (WPS constable) affirms that the police are now focused largely on forming relationships and building trust with sex industry workers, in hopes those workers will share intelligence that the police can potentially act upon.

REJEANNE CARON: I think, as I mentioned before, [police should take care] not to revictimize the victims. I think that's a critical piece of it. And working with [survivors] to gather intelligence, to understand who are the predators. And then, from there, creating – whether it's projects or initiatives – because those girls are a plethora of information. So, really, it's working with them closely, and engaging them in understanding what's out there. And go from there. And then, of course, directing them as best to the right service agencies. And us, as a service, dealing with a lot of the agencies. To work with each other – whether we identify somebody and pick up a phone and say, "I've got a girl that you may want to meet," depending on who the resources are, and work collectively with each other.

Anna Janzen (WPS constable) agrees, but adds that front-line general patrol police officers need more training in how to spot sex industry activities and react swiftly to protect young prostitutes, and in the importance of gathering intelligence. She points out that in the course of their duties general patrol officers come across sex industry survivors regularly, and they miss opportunities to gather and submit intelligence that could be useful to other investigators.

ANNA JANZEN: I would say intel, intel, intel. That's what the police should be doing. It's so many times it's uniform officers – and I'm guilty of it myself – but we would come across somebody – because we're busy, the call queue is piling up – if you see someone get into a car, if you don't have time to pull them over then, put an intel [intelligence report]: "I saw this suspect and sex trade worker get in this car at this time." And you may be on a call to a robbery, but just jot it down in the notebook. I just think the more intelligence the police can gather on this, the better. And, like I said, treating people with respect goes miles.

Constable Janzen's point about treating people with respect connects with all of the interviews in this study. Every participant said in one way or another that the key to helping survivors is being non-judgmental and treating them with dignity and respect. As Constable Janzen and Constable Caron both mentioned in different ways, it all comes down to building trust.

Rose, a senior prosecutor, emphasized that criminal cases against traffickers and purchasers of sex are difficult, and that the police need to work very hard to build trust with sex industry survivors so that witnesses will come forward with information valuable to a prosecution.

ROSE: I think policing in Manitoba has moved in a really important way, focusing on the people buying the services. I think that's the right move. The penalties are there but there needs to be creative investigations. We also need follow-up. I don't see many victims coming to the police and making police reports. Police need to be seeking them out, identifying them, and giving them the opportunity and then following up. They are tough cases and the victims' vulnerability is what makes them tough. They come with a lot of baggage that we have to deal with in court. We are getting better. But these cases need buy-in from numerous agencies, and that doesn't always happen because there's a feeling at the grass-roots level, I think, that it is a waste of time. So my office has been really reaching out to victims at the grass-roots level to build bridges with them. And I think it is working.

Another senior Manitoba prosecutor, Emma, built on Rose's point by accentuating that police often miss opportunities to gather intelligence by not asking the right questions. Emma relates that the police often have people in custody for other reasons and fail to explore or ask them about sex trafficking, missing golden opportunities to prosecute perpetrators.

EMMA: I think we always need to keep our lines of communication open. We try to keep lines open with the police and other support agencies, but we can always do better. We could enhance this by reaching out more. We are trying to do that with community prosecutors, but would like to see those efforts enhanced. Police and the courts can only play a limited role. If we as a society put more resources into a multitude of avenues – including police, education, life skills, ensuring that people who continue to be exploited have a sense that there are other options. The police [when they deal with organized criminals], the organized crime, they don't even ask about the women. I've seen the interviews. When [we] have informants, when we have people that are talking, it's like all they care about is drugs and guns. A lot of people have felt betrayed by the police so they don't come forward.

According to Emma, the police must ask the right questions, gather the right evidence, and share intelligence between agencies and across jurisdictions. Her comment about feelings of betrayal goes to the need for the police to build trust with the victims of the sex industry. This can be challenging when survivors were arrested numerous times in the past, before police strategies changed, and thus see the police as an enforcement bully.

Emma recommended that the police, on top of trust building, should focus their resources on the investigation of crimes related to sex trafficking. In her view more emphasis should be placed on developing undercover investigations and in gathering information on sex trafficking activity at every opportunity.

EMMA: Laws are important to maintain the expectations and standards of acceptable behaviour. Laws need to be enforced and support exploited persons. Laws tend to reflect society's acceptance of the need for social change. We do see law enforcement as important. Police strategies have changed, offering exploited persons support. It would be helpful if there were more effort put into undercover operations. There is often poor communication across jurisdictions, so it would be helpful if there was a Western alliance of officers that were working in this field that people could connect with and would support officers working in this field. In terms of law enforcement, we know that some exploitation is organized and occurs in organized crime. When people are willing to share with the police about guns and drugs and organized crime and murders, we assume that they could also disclose about exploitation, but it doesn't occur. It would be helpful if support agencies asked questions and gathered information to share with the police.

Joy Smith built on Emma's point about providing resources for investigations, asserting that the police need to develop greater capacity for cross-border intelligence gathering and sharing through agencies such as Interpol. Ms. Smith talked about sharing information internationally, and suggested the police could explore more intelligence-gathering capacity to develop greater awareness across police agencies, pointing out that efficiency is greatly hampered when those working towards a common goal refuse to work in teams, collaborate, and learn from each other.

JOY SMITH: The question is, Why aren't the police forces aware of what is going on? What has prevented them up until this time? I was at a meeting the other day, and they were talking about – there was a common thinking, "Oh, there's not much trafficking from the US." They live in la-la land. There is a lot of trafficking, major trafficking is between the US and Canada, Canada and the US, and the police don't know that.

So what component is missing? I would say probably between the border patrols not asking the right questions, not seeing the red flags, because at the border, when the trafficker victims come across, they come across with their boyfriends. There can even be a man and a woman in the car saying, "Oh, we're going across to do shopping." But that's how they got into Canada. That's how Mia got into Canada. And then they disappear. And there's no resources to find them. I mean, she was found seven years later. So I think there needs to be some intelligence around – Why is this not happening at our borders and with our police forces? There's a disconnect there.

Ms. Smith had several practical suggestions: that the police develop expertise by being stationed in other jurisdictions and countries in local anti-trafficking units, and that officers be allowed to stay in positions longer for continued development of their skills and expertise in this complex area. She highlights that no one person is the ultimate expert on this complex topic.

Research participants spoke of the need for the police to be the eyes and ears of the anti-trafficking and exploitation system. The police can compile the right evidence for successful prosecutions, as well as gathering the right intelligence and sharing it more effectively. This requires the police to be vigilant and aware of opportunities through specialized training, to build trust with potential "informants," and to gather vital information for prosecuting organized crime networks and for sharing effectively with other agencies. Many of my participants generally felt that the current police approach of relationship building and intelligence gathering is the right thing to do. They also stated that there is much room for improvement in the information that the police gather and how it is shared and used.

The following nine significant findings emerged from analysis of interviewee's perceptions and experiences regarding to anti-trafficking laws and enforcement related to the sex industry.

First, survivors should not be criminalized. Research participants argued that survivors are victims, not perpetrators, as they were widely viewed by the criminal justice system in the past. In a complete change in the philosophy and approach of policing in the province, in Manitoba new intervention approaches have incorporated this view, and the survivors and practitioners I interviewed universally said that they approve of the new approaches in law enforcement.

Second, greater deterrence is needed. Respondents indicated that more deterrence of sex purchasers is needed. The majority of interviewees strongly emphasized the need for the justice system to focus on investigating and prosecuting sex purchasers and traffickers, not sex sellers. Participants said that johns are not likely to attend john schools, which are humiliating for them, unless they do so under duress. Many, including Hennes Doltze, who runs the john school at the Salvation Army, strongly endorsed the value of educating johns and making them aware of the psychological and physical damage they inflict on many sex industry survivors. On the question of harsher penalties for johns, there were strong voices on either side, with some arguing that humiliation and harsher penalties do more damage than good, and others arguing that harsher penalties are required as a deterrent for men who prey on young women. These are both significant arguments. Several participants also referred to an apparent wilful blindness within society over the john's role in the problem. Some participants observed that no one seems to want to gather intelligence and prosecute johns.

Third, global laws and proclamations often do not translate to the ground level. Some interviewees suggested that the police and local agencies in Manitoba do not draw upon international laws and global anti-trafficking programs to buttress their work and support survivors. Most of my research participants didn't bring up national tribunals or UN proclamations, let alone national programs, when discussing the impact of anti-trafficking laws on the sex industry. Nor do local practitioners and survivors substantially draw upon these guiding global authorities and international laws to supplement and support local, national, and global efforts to stop the violation of young people trafficked in the sex industry. This finding has significant implications for national programs, which might be lost in the ether without a strategy to deliver them into the hands of front-line practitioners in local contexts.

Fourth, people aren't aware of the degree of exploitation going on. Respondents pointed out that there is a complete lack of awareness about international trafficking in the city. Several participants maintained that even those in law enforcement are largely unaware of the extent of international and national trafficking of young people that is underway in Winnipeg, Manitoba, Canada, and globally. They suggested that increased awareness, training, and education are required for practitioners across sectors and disciplines that might recognize and intervene in cross-border trafficking. Multimodal and multilevel training should be delivered on these issues for the judiciary, political leaders, prosecutors, social workers, and the police. These groups should all be represented at the training sessions in order to foster a multimodal learning environment and multisector team building.

Fifth, existing laws could be used more effectively. My interviewees were of the opinion that provincial agencies could use existing laws that are easier to prosecute as well as having stiffer penalties in their arsenals. Several participants pointed out the low numbers of successful sex trafficking prosecutions, stressing that legal and political authorities must consider using existing laws such as kidnapping and rape, which often have more straightforward applications for gathering evidence to be used in prosecuting sex traffickers and pimps.

Sixth, police should focus on trust building. Interviewees endorsed the police approach of building trust and supporting sex industry survivors. They universally expressed their support for the current approach of having police officers on the streets seeking to build relationships and trust with sex industry survivors in order to help them in any way they can. This major paradigm shift in policing has opened up many opportunities to help survivors. Some police leaders outlined the challenges of deploying scarce overall resources in this specific area, especially when one considers that the demands put on policing from other sectors, such as child welfare, are continually increasing. Placing more resources into counter-exploitation necessarily requires redeploying officers from other areas that are also critical. However, there was universal support for having some police resources deployed in this way.

Seventh, practitioners need to be more aware of and vigilant about the signs of trafficking. Respondents were adamant that front-line practitioners, including social workers and the police, should be more vigilant about the tell-tale signs of sex trafficking and ask more questions of the young women they meet daily on the streets. Several participants, in particular prosecutors and politicians, stressed that investigating sex trafficking is still not a top priority for many police officers in their day-to-day work, that gathering evidence of trafficking should be a higher priority for all officers, and that more counter-exploitation training is required in this area.

Police and social workers are the ones who are most likely to encounter perpetrators and sex industry survivors and, therefore, are in the best position to take action to stop victimization. Respondents also viewed police and social workers as most likely to come in contact with survivors when they are at their most vulnerable and in crisis. Therefore, the two should be trained to act effectively when these windows of opportunity present themselves. Several respondents stated that investigators who are in contact with organized crime suspects are in the best position to take advantage and gather vital intelligence. They need training to recognize and take advantage of these opportunities.

Eighth, we need to consider how to deliver to survivors the supports they need. My interviewees had mixed opinions about forcing women into addictions and counselling programs. This is an area that demands an in-depth policy analysis and further research, to allow a solution to evolve beyond just using force to assist young sex industry survivors. Police officers specializing in counter-exploitation, as well as survivors and other front-line practitioners, fully understand the oppressive aspects of the sex industry, and my research participants universally view the survivors as victims of disparity, oppression, and violent predation. At the same time, some police officers view apprehension as sometimes the only tool available to help survivors. Several survivors also said that the only reason they are alive is that they were arrested and taken into custody by the police.

One unique suggestion came to my attention during my research on this topic. Senator Vern White, who was previously chief of the Ottawa Police Service, suggested that one way of addressing this problem is to implement an act allowing police and social workers to force trafficking survivors into treatment, but with none of the repercussions that criminal charges bring for these young women. This is currently done in Manitoba for drinking: the Intoxicated Persons Detention Act (2016) gives police the authority to detain intoxicated persons temporarily for their own safety, so they do not freeze to death or get hit by a car. This is not a criminal charge arrest, but is a temporary detention that does not create a criminal record for people. Perhaps the law could give social workers and the police, as Senator Vern White pointed out, the parallel authority to forcefully apprehend sex industry survivors for their own good, while not charging them criminally and therefore avoiding the negative effects of being arrested for a crime. This measure might provide a way to assist someone, for example when they are high on drugs and need assistance to dry out, by force if necessary yet in a constructive and compassionate way.

This naturally brings up the topic of resources for sex industry survivors, the need for greater availability and accessibility of which is critical. A resource hub could potentially serve this function. If a sex industry survivor decides that she wants assistance in exiting the sex industry, but the required addictions and trauma counselling is not available, a golden opportunity for her to place her life on a different trajectory might be lost. It needn't be if a resource hub has been established to provide centralized resources, 24/7, to coordinate sex-industry-oriented resources locally, regionally, nationally, and internationally. There is no question about the utility of such a measure: my respondents and previous research on trafficking have highlighted the need for greater coordination of resources (Dandurand, 2017).

Ninth, practitioners need the authority to do their work effectively. Respondents contended that the police and social workers' authority could be adjusted to empower them and to enhance their roles when they are assisting sex industry survivors. One participant made the highly unusual suggestion that police and social workers both need expanded authorities that include adjustments to the laws pertaining to their duties in supporting sex industry survivors. For example, currently the CFS Act (2016, section 52) allows for a mandated social worker to enter a premise, by force if necessary, for the protection of a child. A social worker can call the police to assist in the protection of a minor. Perhaps, as some of my respondents suggest, such acts could be adjusted to empower police officers with that authority as well, so they would not have to call and wait for a social worker to arrive in an emergency. Conversely, social workers do not have the investigative powers of the police, such as obtaining search warrants to gather evidence. On the efficacy of Canada's new laws regarding sex trafficking and exploitation, Schwartz (2014) has written: "don't expect court challenges or big changes in enforcement any time soon." He goes on to say that the Harper government's Protection of Communities and Exploited Persons Act did not immediately affect police approaches to the sex industry, nor do they currently affect that industry, as activities such as the advertisement of escorts continue in platforms such as Backpage.com. Lawyer and Osgoode Hall law professor Alan Young, who launched the case that resulted in the Supreme Court's 2013 overturning of the Criminal Code's prostitution-related provisions, states that the sex industry "can pretty much continue to do what they do by running ads for independent sex workers" (Schwartz, 2014). He adds, "it's really bizarre to say that a sex worker can advertise and then when someone answers that ad, they become a criminal."

University of Ottawa criminologist Michael Kempa has commented that the police have some discretion about how they apply and prioritize enforcement of the laws (Schwartz, 2014). My respondents reinforced this view. Initiatives such as Project Return in Winnipeg (Prest, 2016) and Canada-wide Operation Northern Spotlight ("Five charged," 2016) involved new approaches focusing on enforcing the laws against johns and viewing prostitutes as victims rather than criminals. In Northern Spotlight, thirty-two people were charged with seventy-eight offences across Canada, and sixteen minors found working in the sex industry were brought to safety ("Five charged," 2016). While some of these charges were newly created offences, the general approach of targeting johns rather than sex industry survivors had begun across Canada, as police respondents described, a decade before. At this point, in 2017, the overall effect of the new laws or of enforcement in general on sex trafficking and the sex industry is still difficult to judge. Future research on the outcomes may shed more light on the effect and efficacy of laws designed to reduce sex trafficking.

7 Getting Out Is Harder Than It Looks

PAIGE: Meet them where they're at; they're stuck, you know. Had I not lived what I have lived I would not understand, I really wouldn't understand it. I've struggled around addiction; I hitchhiked to Vancouver for the first time when I was fifteen. So I was in and out and that was where it was first turning out in Vancouver and that was years ago. I've always thought so less of myself. Really, looking back, I did not love myself, you know. I did not believe [in] myself when I came in and I would sit in the [program] room.

    I would go to escort [program] group twice a day because I didn't know where else to go. I didn't have my own place. Now, I've gone to rehabs, I've gone through residential and I relapsed, and I've gone through another residential and relapsed. Where am I gonna go now? And one of my counsellors said, you go back to AA, because you know what you gotta do, and she said you go every day, so I went twice a day. I thought I didn't even know how to get there twice a week and I ended up going twice a day for about six months. But my mind was so closed, partly from, I think, the drugs, partly from maybe the abuse, partly from just having never learned.

Paige's was one of the interviews that really affected me; she has lived this vulnerability and articulates the helplessness but also the toughness that these survivors have. It became clear early on in this study that one of the significant challenges in addressing sex trafficking and exploitation in Manitoba is the complexity of the issue and the trauma that survivors endure. It is a unique trauma, compounded by the fact that survivors are coerced into and entrenched within the sex industry subculture and, consequently, service providers have the unique challenge of trying to help people that don't want to be helped. The survivors' challenges are frequently exacerbated by severe substance abuse issues and the fact that traffickers often arrange that survivors have no home or support system when and if they do try to escape.

My interviewees described the layered challenges that survivors struggle with, including substance abuse, childhood trauma, post-trauma stress, and other mental health issues that are exacerbated by the daily trials of violence they encounter in the sex industry. Here Kaitlin talks about the psychological challenges that accompany efforts to escape the sex industry:

KAITLIN: When I came to [–], I was still seeing a couple of them [counsellors] and I was open with my social worker. I was telling her, like, "Ya." I learned in addiction, from going to these treatments, and that you have to be honest. If you lie, it's just going to keep you in there. So I told her, "Ya, I'm still seeing this guy" and that. And she said, "Well, the only way you're going to help yourself is if you completely stop." Once she said that I started to notice that I still felt dirty and cheap. Even though he's a friend and that, I still felt gross. And, you know, had hot showers and all that. I used to feel gross, but I wasn't using.

And I know why I was using so much. It was to hide that pain, to hide that feeling.

Kaitlin tells a typical story that most of us would prefer to not hear, yet tragically, it is the modern-day context of an ancient problem.

Trauma and PTSD are part of everyday life for survivors of the sex industry. Most struggle with complex multilayered issues that call for individualized treatments and supports. Grace, a survivor, describes the trauma she endured in the sex industry and how she didn't really want to leave because she was so enmeshed in that culture:

GRACE: It started out [selling sex] to have food and clothes because I was in Child and Family Services. But the more you have to perform those, the more you work – no, it's not work – the more that you are abused, the harder the pain. So it started with crack, and then it went to meth, right? So it's like you can't – when you are that age – you need to be able to kind of provide your way, so maybe I would show up to a flophouse, I guess you would call it, where like a whole bunch of kids hang out with money. But I'd show up with drugs, and they would be like I was taken care of and fed and clothed because there was a group of us. There was one time this fucking asshole – sorry, pardon my language – he was going to save me, and he took me – I was maybe thirteen, maybe fourteen – and he took me to St. James off the street. And he's, like, "Oh, let's get better, blah, blah, blah." And then it was like three weeks later. I got sober for three weeks. Then he asked me to go and work. So I went and worked, and I made about three hundred dollars and I got groceries. But I don't want to do that sober. So a couple of days after that I headed back to our core of Winnipeg and, ya, it's mostly for drugs to survive, right?

Grace is clear about how post-traumatic stress has affected her. The survivors I interviewed all described their intersectional challenges, explaining how difficult it is to escape life on the street. Participants believe it is critical that people working with survivors maintain a non-judgmental attitude that does not create feelings of guilt or shame. Arousing these feelings in young people, it can cause them to regress and fall back into the problems they are trying to overcome. RCMP deputy commissioner Kevin Brosseau, for example, said how people feel about themselves determines their next steps; therefore, people trying to assist survivors must be nonjudgmental and supportive.

KEVIN BROSSEAU: It becomes a self-perpetuating and self-fulfilling prophecy. If you feel bad about yourself, you're going to continue. If you continue to be told you are – you're less of a person because you happen to be a street worker or you happen to be a sex trade worker, you know? It's often the case. And you'll hear sometimes – you'll read in the paper that somebody's gone missing or somebody's been murdered. And the third line will be that person worked on the street. And it's almost, like, "Okay, they're either being blamed for the situation they're in. Or, they're being thought less of because of the manner in which they've been exploited or the lifestyle choices they've made along the way." So, I think, to me, resource-intensive, culturally appropriate supports, and quickly, would be really important so that engagement that happens – either in, you know, the areas that are commonly understood where this type of activity occurs, or you know, with those who are known to be engaged therein – [support workers] would be able to deploy and be able to be there in a trusting, caring environment where a person is able to be removed.

DC Brosseau believes that survivors who wish to exit the sex industry should be wrapped in a blanket of vital resources in a safe and nurturing environment.

Some participants noted that a significant component in determining survivors' needs and being client centred includes deep listening to their often-painful stories. Jennifer Richardson (StreetReach) said, "I hear once a week from experiential people that they don't feel very heard." An "aha" moment occurred for me as a researcher while completing the field interviews: I realized that several participants – Dianna Bussey, Jane Runner, and Jennifer Richardson – all said "meet them where they are at," and a light bulb went off for me. I understood that we need to meet survivors where they are at in the moment they are seeking assistance, because circumstances are always changing.

My participants also stressed that everyone is different, and so where they are at will differ. Daphne Penrose (executive director of Winnipeg CFS), for instance, asserts that there is no single approach that works to intervene with exploited youth, no "one-size-fits-all approach," because every person is so different.

DAPHNE PENROSE: What needs to happen is the coordinated response so that folks can access different resources depending on where they're at. If you ask somebody who has a ten-point-a-day meth addiction about what's going to help that person exit the sex trade – nothing until they get sober, nothing until somebody intervenes with them.

Jane Runner (executive director of TERF) also points out that nothing happens for women trying to escape the sex industry until their basic human needs are met. This same principle applies to assisting victims of many types of violence, including domestic violence and rape. Here we encounter an overlap with the need for safe houses, in which women can feel safe and access the resources they need. Here is Jane Runner's view on providing for young sex industry survivors' basic needs:

JANE RUNNER: So it's education and being able to understand and see it [signs of sexual exploitation] for what's probably going on, cause a lot of people miss it, right? If you don't know it, if you're not enmeshed in this and know kind of what's going on, people miss it. Or, if you're too busy and overwhelmed, like a lot of teachers in schools, they're busy and they've got maybe ten kids acting out in their room, and the little quiet one's getting missed. So, preventing it is just going to take a lot more work and resources to get in supporting families, educating people who work with kids to be able to identify it and know what the indicators are. And you've taken the [Sexually Exploited Youth] training. We talk a lot about the indicators there and what people can look for. It's education. The main thing – and again when you're looking at people's basic needs we always refer to Maslow's hierarchy of needs – and the main thing people need right away is stability, like, with food, shelter, clothing, like, just the basic needs. That they feel safe and secure. And once that's in place for people, they have a better opportunity to then try and get to programming, get to school, go to counselling, you know, whatever they're needing to do. So, having a good stable home environment, or good stable foster parent, you know, whatever it is that can help somebody feel secure and safe.

Ms. Runner's comments about providing for young people's basic needs and safety align with other research participants' experiences.

Krista Dudek, a WPS staff sergeant with extensive experience working in the Sex Crimes Unit, is less positive about the efficacy of programs. According to her, services are generally ineffective in getting people out of the sex industry; however, programs like the prostitution diversion program at Salvation Army do offer survivors a reprieve from the street, if only for a few days at a time.

KRISTA DUDEK: I know we have different organizations out there. I mean there's Sage house. The Salvation Army's there. Well, when I was in Morals [Vice Division] it was called "prostitution camp." I know it's going to be called something else now. There's the diversion program for the johns. I mean those have existed since I was in Morals, so this is back in 1999. And has it gotten better? I don't think so. I'm not saying that what they were doing is bad. You know, I was able to participate in quite a few of the camps, and when you see the girls when they're not on drugs and they're in a safe place like the camp, you can see that they're all relaxed, they're all laughing, they're all having fun. And that was the one thing that Ms. [–] and I always would comment on. And it's, like – it's too bad, they're actually having fun, and it's only three days, and they're basically thrown back into their reality.

Ultimately, despite all of the problems in the existing anti-trafficking programs and systems, Staff Sergeant Dudek stresses that we need tenacity to hold out a lifeline for those youth who reach for one. This requires flexibility in the availability of resources and support because every person's needs are different.

Michael Richardson (Marymound) believes that there is one thing, a very important thing, that all people need in order to quit the sex industry: hope.

MICHAEL RICHARDSON: I would say people try and exit an average of seven times. I would say it would be fewer times if there were some resources on the other side – housing opportunities, education opportunities, mentorship opportunities, job opportunities, all those things that help people exit the sex trade. Until we can make them feel safe – I think sometimes people want to leave or want to get out of the sex trade, but there's nothing on the other side that they can see promising them a better life and all of that. And we are responding quicker for them to exit. When we talk about people exiting the sex trade, and all that entails – giving up their offender or their pimp or what have you, I bet, there's not enough safe houses or we can't keep them safe. There's no commitment to keep them safe because it costs money. And then there's no witness protection for exploitation. And that's a strong one because the sex trade operates on fear and the manipulation. And the people that's involved in it, they are, they're fearful. So I think protection would be a way to help people feel safe, but also help them exit. And I think the police can provide some of that.

Mr. Richardson describes a bleak reality: that many survivors see nothing for them outside of the sex industry.

As I reflected on the stories related to me by participants, it became clear that survivors of the sex industry do not simply wake up one day and find they are out of the nightmare. They most often experience a crisis or a critical event that forces them to seek help and want it desperately, or they are lucky enough to have a significant person influencing them and supporting them to quit. Even then it is difficult; most people relapse numerous times in their journey out, and some never make it out at all. Many who finally do escape the sex industry dedicate their lives to assisting others do so as well.

Survivors spoke of a gut-wrenching long-term battle with substance abuse, historical and new traumas, and numerous attempts to escape and multiple relapses. Several of the survivors I interviewed said they did not finally escape for good until they became pregnant or saw someone close to them die or get murdered.

One survivor, Paige, was trafficked all over Canada for over twenty years. She described the critical events that finally led to her opportunity to escape the sex industry.

PAIGE: When we talk about this, I always think, "What's personal to me? What happened for me? How did I get out?" I said, and at different times, "It was the police that saved my life." Had I not been scooped and my warrant be put out there for arrest in other provinces, I may have died where I was. I was brought back on a warrant. I was a witness in a murder trial, and I really believe my life was spared. But, for me, I didn't do anything. People came to me. It was almost, like, I am a believer. I believe there is a force greater than myself and I really believe that when I was escorted back from [–] to Winnipeg and east to [–], I had nowhere to go. So I went to 180 Henry [the Salvation Army

Booth Centre]. And it was there at 180 Henry – I had charges on me out of [–]. I was there and met [–] at Booth Center. And that began the healing journey for me. It got me into the prostitution diversion program. So I didn't even know where I was going. I really did not even know what kind of camp I was going to, because another girl was going. From that camp I was introduced to so many different programs here in Winnipeg, such as TERF, Dream Catchers, Sage House, all of these programs. And they were all little stepping stones for me.

Paige's description of the various programs as stepping stones further illustrates that a wide array of choices must be available to young people trying to escape the sex industry, because different people need different stepping stones, and those needs are continually changing along with people's personal circumstances.

Friederike Von Aweden (Klinic) also notes that critical events in the lives of young sex sellers often precede their "getting out." She stresses the significance of the person's environment and the relapse that survivors often experience when they re-enter their old triggering milieu.

FRIEDERIKE VON AWEDEN: When I see people making amazing changes, sometimes it is with pregnancies where they feel like they are responsible to their fetus. Lots of lifestyle changes happen. I think with pregnancy, they are great lifestyle changes, but it's often not enough to keep a mother with her baby. Sometimes critical news like a new diagnosis of HIV or HEP C, I think, is important. Losing a friend to an overdose. But nothing easy, nothing quick. Wide access to treatment programs. With treatment programs, I see so many women work so hard and do so well in treatment programs. And when they release into the old environment they lose all the [progress] that they made.

Other respondents also describe how various events could jar women into wanting to escape.

Diane Redsky (Ma Mawi Wi Chi Itata Centre) summarizes the need for an effective anti-trafficking and sexual exploitation system to be client centred, flexible, and adaptive. She also stressed that counselling and addiction resources must be available to survivors when they need them, which might be immediately, without wait lists. Ms. Redsky noted that these women walk a fine line, always on the verge of relapse into addictions and/or the sex industry, and that they require a safety net that doesn't currently exist.

DIANE REDSKY: Some consistent things that we've heard [are] that, first, women don't have a safe place to go. And if there was a safe

house or a safe centre or a place to go that is non-judgmental ...
That's what needs to be there that we don't have. What they rely
oftentimes on right now is other women who have exited. And they
hang out in their house. And that's always not a good idea because
there's a woman trying to rebuild her life. So we don't have a safety
net. Another thing that women will talk about is that "I need addictions
[counselling]. I need to deal with my addictions first and foremost."
Like, "I want detox right now, and I want to do it this second." And then
you get into waiting lists. And then you get into a process. And then
you have to be drug-free for two weeks before you can get into this
program and that program. And it's not realistic for women who are,
like, "Now. I want now." And we don't have a system that can respond
to "now." And that's part of the problem.

My interviewees repeated that no one wants to be out selling herself
on a street corner. WPS constable Anna Janzen describes the cycle that
many women struggle with, almost always including a roller coaster
of substance abuse and addictions. She has found that 99 per cent of
people who are out selling sex on the street wish they were doing something else; they are doing it for survival.

ANNA JANZEN: Anyone that I've dealt with in the sex trade, all want
to get out and there's not one person I've ever met that wants to be
standing on that corner for twenty dollars or a rock of crack cocaine
or whatever they're doing. They're all out there because they need
to be out there. And even with the kids, they want to be out there or
they don't want to, but they're out there because they would rather
be getting paid than being home getting abused and not getting paid.
It's reality. An awful thing, but I just think, from a policing perspective,
I found even if it's for one day, if I can tell a girl to get off the street for
one day and be compassionate and non-judgmental – like, I've never
walked in their shoes, I don't know. What they're doing out there, it
definitely is wrong, and they're out there doing something illegal,
they're going to be using drugs and selling themselves, but if you can
be non-judgmental and compassionate and just treat someone like
a human being instead of being disrespectful or abusing them even
more with your language or your position or whatever, that can do
wonders.

Here again, Ms. Janzen highlights the critical importance of service providers, including police and social workers, being non-judgmental and
caring about survivors' safety and well-being.

Another survivor, Elizabeth, says the damage is permanent and that one can have setbacks even decades after leaving the sex industry:

ELIZABETH: I'm experiential, identify as experiential today, even though I exited over twenty years ago. I'm still experiential. I'm no further away from that curb than any of the other women that are out there, just because it's been twenty years – the triggers are still real for me today. The work that I do is extremely rewarding, but it's also hugely triggering. And anytime financial insecurity hits, stinky thinking does too. Yeah, it's easy to go back to that frame of thinking. I used to start my story by saying I was twenty-one years old and I left a relationship. I was violently raped. And then I started working in the sex trade. But over the last few years, I started recognizing the fact that I was groomed for the sex trade long before that. And I actually turned my first trick when I was eighteen. And I had been primed for it for a number of years prior. And just the people that I associated with and people that I considered to be normal everyday people were folks that were either in a place of exploitation or drug dealing or some kind of criminal activity. But at that point in my life, I thought it was normal life.

Elizabeth's insight has significant implications for developing sustainable resilience training for survivors. They need effective responses for when they feel triggered, to avoid relapse. This is pertinent to the large number of survivor/practitioners working to assist young people to escape the sex industry. Organizations that employ survivors should be very cognizant of the danger that these people could suffer from triggering experiences as a result of their work. Trauma programs for dealing with PTSD and triggering experiences could save people from relapses.

Bill Fogg, WPS superintendent (retired), perhaps best sums up the challenges that survivors face while attempting to escape the sex industry:

BILL FOGG: I think the biggest thing, and it sounds really generic, is viable alternatives. People don't – I don't believe people enter the sex trade because they want to, especially in a place like Manitoba and Winnipeg. And I think you know it may be different for different people, but addictions are certainly one of the big problems.

I think once you stabilize the addictions, what you find is that there's some underlying trauma and mental health [issue] that has probably driven the addictions in the first place. So you need to be able to get at the root of those things and be able to provide support. So if you give those kids an opportunity to live some place safe, and stable, in a realistic environment – it can't be a sterile environment because they're

really not programmed to be able to walk into [a] "Father Knows Best"
1950s environment. I think that what they need to have is that opportunity. They need to have the hope and believe there's another way for
them. I think that has to be, to some degree, tailored to the individuals.

Inspector Fogg's analysis is similar to the views expressed in my
interviews of survivors as well as other participants. Survivors first
require that their basic needs be met in a safe, secure environment; then
they need support coupled with hope for the future.

One finding of my research was the disproportionately high number
of sex industry survivors working in agencies and programs oriented to
assisting survivors of the sex industry. As the interviews progressed, it
became abundantly clear to me that survivors who flee the sex industry
often feel indebted to the people who helped them escape, and they feel
compassion for those still trying to extricate themselves from this brutal
and violent culture. Helping others is also one way that the person can
derive some value from their horrific experiences in the sex industry.
One survivor, Paige, observed that it is meaningful for those striving to
escape the sex industry to see others who have successfully escaped. In
this respect, experiential people play a critical role in supporting other
survivors.

PAIGE: Based on my twelve years' direct experience of being trafficked
and having previously participated in programs with staff who were
not experiential and those who were, I preferred to talk with professionals who had similar experiences as me because I knew they really
understood what I was going through and genuinely wanted to help.
When a survivor is working at an agency that meets the needs of
those who have previously been trafficked, victimized by predators,
it can make a big difference in the lives of the women they work with
because [the women] see someone who has gone through what they
had and found a way out. From my own personal experience, currently
working with other survivors, I've had the opportunity to be the role
model to women who went through the same things I did. One woman
said to me, "If you can do it, I know I can too." This is why it is so important for survivors to work with other survivors. And it is important for
survivors to have an input in the decision-making processes at front-
line organizations.

Paige and two other survivors, Elizabeth and Grace, described their
experiences of transitioning out of the sex industry and becoming

counselling and supporting practitioners helping others going through similar exiting processes. Elizabeth, a survivor/practitioner who has worked for twenty years helping others as a support worker, said:

ELIZABETH: Okay, I myself am a former sex trade worker. I transitioned out of the sex trade over twenty years ago. I was involved in both street-level as well as indoor trade. I worked for pimps. I worked independently. I worked for escorts, a massage parlour, and I was trafficked across Canada. I put two pimps in jail for living off the avails, prostitution and conspiracy, and murder, and I started my healing journey twenty years ago in a program called [–]. And I stuck around long enough that they hired me. And I've been working in the field now for many years as a peer support worker. I'd like to say it's [selling sex is] all a choice, but I feel that there's a lot of survival sex that's in the sex trade as well. Some folks feel that they've made the choice, and don't realize the amount of involvement that they actually get into. As somebody who chooses to identify as a victim of exploitation – I usually identify more as a victim of exploitation although some people I know identify as survivors of exploitation and I have identified myself on occasion in that frame.

Similarly, Grace, another survivor/practitioner, describes a sense of giving back to the program that helped her:

GRACE: It's kind of funny because I never talked about it, but it was like I needed to talk about it to get into this program, because it's for experiential women. It's an oxymoron because it's like exploiting my experience to get to the next level, but things are so much different. I don't even have to identify in my workplace as being experiential anymore because I have the credentials. Like, I always had the ability to have a different lifestyle, but I never had the opportunity presented to me to make it different. And so it's been a journey since 2010 when I finished this program. And I went on into second year and people actually wanted to listen to what I had to say and incorporated my opinions and ideas into working with children in care themselves.

Paige, like Grace and Elizabeth was drawn towards helping others. She made a lot of interesting points about her work with sex industry survivors. Having "lived the experience," she says, she knows what it was like to stand on a corner selling sex and is able to fully understand the value that she brings to helping others. Here's how Paige describes working with survivors:

PAIGE: I come to the table working in the field, here with sexually exploited women and transgendered females, as a result of lived experiences of my own. With a past of addiction, which my addiction took me down to the point of being homeless, I often say that when I got well or began to get well, I was almost emotionless – and no place to go. And that was pretty much the way it was for me. So having lived experience was knowing what it was like to stand on a corner, if you will, jump in a stranger's car only with one thought in mind, and that is to pay in cash to supply a habit. Looking back now, I also see those periods in my life where I was able to pull it together. It took a number of times but I was able to go back to school. And able to maintain and get my grade 10. And then I did the GED and got my grade 12. And jumped back in and took a nursing program. And was able to work as a nurse for a little while, and was able to maintain sobriety on my own.

I wasn't happy, but I was sober. So I had successful periods, but I would always end up back there somehow. So even back then I always knew I wanted to work with women. I did not realize then I would be involved [working with those] in the sex trade. I still feel it is women who are involved in the sex trade that I am involved with. But I feel that I would be there for any women with pain. I know who I am, wanting to help people, yeah.

After hearing Paige, Grace, and Elizabeth's stories, I understood that no one can know what these women experience, or what it takes to escape the sex industry. Therefore, they are a priceless resource for service agencies and people who are reaching out for help.

As further testimony to their value, Diane Redsky of Ma Mawi Wi Chi Itata Centre discusses how important it is to include survivors' voices in programming, working in the field, and advocating around sex trafficking and exploitation issues. She emphasizes that survivors' voices should be amplified.

DIANE REDSKY: Building on certain resources is one thing, but one of our main priorities is increasing the voices of experiential women. We're all past sharing the horror stories. Now we're so far advanced in this province that we're looking at real exit strategies for women, which we actually don't have here. We don't do that really well. For women who want to exit, it's still an uphill battle for them. And we can do things well and keep them safe when they're under eighteen. But once they get eighteen and over, there's almost nothing available. So the coalition – that's another one of our key priorities, is we're not expanding our mandate to adults, both men and women.

She makes a very important point: that effective exit strategies for adult survivors are not established anywhere in Canada.

Another survivor, Julia, describes how some people wind up working with survivors despite their best efforts to avoid it. She avoided the work and then seemed to gravitate back towards it.

JULIA: When I first went into social work, I went to work with addictions, and I didn't want to work with exploited people. I just wanted to stay away from that. And it just ended up everywhere I went, I ended up being the person that ended up with those kids, or those women. I think, unfortunately, a lot of exploited people, or people that are trying to exit now, the only legitimate thing they can do is work with kids or other adult women. And not all of them want to, but they don't have any other real avenues to gain employment any other way. And that's sad because then they sometimes end up doing this work and they're not ready, or they end up relapsing, or things end up happening because it's too close, it's too much for them to cope with. If there's other opportunities for them to choose, then they might not [do this]. I've just seen a lot of people relapse. And they've said, "I don't want to do this work. I didn't really want to work with kids but there were no other jobs."

Julia went on to explain that she was drawn to the helping industry, but others are guided into it, perhaps because it was an opportunity that was more available to them.

Ed Riglin (RCMP sergeant) has devoted most of his career to counter-exploitation. He was also involved in establishing the Joy Smith Foundation, which is focused on reducing or eliminating sex trafficking in Canada. He points out that numerous agencies focused on advocacy and assisting survivors to leave the sex industry were established in recent years because of the high number of survivors available to work in them.

ED RIGLIN: Of late, I would say that a lot more NGOs have popped up, primarily driven from girls that have come out of the sex trade, the human trafficking trade, sexual exploitation, have evolved from there, have come out there, and have tried to get other girls to come out. I would say this is a relatively new thing that has come out around sexual exploitation. From a criminal aspect, I think, you can look at it by simply looking at the dated criminal codes in your research, from what it used to look like in 1988 to what it used to look like in 2000. You have to look at it thirty years ago. My view is that we are at the forefront of starting to evolve both with policing and society with NGOs, social services. All of these areas are starting to become more aware, more educated. We're on the front end of this.

Sergeant Riglin, in addition to his point regarding survivor-centred NGOs driven by experiential practitioners, provides valuable context, contending that we in Canada are just now on the edge of making real change in counter-exploitation work.

The consensus among those I interviewed is that the survivor's perspective is important and that they do great work to empower other survivors. Claudia Ponce-Joly, former executive director of Manitoba's Child Protection Branch, emphasizes the important role that survivors of the sex industry play in assisting young women on the streets, as they are aware of the dangers they live with as well as their needs.

CLAUDIA PONCE-JOLY: I also think that one of the most successful approaches and strategies in place today that's growing is experiential workers, people who have exited the sex trade. They successfully are being empowered to tell their stories, to share their knowledge, and to reach out to those who may be at risk or are entrenched. I believe that the information that they're providing is also helpful for all kinds of research, learning, and investigative approaches. But I believe giving those women and men a voice helps empower others in addressing and combating sexual exploitation, and even at times being able to recognize it and step out of it. Those experiential workers, I believe, are a key strength and strategy that are in place today. I think it also serves [as] a deterrent for those who are exploiting others, for them to share. People who were once victims become ambassadors of hope and change, powerful, and in that capacity I believe will help deter others.

Ms. Ponce-Joly's description of the role of survivors in the helping professions is profound and inspiring, as are the stories of the survivors I interviewed.

There is room for research into whether survivors are more effective than non-experiential practitioners at supporting other survivors of the sex industry. However, there is little question that they are a valuable resource that is appreciated by the clients they serve. A second question that should be researched is the impact that doing this type of work has on survivors. Several of the survivor/practitioners I interviewed stated that working day in and day out on the very tough issues that these young women encounter is very difficult for them, often triggering emotions that they must cope with.

Speaking more generally about needed services, Sada Fenton, manager of the prostitution diversion program at the Salvation Army, notes that it is important to recognize that survivors' situations are continually changing:

SADA FENTON: I think basically for me, right now working in the field I'm working, it's just meeting girls where they're at and being there and just encouraging them, believing in them when they're unable to believe in themselves. We can't do it for them, but we sure encourage them to do it. Give them hope.

A large number of my interviewees emphasized that services must be client centred, as everyone has different requirements at particular points in time. Jane Runner, for example, agrees with Ms. Fenton's point that service providers must meet each survivor where she is at in her life to provide hope, and each person's experience is radically different.

JANE RUNNER: I think people need to work where kids are at. The approaches that we use here [TERF, New Directions] that I think are really effective [are] really being person centred. So that's really supporting the person to drive their own bus. Not for us to be directive and tell them what to do. And to make sure that we are working from their cultural lens, not our own. So whatever it means to them, on how they want to move from there, and other strategies and working from [a] harm reduction perspective, working from the stages of change.

Kim Trossell of the Dream Catcher program at Klinic agrees that programs must be client centred, focusing on the unique requirements of each individual.

KIM TROSSELL: Number one, I wish and I hope that one day it will be a reality that all services will be client centred and [client] focused rather than the need of the government to create funding and hoops for people to be jumping through. I think it's extremely important that people are treated as individuals, that the amount of trauma that has been experienced out there has an opportunity for healing. I think that the biggest piece was getting everybody to play nice, not competing against [each other for] funding, but working together to collaborate so that we're not repeating the same – or reinventing the wheel, that the needs of the clients are met. It doesn't matter who's getting the funding for that. It's collaborating together as a community, working together to be able to provide this support for the women.

Similarly, several of my respondents noted that providing services is more about building good individual relationships.

A number of service providers talked about the challenges of having only a short period of time to work with survivors due to the structure of their programs, and in trying to connect survivors with effective long-term, flexible resources. Chelsea Jarosiewicz (Marymound) stresses the importance of providing critical resources for young women who are desperately in need.

CHELSEA JAROSIEWICZ: There's always an initial crisis where some-one out there is brought to the Crisis Stabilization Unit, which is a short stay of three to five days. And I think what would need to hap-pen, though, is that either they stay there longer or there is some sort of plan as to where they go afterwards, where they stay with us until a new placement [in the child welfare system] is found, and one that actually addresses the sexual exploitation and the root causes of that and what's going on with that child, rather than "Okay, your five days are up, and now you're going to this shelter." In the last year, I can only think of one girl that was on an extended stay due to a sexual exploitation disclosure that came out. And even that was just a sev-en-day stay. And then they had found her a rural placement, which I definitely think does help, but in the end the kids just got to find a way to come back to Winnipeg [where their supports, friends, and family are]. So in the end it's almost backwards in itself because it's not helping the child. It's just moving them physically and not addressing the true issues.

Ms. Jarosiewicz remarks that her agency works with a child in crisis for a few days, often with little or no input in the longer-term intervention plan. She also viewed the lack of coordination between service provid-ers as problematic because often the best resources for multiple issues a youth is facing might reside in different agencies, which often do not coordinate resources for the client.

A message that comes through loud and clear throughout all of the interviews was the compassion that practitioners generally feel for the sex industry survivors they work with. They repeatedly acknowledged from every perspective that being client centred means thinking of sur-vivors as valuable human beings, loving them, and treating them as individuals with dignity and value. WPS constable Trevor Bragnalo considers every client important and valuable, and took a compassionate approach to assisting them:

TREVOR BRAGNALO: It is unfortunate, because a lot of these girls are really great people, you know. You talk to them, they're smart. They're funny. They're intelligent. They joke around. And then it's this other side, you know. They get slowly pulled into it. And it gets to that point almost of no return, where the addiction, the crack addictions – And, yeah, you could put girls into a treatment facility, but after the treatment facility there has to be supports on the outside where they can go and be safe, away from that group that they originally had contact with. But then again, those are their friends, and they, a lot of times you know what, they get dragged back in. But if you could just save one, that'd be great, you know.

Constable Bragnalo's words show how much he cares about the children he has tried to help over the years. Patricia Haberman (Rose Hall, Marymound) is another example of a compassionate service provider who really cares about the young people who cross her threshold every day. Here is what Ms. Haberman says about her "little girls," as she calls them, whom she works diligently with to see them through hard times.

PATRICIA HABERMAN: I love 100 per cent what I do. I love all the sassy little girls in my home, in my group home. I'm trying to say to my staff, and this is what I say to you and my team, "This week we do what we can do on a daily basis." I walk in every morning, and the first thing I say, I say, "Good morning." And then I say, "Who's in their bed?" Not "Who's not here?" It's "Who's in their bed?" If they didn't go to school four days this week, did they once? All right. We give them a high five on that one because they've had enough people telling them that they're pieces of shit and they're tired of life. They don't need us telling them that they're failing, too. That's from my standpoint. Yeah, we need to hug them and love them, and tell them to keep coming home and we'll feed them.

Ms. Haberman is passionate as she describes the spirit of the survivors in her group, their potential to make a difference in the world. That same compassion for others came through in RCMP deputy commissioner Kevin Brosseau's words above as he discussed why it is important to be non-judgmental with survivors.

My respondents stressed that relationships are important. Very rarely do survivors say they escaped the sex industry as a result of a particular program or agency. More often they report that they were able to free themselves as a result of the support of a certain person, whether from a program, an NGO, a social work background, or policing.

Rejeanne Caron (WPS constable) emphasized, as most participants did, that practitioners and supporters must be tenacious and non-judgmental in supporting youth in their struggle to escape the substance abuse and other factors that draw them continually back into the sex industry, so that they can pick themselves up and try again each time they fail. Here is how Ms. Caron described one survivor she worked with:

REJEANNE CARON: I think the supports, having the supports there, and realizing that you're going to fall off the wagon a hundred times, and having people there to help you to get back on. I've seen it happen where I had a young girl who was sexually assaulted over a period of seven hours. And we go to court, and she had to write a victim impact statement. This girl was, I didn't know her level of education, was absolutely brilliant, what she wrote. And I told her you should get your grade 12. You're a very smart girl. And that sort of planted a seed, like, "You can do this." Through a period of, like, two years in my time in the Sex Crimes Unit, she fell off, I'd pick her up off the street. She was, you know, full of drugs. But I kept trying and kept trying. And about a year after I left the Sex Crimes Unit, she called me. And she was so happy to say she did get her grade 12 and that she had been clean. So I think to just keep at it and knowing there are people there and people care and there are resources there.

Constable Caron's point is critical: an advocate's tenacity and non-judgmental support could sometimes be the key to helping people escape the sex industry.

In a related vein, Leslie Spillett, executive director of Ka Ni Kanichihk, refuses to label people: they aren't "trafficked" and "exploited" people, they are just *people*.

LESLIE SPILLETT: I don't differentiate, Bob, between "you're a sex trade worker" and "you're this" and "you're that." That is not how I conceptualize people. They're my people. They're my relatives. They're my kin. These are my family members. These are the remnants of great nations that have survived here. And we are – we might be a little bit bruised and weary, but we have survived several centuries now of pretty sustained attack on us. And so I celebrate our survival through the people that I relate to. So, in my mind, I never see a sex trade worker. They're my relatives, and that is a very different way of relating to people. It's within a very much more culturally safe or culturally appropriate way in many ways than to categorize people by how oppression has impacted their lives.

So that's kind of how I see this. And, in that capacity, I know women that have had no choice, no choice – be it by what they understood, and it comes down to where they are. How can you condemn somebody? And sometimes I give this so much thought – that people have done what they had to do to survive. And sometimes, because we are so outside the system that wouldn't respect us in terms of the economies [street-level economics], I see survivors. I know that they call themselves "survivors" and I know there's no big debate over it.

So if you want to stop the sex trade, you have to go back and start figuring out the structure, and dealing with the structural conditions that hold that in place. I mean we have the United Nations that have the Declaration of Rights for Indigenous People. We have the [Royal Commission on Aboriginal Peoples], their rights, human rights, Indigenous rights. They're going to cost, because Canada's growing rich off of our resources and our removal from those resources. There has to be some deep structural changes made and also social changes. But I think that if we don't change the structure, the social conditions just continue to replicate themselves and you – Really, if those structural changes don't happen significantly, then again it's just people are going to pay a price, our people paying the price for it.

As Ms. Spillett points out, labelling people tends to limit one's view of the whole person. The larger context that Spillett describes views survivors as victims of the poverty they were born into. Yet despite being victims, they are often blamed for the conditions they live in, for example when prostitutes are viewed as perpetrators rather than victims.

Kelly Dennison (WPS inspector) notes that people need help to leave the sex industry:

KELLY DENNISON: Someone needs to step in, offer a helping hand and give them a different path, show them a better way, experiential people, any individuals that have been there. You don't wake up one morning to be a prostitute. And you don't wake up one morning to not be one anymore either. Someone, somewhere, has to step in and provide whatever it is that individual needs – whether it's getting them into some sort of addictions therapy, whether it's finding them housing or shelter, just getting them set up financially somehow so that they can eat and feed themselves. They're not going to get out of it on their own.

Kerri Irvin-Ross (former MLA and CFS minister) also emphasizes that there must be someone with the tenacity to stay with a person trying to exit, to provide mentorship and support. She has heard survivors who left the sex industry stress that someone believed in them, giving them the courage to leave.

KERRI IRVIN-ROSS: I'll talk about how police have continued to work with vulnerable populations, whether it's through partnerships that they have with not-for-profit organizations or even if it's for the people that officers that are in the patrol cars stop and talk to, the vulnerable people, and [police] know who the women and men are on the street, and perpetrators and predators knowing that there is a presence around them. I think that police are only one part of that solution. I think child welfare has a key [role] to play. I think employment and education. All of that, it's a collective response that we have to work on. It might not have been the first time that that [supportive] person had tapped them on the shoulder, it might have been the twentieth time, but people saw something in them and didn't give up. So, I think it's about relationships. I think it's about ensuring safety because, you know, it's very important, and that ability to stabilize, and employment and education, and that there's a way out.

Kerri Irvin-Ross observes that young women leaving the sex industry require resocialization, and that entails providing them with extensive resources and support systems. A strong theme that arose in my interviews was the system's inflexibility in meeting the unique and changing demands of each individual. My research participants maintained that every individual is different, with different needs, and survivor-oriented programming must adapt to changing client needs. This might mean adaptability within programs, or it might mean having the flexibility within the system to easily move people between programs or allow a person simultaneous access to multiple programs. Chelsea Jarosiewicz (Marymound) talked about the need for long-term wrap-around approaches:

CHELSEA JAROSIEWICZ: I think longer-term programming, more wrap-around services. A lot of programs are shorter term, go for a few days,

then you go back out, and it's quick to lose [women] to their previous lifestyle. So I think that programs need to be longer and more in
depth, [looking] at the root causes of what's going on. What I see a lot
from girls who have come to the crisis stabilization unit, rather than
having the root issue as to why they're in the sex trade be addressed,
they get put into rural placements, which doesn't change the situation. It doesn't change how they feel about themselves, what they've
gone through. So, I think there needs to be longer programming which
addresses their self-esteem, self-worth, housing, all the kind of things
that lead to somebody being vulnerable.

Ms. Jarosiewicz concentrates on the point that programs should address the fundamental causes of each individual's needs, and this takes
time. Some of my interviewees also noted that not only must the system
be flexible, but survivors must also be actively involved in making decisions on the treatments they participate in. For example, Sheldon Beaton (RCMP EPPS) and Friederike Von Aweden (Klinic) both mention
the need to meet people where they are emotionally located. Mr. Beaton
describes how "Snow Night" at the Salvation Army allows people a
reprieve from the street, if only for a night. He stressed that multiple
resources need to be available in situations like this, so that something
useful might appeal to different survivors, depending on their requirements and their state of mind.

SHELDON BEATON: Snow Night is a perfect example of how the
Salvation Army – It's one night a year where they try to get – the
last few years I've been involved, there's been about eighty to one
hundred people come for the night. And there's prizes for people
and pampering and that, so that's a draw, too. But at least there's
one night to get off the street. And the resources are there whether
people want to take them or not. It is hard because you're battling
with mental health issues, post-traumatic stress, traumas from back
and to whenever, past sexual assaults. So it's not like someone wants
help with just one thing. I've always said you need a one-stop shop
for everything. If someone with an addiction – if they want to – they
only stop if they want to stop. Anything from smoking or drinking
to drugs, you can try and you can say it's there, but if you are again
[forcing them] with probation orders, if someone is forced to do
rehab – Like, I talked to one young girl once where she wanted help
but she didn't want to be forced by a court order to go there. So we
actually liaised with the Crown and they said, we are going to set her
up, get her the help.

Here Mr. Beaton articulates the need for one location where young sex industry survivors have access to multiple services at the same time, an idea that came up repeatedly in my interviews.

Friederike Von Aweden also notes that multiple agencies should be working together to provide the right resources for survivors:

FRIEDERIKE VON AWEDEN: I sometimes hear especially the youth telling me that you have to be cautious of social workers. You have to be cautious of some other programs, with how they make choices that are deemed not appropriate by other organizations. That aspect is not appealing to them [youth]. So if a fifteen-year-old wants to get pregnant, it would probably help her more to have someone work with her in those choices than [to have] someone direct her. The other thing that I think works is the combination of several disciplines working together. So when I work at TERF I don't have to do a lot of the social work. That's all done by people that know best how to help women, with resources, with choices, with personal safety plans, [and so] on, so I feel like I can just direct my care at whatever women want in terms of medical care. The other thing that I think is really helpful is that even though sometimes we get information given that is highly disturbing ... we never pass on any information or specifics where women's partners could get incarcerated or something like that.

Ms. Von Aweden believes that women need a sense that they are in control of the direction they are taking; it is not effective to press resources on them if they are not part of the decision process. She is the sole contributor that stressed the importance of creating opportunities for survivors to reap the benefits of participating in sports:

FRIEDERIKE VON AWEDEN: We under-capitalize on women's athletics, women that are sexually exploited, on their athletic abilities. If we had more women involved in physical activities, I think that it would help their mental health. It would help their anxiety. It would help their risk for diabetes. It would probably make them stronger on the streets, and less at risk for drugs. Introducing sports at a young age, specifically for Indigenous kids, would be huge. Making it appealing, making them realize how much potential they have, because I think there's a lot of genetic potential. Yeah, I think we're not doing a great job with engaging First Nations physical activity or making it appealing.

Ms. Von Aweden specifies that both sports and education should be made available with flexible hours so that survivors can take advantage of them on their own terms.

Michael Richardson (program manager at Marymound) notes some of the funding challenges faced by service agencies. He finds, for example, that there are effective survivor-oriented programs that struggle continuously for government funding, and he wonders why this is the case.

MICHAEL RICHARDSON: Marymound is a unique organization. We have a full wrap-around service here. A kid can come to us and have services right until they're twenty-one years old. We have unlimited opportunities. We have specialized homes for at-risk kids, kids that are involved in exploitation. We have an addictions facility. We have a crisis facility. We have an assessment and stabilization facility. We have a sexual abuse program. We have a school. We have a number of resources here. We have behaviour specialists. We have a number of opportunities to engage the population. Some of the barriers are funding. Marymound starts every year off in the negative, and that's based on the funding models that are passed down from the Province of Manitoba. The funding models are outdated, which affects the service that you can provide. We have, when you think of 680 kids, it's a constant fight of trying to get the funding, or all these hoops that you got to jump through. There's so much criteria in order to get money to actually provide the service. But then a kid dies and then you're screwed. So to be in this work is a risk to provide services. It's a risk.

Mr. Richardson astutely observes that the funding models used by government are outdated and cause important programs to start each year underfunded. Like many other research respondents, Mr. Richardson points out that effective services exist and that we need more support and funding for those that do work, such as the Marymound programs he described.

My research participants consistently reinforced the idea that the system must be flexible and adaptable, and one size does not fit all when it comes to the complex issues surrounding how young people are victimized by the sex industry. Survivors must have a say in their own treatment, and this requires policymakers and practitioners to listen and be sensitive to their desires. Participants also stressed that service agencies must go out of their way to be flexible in how they protect each client. We know from participants' stories that services are not well coordinated and that survivors and practitioners often don't know all of the programs that exist or how to access them.

Leslie Spillett provided some important insights into the context in which the social phenomenon of sexual exploitation occurs, foregrounding the importance of seeing survivors first as human beings with dignity and value; as I wrote above, interview participants and previous research have stressed the damage that labels can cause for survivors. Ms. Spillett also highlights, as did Chief Ron Evans and numerous others interviewed for this research, that poverty is at the root of the lack of resilience that makes girls and women vulnerable to engaging in survival sex, and can make escaping that life very difficult.

The following seven prominent findings emerged from my analysis of my respondent's experiences and perceptions of what they described as the multiple and multilayered challenges individuals face in attempting to escape the sex industry.

First, survivors want to help others. Respondents noted that a significant number of survivors become helpers to others who are still trapped in the sex industry. Many people who work as practitioners, assisting and supporting sex industry survivors, are themselves survivors of sex trafficking. Survivors reported that becoming a helper and a support system to others is one way of deriving value from their own horrific experiences. Others reported that despite their best efforts and intentions to avoid having anything to do with the sex industry, they gravitated back into helping roles working with survivors. Survivors in particular stressed the value that people who have been trafficked bring to assisting young women entrapped in the sex industry.

Numerous experts I interviewed also stressed the importance of involving survivors in developing programming and child advocacy such as public awareness campaigns and trauma counselling. This is important for the credibility and effectiveness of programs, and also for ensuring they are effective and don't further traumatize survivors. Survivors who are stabilized and working in survivor-oriented agencies are well positioned to play a pivotal role in program development to ensure that survivors' voices are incorporated into anti-trafficking and forced prostitution programs.

Second, intervention and supports must be flexible. Interviewees strongly emphasized that there is no one-size-fits-all intervention and prevention approach, as every survivor typically has multiple layers of issues that have compounded over a period of years. A large number of research participants highlighted that we must guard against the tendency to essentialize or label survivors because they all have different experiences, backgrounds, and needs. This finding has important implications for developing services and programming (see next section).

Several of my interviewees related that severe substance abuse and addiction problems probably need to be addressed before other counselling and resources can be effective. Others might need an entirely different combination of resources. As Dianna Bussey (Salvation Army),

Sada Fenton (Salvation Army), and others said, we must "meet them where they are at," seeing every person as an individual and never succumbing to the tendency to think of them as all the same (see Wilson, 2008). We also must consider this issue in relation to the tendency to view people from one cultural background as the same.

For these reasons, my contributors stressed that people must be treated as unique individuals. They should also have a voice in what treatment or supports they wish to pursue. Several participants also stated that not only must every individual's needs be addressed as unique, but the system must be flexible so that they can seek different resources as their needs change.

Third, survivors have multiple challenges, and supports must be coordinated. Respondents argued that survivors are intersectionally challenged and require multilayered support. A sex industry survivor is also, in most cases, a victim of childhood abuse, a severely addicted substance abuser, and may be developmentally delayed, all the while potentially being criminally harassed by traffickers. All of these interrelated challenges require different types of support systems, and the overall intervention must be coordinated expertly if it is to be effective. All participants stressed the importance of having multimodal and multilevel intervention and prevention approaches for survivors.

This need for coordination of processes has implications for service delivery, as many survivors have difficulty completing seemingly simple everyday tasks. One cannot just make a doctor's appointment for these survivors and anticipate that they will show up. As one respondent pointed out, how can we expect these young women to show up at a medical appointment or pick up a prescription if they are homeless, living in the grips of severe substance abuse, and do not even know what day of the week it is? If supporters do not take this intersectionality and complexity into account when dealing with sex industry survivors, they are setting them up to fail. This seemingly simple observation actually points to major structural issues that challenge a lot of people in society.

Fourth, escaping the sex industry is difficult. Interviewees observed that it takes most survivors repeated efforts to get out of the sex industry. They stressed that most survivors walk a tightrope, only a remission trigger away from relapse, even twenty years after leaving the sex industry. They also note that when survivors work with survivors, this can act as a retraumatization trigger for the helpers. Therefore, the anti-trafficking business is dangerous for survivors to work in. It is critical that survivors be involved in the oversight and design of survivor-oriented programs to ensure that they are evidence based and effective, and that they are not traumatizing for survivors.

Fifth, relationships are critical. Interviewees were adamant that people and not programs make the difference in survivors' recovery. A significant number of participants stated that survivors rarely talk about how a treatment program or agency saved them; typically, they name a person within an agency who made all the difference for them. Participants pointed out that having a pivotal person or mentor is often key to a survivor's successfully escaping the sex industry. Relationships are critical, and trust is critical for relationships to be effective. Respondents emphasize the importance of building trust with a police officer, a parent, or a social worker that is trying to assist them. If the survivor does not trust the caregiver, then she is unlikely to be able to take full advantage of the assistance offered to her.

Sixth, escaping takes a critical event. My respondents were aware that it often takes a critical event to move the survivor to leave the sex industry. A significant number of survivors and practitioners I interviewed highlighted that despite numerous attempts to escape the sex industry, many people are not successful until a critical event or crisis occurs to spur them to make substantial changes in their lives. Of course, "critical" is a subjective term, yet the events described to me by survivors would be considered horrific by the average person.

Most of the survivors I interviewed have experienced being beaten, tortured, and raped, and many have friends and acquaintances who were murdered while selling sex. This finding has implications for anti-trafficking and sexual exploitation treatment programming, in that it could cue the government's implementation of special resources when survivors are observed by one of the intervening agencies as having a critical event unfold in their lives. A tragedy could be an opportunity for the intervening agencies to assist the person to commit to leaving the sex industry for good.

Seventh, resources must be accessible at the times they are needed. My interviewees repeated the theme that resources are often not available at the time of day and day of the week when they are most needed. This is a significant problem with relatively simple solutions. Practitioners I interviewed observed that often when a survivor finally decides she wants help in leaving the sex industry, she needs certain resources connected with severe substance abuse problems and trauma counselling, among other services. Then she finds out that the services are closed at night, when her needs are greatest; or she finds that there is a wait list of days or weeks until she can get into the program she needs. It is then explained to her that she has to be sober to get into a substance abuse program.

While I understand the rationale behind demonstrating the will power to remain sober for a period before receiving addictions counselling, the logic is akin to requiring that someone lose fifty pounds before being admitted to a weight loss program. Some people with severe addictions problems don't stand a chance of remaining sober for several weeks without serious help. Survivors sometimes told me that they are only alive because they were arrested and put in jail, where they started to come down from the street drugs they were self-medicating with. Having a person ask for help and then be told they have to wait seems like a tragic loss of an opportunity that could save a life. None of this bureaucratic inertia works for survivors with addiction problems. Prevention and intervention programs must be tailored to fit intersectionally challenged women and children, "meeting them where they are at," or they are a waste of time and taxpayers' dollars.

As this chapter outlines, the challenges faced by survivors struggling to escape the sex industry are formidable. The most salient finding is that even simple daily tasks are difficult for intersectionally challenged survivors. Every person is different, and survivors all have different — requirements, so each case must be dealt with on its own facts and merits. Ensuring that the right people are involved in intervention and prevention can make all the difference for survivors trying to escape the sex industry. Resources in the system must also be flexible and accessible for survivors. This might be achieved by having survivors involved at all levels of treatment development, from design to implementation.

8 Challenges and Opportunities: Intervening in Sex Trafficking

MARIE: Once we know the kids are exploiting themselves, there should be a process of getting them out of the city and getting them into treatment – treatment that will heal them from the trauma of being sexually exploited because it's just like molestation. It changes the way that you think. It changes the way that you see yourself in society. It changes the way that you think that people see you. So, it's a whole breakdown of who you are on the inside. I think it takes a lot longer to recover from than the actual work. It's the damage that's done to your thoughts and your mind and your spirit. So, for me, I'd like to see them all go to a camp or have specialized programming for kids that have been sexually exploited.

Marie makes clear that sex trafficking and exploitation is a unique trauma and calls for special measures. This chapter is devoted to some of the specific ideas my research participants identified concerning the spectrum of services and resources related to counter-exploitation and sex trafficking. My contributors made numerous suggestions regarding areas that could be improved, including safe houses, more facilities for at-risk youth, better coordination between existing resources, and better collaboration between agencies. Here, I explore these challenges and opportunities to prevent recruitment and intervene more effectively in sex trafficking.

A number of interviewees strongly suggested that effectiveness could be enhanced through improved cross-sector collaboration, and that no one agency can be effective on its own. Political leaders and senior bureaucrats are often well placed to see how the elements of the system fit and work together. For example, Kerri Irvin-Ross (former MLA and CFS minister) says some initiatives look more collaborative on paper than they really are.

KERRI IRVIN-ROSS: You can look at a number of initiatives that on paper look very collaborative and cooperative, but in practice, we're not practising it. And I think that we need to use our resources that we have, our limited resources, and coordinate them better and make sure that we're making a solid attempt to provide that safety net for people.

And I think that, with the initiatives we're making around poverty reduction, the mental pieces, the supports that we're working really hard to implement in family services around the complex kids – and those, I would say, would be our high-risk kids to be sexually exploited – the better we get at serving that population, I think the fewer opportunities, the [less the] predators will find victims. And that really would be my ultimate goal.

Ms. Irvin-Ross points out that collaboration among agencies is needed on paper *and* in action.

Similarly, Joy Smith (former MP) maintains that the next thing we need across Canada is improved strategy and collaboration around counter-exploitation and trafficking. She notes that nowhere in Canada has she seen the kind of teamwork that is needed, not in any of the provinces or territories. There are a lot of programs, yet agencies still continue to operate in isolation.

JOY SMITH: Well, no matter what anybody says, the two things, education is our greatest weapon, and the collaboration between all the entities. We have to get out of the silos and go into a concerted effort. And there's been no program that I've seen in this country and, you know, I've written lots of programs. I've written the National Action Plan, I've done everything. But you know, this is the next thing that provinces have to do.

Kevin Brosseau (RCMP Deputy Commissioner) states that organizations must have "skin in the game," working together collaboratively while providing front-line workers the tools they need to do their work. He elaborates on what is required to fight exploitation:

KEVIN BROSSEAU: You know, Bob, I think there's a lot of room within the current structures of policing to be able to improve the work. It needs a redirection or a re-profiling of some of the resources. We have to ensure that we're there, that we can be trusted, and that these aren't just words, but that those who are being exploited, those who are vulnerable, can turn to the police. And the police will be able to be there. But I don't want my guys and gals out there, young people in uniform, to be without the tools for them to be able to help those who need help. They need to be able to turn to agencies and supports that can then really step in and say, "We've got it." This person will then be provided the opportunities that they need to be able to grow and continue to do all the things they want to do in life. To me that's a big thing. And I think we've reached the point where there's much clarity in the law, maybe not to the extent that some want to, but taking the purchaser out of the equation is a really important piece.

It is important, Deputy Commissioner Brosseau notes, that government departments work collaboratively with community-based agencies for better effectiveness, and it is critical that agencies and service providers earn the trust of sex industry survivors.

Ed Riglin (RCMP sergeant) suggests that it is vital to create a communications hub for all of the different sectors – health, education, social work, and police – to meet, exchange information, and create coordinated approaches to community problems.

ED RIGLIN: If money wasn't an object then we could set up places that girls could come to and feel safe, and a better environment, better than the johns and the handlers give. We would be better ahead if we actually had money, here in Winnipeg, if we actually set up in a table like this boardroom here. We meet up every week between all of our agencies: here is our high-risk places; this is what happened this week; this is our patrolling units; we were sent to this house fifteen times. There's ten kids in there, they're all doing their thing, we need to get out there, and we devise an approach and do it together, everything. One of the key issues in here, that I haven't mentioned much but leads with all of these questions, is there has to be the mental health component, a hub or a joint unit if you want to call it that, [that] attacks these issues.

Liz Kaulk (RCMP EPPS constable) also stresses that more effective intervention and prevention teams could be built through collaboration, to eliminate wasted efforts.

The communications hub suggested by Sergeant Riglin could fill these interagency gaps. Constable Kaulk calls for specialized multisectoral, multidisciplinary teams that could respond more effectively to sexual exploitation cases, and notes how such teams might work:

LIZ KAULK: I would love to see, for lack of a better word, not crisis teams but trafficking teams, or something where it could be integrated teams with different police forces with representation, and when something happens that we could go there and actually deal from beginning to end with that situation. Even the victim management part is from beginning to end, because it just seems to pass through so many hands.

And it's difficult then to figure it out, what have we missed and what can we do better. So, that team of people would be great in almost any region, not just one team for Manitoba. Manitoba is huge, there is lots going on all over, it needs to be like regions of teams, and maybe it's not their full-time duty – But it's something that is their responsibility to know what to do, and to help when they're called, like an earth team or something.

Ms. Bussey suggests that private business partners could play a larger role in the collaboration around the sex industry:

DIANNA BUSSEY: I think wanting to see departments more than any other issue, with the human trafficking piece – it can't just live in one government department or one organization. I think that it is something that can go across not only NGOs but the corporate world as well, and it is something that everybody can get aboard on. It's not a tough sell, but it's kind of how to manage that whole thing and manage the communication of it all, so I think that would also be something, a strategy or approach could include something. I think that there is a way for the corporate world to get involved, whether they're Crown corporations or not, right? Just, the business community is willing, so I wanted to include that and then to hear from people who have certainly been there and dealing with that.

Gord Mackintosh (former MLA) suggests that some such work has already gone on in the private sector, but has not been integrated with government efforts: "We've seen engagement, a welcoming engagement from the Manitoba Hotels Association for hotel workers to watch out for what's happening." This makes sense, as hotel staff are often in a position to see sex trafficking going on where they work.

Jane Runner (TERF, New Directions) also notes the importance of learning from each other and not letting politics get in the way of partnering between agencies in all sectors.

JANE RUNNER: I think we've done a lot of work, especially in Manitoba in groups coming together and educating with one another. So, working with the police, probation, social workers, and that does take a lot of work because you're all coming from different approaches and training on how you have to deal with the issue. But I think there's been a lot of work done in Manitoba where there have been great partnerships in dealing with the issue. And then, as we talked earlier about Vice even changing [its focus] to counter-exploitation, that whole shift; that works. The biggest thing is building relationships. So, whether it's with people in the community, with families, with people you work with, it's all about relationships. I could go on and on and on. Everybody needs to work together on this issue, you can't segregate it, you just can't.

Ms. Runner's comments regarding the need for more inter-agency collaboration echo those of other interviewees. For instance, Hennes Doltze (Salvation Army) describes how the whole system might work better together:

HENNES DOLTZE: I think a major concern is the fragmentation of services. There's a lot of good services in the city and they do amazing work, but sometimes they struggle because it crosses over to so many areas. You have the housing unit, EIA [employment income assistance] for financial support, you have trauma care, which comes from a different agency. And I think the struggle is the fragmentation. It's hard sometimes to have this one-stop shop where people can get the help they need on different levels to cover all of their needs. So, what should be done going forward, I think, is to streamline the services and truly collaborate with each other and cut down on certain red tape that prevents people from getting the services they need when they need it. I think that would be something with full coordination that can be achieved in the future, I would say. And that's I think where all of the agencies have to put more effort in, not that they [don't] already do, but even more so.

Mr. Doltze makes the key point that improved coordination not only could offer survivors better access to services, but could allow those services to work better together as a system, ending duplication of efforts. Overall, the consensus among my interviewees was for greater collaboration, whether it be forging new teams and sharing resources, or bringing parties around the same table and widening it to include a broader range of participants to share valuable information and work together.

Several interviewees noted that the system of resources available to sex trafficking survivors is insufficient, and it is the clients who suffer. Jay Rodgers (Deputy Minister, Manitoba Department of Families) suggests that the needs of women and children should be considered first and foremost when coordinating resources to assist them.

JAY RODGERS: I think that my experience with this is that there seems to be a fair number of resources devoted to this issue but the responses seem to have been somewhat piecemeal over the years. I don't think that there is a coordinated, coherent strategy to respond to this issue.

As well as lack of coordination between existing services, Mr. Rodgers pointed to loopholes and pieces missing in the system, and suggested existing resources could be better utilized.

Several interviewees further described how clients/youth get lost in the bureaucracy, shuffled between agencies, and said that people working within various offices often only know their own organization's mandate, so they are unable to coordinate with others to find the most effective response for sexually exploited youth. Chelsea Jarosiewicz (Marymound), for example, spoke of how children fall through the gaps between agencies because of inefficiency, lack of knowledge, and lack of communication:

CHELSEA JAROSIEWICZ: I think when it comes to working between organizations, if we could do it that would be great. There's tons of different programs, and I think there's a lack of everybody knowing what's out there and how can we work together to provide the best service for the youth or the women. At the same time, though, the organizations, they're fighting for the same resources a lot of the times.

Ms. Jarosiewicz also mentions that practitioners are sometimes biased and don't wish to work with certain other agencies. Her major point is that there is much need for training to make practitioners aware of treatment resources that they could draw on for their clients, and for overall coordination of an intervention strategy that triages the cases in order to make the system more client centred and less fragmented.

Diane Redsky (Ma Mawi Wi Chi Itata Centre) also calls for higher-level coordination, including public awareness, regulation, and coordination of a safety net of service agencies for high-risk youth:

DIANE REDSKY: Manitoba has a provincial strategy to work within. We have a provincial department called the Sexual Exploitation Unit, and in a perfect world, when there's good people that work there, that work with community, it was really strong. It's a little sidetracked right now, but we'll get it back on track. So, when that's going well, then there's lots of coordination at the community level and at the government level and it's all kind of a working machine. And that works as long as that's working well. I would say the best thing that could happen is if we actually pulled off a simul–, I can't say that word properly, a whole bunch of things happening at the same time where we're doing public education, we're going after the demand, and we have the service safety net. I believe that if we can make drinking and driving not cool, smoking not cool, like in my generation, we can make buying women for sex not cool. It just, it takes a combination of laws, public education and awareness, stories, prevention programs. It was a whole concerted effort of everybody, and that's what we hope our coordination centre will play a role in. Even at the local level, let's pick some communities that are like, "nobody's buying sex in here, our boys are not wanting it and our girls are not putting up with it," and, you know, "we're a community that does not have sexually exploited women."

Ms. Redsky is fully aware of the need for the multilevel synchronization of services, public education, and the training of personnel. Some define this type of multifaceted harmonization around social problems as collective impact (Byrne & Keashly, 2000; Chrislip, 2002). Several respondents called for more national, as well as local, coordination. For example, Marie, a survivor whose words lead off this chapter, noted that greater national coordination could accommodate better safe housing for those trying to escape the sex industry. Her goal is to "see a Canada-wide service that provides first-, second-, and third-stage housing."

Similarly, Darryl Ramkissoon (WPS staff sergeant) identifies the need for both provincial and national strategic coordination in anti-trafficking and sexual exploitation of children and youth. He describes the challenges of working across different regions and suggests a national coordination centre might help that particular effort:

DARRYL RAMKISSOON: We almost need a central place like the Polaris Center [an anti-trafficking program] in the USA, so if we deal in Winnipeg with a trafficking victim we can deal with counterparts in the unit where the person is from and [can] coordinate responses. We need a provincial coordinator or national coordinator so these things don't fall off the table.

In addition, Christine Kun (WPS detective) emphasizes that national coordination of an effective anti-trafficking and sexual exploitation intervention strategy is required because some offenders travel nationally, or internationally, and police agencies need to be able to work together to track and prosecute them to the full extent of the law.

CHRISTINE KUN: I think in terms of policing, putting our resources in an efficient, effective way, and coordinated way, is important, and I think that we're moving in that direction. I think that funding that supports coordination, communication for the long term, because this isn't something that is just going to go away. If [there's] anything that I've learned from working in ViCLAS [Violent Crime Linkage Analysis System, a crime analysis tool used by police across Canada], it is that we have transient people that move all over the globe, and to be able to catch or track these individuals who are committing these crimes we need to be coordinated with other agencies, we need to have that communication, and if we are willing to invest the money, again in a collaborative, informed way, then I think we can be very successful. But I don't know, because I don't work in that area now and it's changed, possibly, since when I worked there.

Sergeant Kun recognizes the transient nature of the sex industry and that better national coordination is required. Interpol could work with local police agencies to attack the global sex industry. Joy Smith also mentioned that cross-border sex trafficking happens much more than even Canadian law enforcement agencies realize.

Some of my participants pointed out that formal structures and processes, such as acts controlling the sharing of information, hamper coordination between agencies. WPS superintendent Bill Fogg (retired) describes how both compartmentalization and insufficient communication are often barriers to effectiveness within organizations.

BILL FOGG: Well, [lack of] communication's always a barrier within organizations and a barrier between organizations. One of the biggest problems is even inside of our organizations. We're compartmentalized. So the Child Abuse Unit does child investigations. The Sex Crimes Unit does adult sex crimes investigation. If you go back a little bit, our Morals Unit dealt with morals. So what it depended on is the relationship between the people running those units, whether there was enough information sharing or cooperation. And we've been fortunate in the last couple of years, but generally speaking, we've had good-functioning relationships. You need to formalize those. So, an example is when we brought the Morals Unit and the Missing Person

Unit [together] to become part of the Anti-Exploitation Unit. That's the kind of collaborative piece. We can afford to do more of that.

In essence, study participants, and in particular practitioners such as Bill Fogg, asserted the need for increased communication at all levels, internally within organizations as well as between organizations, locally, provincially, nationally, and internationally.

Research participants observed that increasing numbers of survivors of the sex industry often struggle, operating psychologically and socially at younger ages than their biological years suggest. As we have seen, commonly they are abused and traumatized, never having had the opportunity to just be children and grow up in a healthy way.

Several of my participants highlighted that a major barrier to services for youth occurs when they turn eighteen years of age. Jay Rodgers (Deputy Minister of families) advised me that most if not all of the twenty or more child welfare agencies operating in Manitoba have legal provisions to continue providing services after a client turns eighteen. However, most of those agencies choose not to use that authority (personal communication, 14 June 2016). Michael Richardson (Marymound) considers it untenable that youth are forced to negotiate bureaucratic obstacles in order to gain an extension of resources beyond the age of eighteen:

MICHAEL RICHARDSON: In child welfare the kids can get an extension of care till they're twenty-one, but in order to get that extended they have to jump through a number of hoops. And we're asking kids that are highly addicted with low-cognitive-function issues to jump through hoops in order to continue to be in services, and that's, to me that's backwards in a way. You can't get an extension in care for a kid that's exploited, but we know that we need to be involved with kids that are exploited a little bit longer because they missed out on life, and want to build a life. We find kids right at the end of their time in the child welfare system, just starting to realize the opportunity, and before they exit the system they don't get the proper [education] scales, or the proper mental health services that they need. We've missed the transition period to actually have a kid for those services. I think the continuum of services need to start looking at, I don't know what the answer is, but it just seems like we're constantly, we're a day late.

Mr. Richardson points out that youth addictions counselling and other services must be provided on a continuum. In his view it's asking the impossible for youth with all kinds of problems to navigate bureaucratic obstacles in order to have their child welfare benefits continued past eighteen. He concluded, "sometimes I feel that there is no real commitment to these kids, they're just, I don't think that there is enough commitment to understanding the issue."

As for adults, it is clear from my interviews that they face similar challenges with trauma and substance abuse issues as do youth, as well as even worse structural challenges in accessing services. This is an important issue, as the percentage of exploited and trafficked adults with mental health challenges is high, and these impediments create numerous barriers for them.

Some research participants also talked about resources that are sometimes not available when they are needed. For example, Kaitlin, a survivor, spoke of a great program that was only available to her for limited hours during the day.

KAITLIN: There is Sage house, that does help, but maybe they could do a lot more, 'cause they're only open in the daytime and all the action happens at night. And there are girls who have no place to sleep. They have improved a bit, never used to smudge, now they do, I noticed a lot of my friends go to sweats [traditional Indigenous sweat lodge ceremonies] and get connected with their inner selves, I have not been doing that but when I do I feel better. A lot of girls, if they see a cop they run, they are scared. Not all cops are assholes. Officer Phil used to harass the shit out of me in a good way and then walk me home. I don't know, more programs, more treatment centres, more centres that have counselling therapy, making people more aware of addictions. I know if I wasn't addicted to crack I wouldn't have gone out there and did that [selling sex]. If I had been more aware, no one told me, I grew up seeing my mom do that so I thought it was normal.

Kaitlin offers an important observation that echoes comments of other research participants: that services are not available at night when they are needed.

Liz Pilcher (WPS superintendent) also notes the challenges of not having resources available when they are needed. She suggests that the system requires a place practitioners can call at all hours of the day or night to access information and services.

LIZ PICHER: I think resources; we spoke about this a bit earlier, that even our counter-exploitation team – there is a lack of resources where they can actually, you know, pinpoint some area to go to or call 24/7. I know that there is some programming out west, and we had one case where we had to get some temporary funding because we didn't have the funding to send somebody to an addictions place to help women in the sex trade, to exit it.

So, I think access to local resources, access to funding, and access to resources should be readily available to help people exit. I know there's a lack of housing and just sort of a system where we can refer somebody and they can actually help somebody exit the sex trade. We do know that a lot of our sex trade workers are addicted. Some of them, very few are in it for survival where they have families. We did have a recent case, though, where this lady thought that the only way that she could make ends meet was going to work the streets again, she connected to our Sexual Exploitation Unit, who actually took her to an Indigenous resource centre who helped her out because she had no money for rent or food. Although those are rare cases, most of them are drug addicted. I think that would really assist if we could do something with housing, addictions, and mental health issues.

Superintendent Pilcher adds that the need for access similarly extends to other regions in the province.

Friederike Von Aweden (Klinic) stresses that these intersectionally challenged survivors often have difficulty in accessing the most basic services. She explains that often these seemingly simple tasks are difficult to complete due to personal issues and challenges such as transportation and childcare. I found this when I conducted my field research: appointments were missed and rescheduled and some interviews were never completed. Ms. Von Aweden explains these challenges as follows:

FRIEDERIKE VON AWEDEN: I'm just looking at the medical piece; the one thing that is the biggest barrier to women accessing care is that their lives are so chaotic that it's impossible for them to make an appointment, so appointments don't work.

You have to place yourself in their path and you have to offer services in a safe environment so that women accessing a walk-in clinic can be hopeful, but it is not always sensitive to their needs. Becoming a client of the primary care clinic where you have to have a home, a phone, in order to make appointments does not work for women involved in the sex trade or being sexually exploited with addictions. Even for me, sometimes at work if I ask someone [a sex industry survivor] to just get medications from the pharmacy down the road it does not happen because for variety of reasons it's a big barrier. So, comprehensive services under one roof is helpful, placing services in situations where women already are. I do think that very small incentives like women getting meals, women getting bus tickets, at TERF it almost seems like some of the supporters are grooming women in order to reconnect with TERF if they've fallen off, so if some-one calls someone to go out for lunch they actually re-engage again. I think those are all helpful, broader perspectives in harm reduction.

Ms. Von Aweden's observations illustrate the survivors' intersectional challenges that are constructed within a paternalistic, colonial frame-work: attend this office at this time or lose the benefits. Services must instead be tailored to clients' basic human needs.

Sometimes services are not available to survivors due to impedi-ments within organizational structures, such as long wait times, and sometimes, as noted above, because people aren't aware of what pro-grams exist or how to access them. These are all issues that could be addressed in a coordinated overall strategy.

Kelly Holmes (RAY) describes how jails are often used where other, more appropriate resources are not available. She did rationalize that homeless youth often benefit from being detained for a few days in jail, as at least they will eat and sleep. However, there's no plan in place upon their release.

KELLY HOLMES: I think we have a real opportunity with justice. I've seen kids that are completely out of control, mental health wise; with a few weeks or couple months in remand they're in great shape. They've eaten, they've slept, they've had medical attention. How come, how can't we plan better so that we're planning their exit? So, we're not exiting them into homelessness. So that we're not exiting them into vulnerabil-ity or back into the drug scene, or back into being exploited. So, exit plan-ning, I think, is a real opportunity we all have. And I think it's not just the justice system, it's child welfare, it's addictions places as well. I think we have another opportunity to map, to do some mapping around our ser-vices and our expertise. We do this organically at the community level. I know who to call about gangs. They know who to call about homeless-ness. I know who to call about cultural stuff. You know what I mean? We all know what each other's bringing to the table. Unfortunately, no one at the police headquarters has the same level of knowledge, which I think would be hugely helpful from any new cadet all the way up to the long-in-the-tooth sergeant, you know, that needs to go, "where the hell do I stick this kid, I've been driving around all night, I have nowhere to put them."

It seems that there are disconnects between systems. If, as Ms. Holmes notes, people in the justice system often fall behind other practitioners in their knowledge of available child welfare and addictions resources and who to call in the community, perhaps this indicates an opportunity for training and information sharing between people in all of these systems.

Kelly Holmes pointed out the need for better coordination of effective addictions, anti-gang, and safe housing resources that already exist. Mandy Fraser (Klinic) adds that the government must expand existing resources so that there are more outreach and front-line workers on the street physically assisting vulnerable people:

MANDY FRASER: Well, I also think things like Street Connections [a mobile public health service], like having the van go out. I think that there's some experiential women involved in that kind of work. But definitely, like, community members, you know, who are plain clothed and accessible and just real people who have maybe, you know, been street-involved in some capacity.

I think that's important. And yeah, just handing out tangible, like physical things that can save lives and protect against, you know, STIs and communicable infection and stuff like that. So, more resources need to be put into that, because I know that front-line workers burn out a lot, again because you're working with life and death, you know?

Patricia Haberman (Marymound) has found that if safe housing is not available to survivors they often wind up going to unsafe places. She raises the innovative idea of Block Parent–type places that high-risk youth could go to:

PATRICIA HABERMAN: I had two young ladies in my house that they go to the same sort of address as their street family. But we know that these are not places of safety for them and they are at high risk in these places. But there they feed them, they'll give them cigarettes, drugs, it's all part of the exploitation thing. So, if we can have buildings everywhere with neon signs: "this is your safe place." [Like] the Block Parents, things like that, that the girls know if they're in danger [and] we can't come pick them up, they can just walk to the Block Parents signs and just say, please let me in and phone the police.

This call for more safe refuge was a powerful theme that arose constantly in my interviews. Survivors and practitioners from all corners of the multidisciplinary counter-exploitation and anti-trafficking system all called for the government to provide more safe housing for young girls on the street. Ms. Haberman's description of the survival mode in which many young women are operating is an eye-opener because it forces one to understand that people are going to sleep somewhere, and if safe housing is not available, there are predators out there who are more than happy to provide shelter.

Research participants talked about the need for the government to provide safer refuge and transitional housing for survivors in order to furnish them with a structure and a safe place, so they can take advantage of the resources and programming available to them. For instance, Hennes Doltze (Salvation Army) notes that safe housing is the first basic requirement before other basic human needs can be addressed (see Burton, 1990, and Maslow's hierarchy of needs, Maslow, 1954). That is, people need a safe environment in secure housing before they can access other services. He advises that a safe place also has to involve non-judgmental support and a range of other services, including trauma and spiritual care. It must be a place that creates a routine for people because, as Mr. Doltze points out, without a routine it is too easy to relapse into previous self-destructive behaviour patterns.

HENNES DOLTZE: A lot of the people struggle to find safe housing. It's supportive and non-judgmental relationships they need, just in order to be able to access other services.

A lot of it is trauma care and even spiritual care for the healing that needs to take place, because I think that the people that are involved in the sex trade, there is a lot of baggage that they carry, and they struggle from day to day. I think they need to find the safe space to heal, but also in the end to deal with addiction issues and then to have a different meaning in life, which generally I would say [calls for] employment and educational training.

Cathy Denby (Ndinawe) further notes that safe houses could be set up in rural locales as a means of keeping survivors safe from predators and away from the triggering influences of their urban milieus, which are associated with their exploitation and addictions problems.

CATHY DENBY: Lots of resources, safe places to be for long periods of time to recover from addiction and safety, safety away from the gang, from different players, from gangs. I mean, it's all kind of interconnected, right, especially with youth. There's such interconnectedness with gangs and exploitation and drugs; they all go hand in hand. I would see it, that having a detox component to it, certainly you know, where they can be monitored medically, and just get their strength up, you know, meeting those basic needs.

A lot of the times when they're coming out and coming off stuff, they haven't eaten for a long time; they, yeah, they need medical treatment, right? A place where there's security, so people can't get at them. You know. A lot of the times they've got hits on them or they've been so threatened that they can't even see themselves getting out, right? So, this place I think would have to be really stocked with good resources that meets their physical, their emotional, their mental, and their spiritual needs.

There is an ongoing debate over how youth facilities should be structured. Some feel that youth are not mature enough or capable yet of making an informed choice to stay in facilities that are created for them. Consequently, the facilities must be secure and able to hold them for their own good, to prevent them from returning to their traffickers, to the street, and putting themselves in harm's way. Others feel that any kind of secure setting is counterproductive and damaging to young people because it re-creates the oppressive residential school structure. (As background: there are a small number of facilities in Winnipeg that can hold high-risk youth for three to seven days maximum.)

Most of the police officers I interviewed viewed forced detention as a necessary evil, as these kids need protection from predators and pimps. For example, Cam MacKid (WPS sergeant) argues that the seven-day detention currently available in Manitoba is not long enough to stabilize a youth in crisis and connect him or her with resources required for safety, and recommends the province follow the example of Alberta:

CAM MACKID: We've got several different facilities in the city, but what we really need is – for instance in Alberta they've got the act out there; I believe it's twenty-five days [maximum holding term]. If someone is even suspected to be involved in exploitation, a youth that is, they can be taken into custody and in a locked facility for twenty-five days for their own protection. We don't have that here, and there's a real political push against it for obvious reasons, it doesn't play well here, but it's something we desperately need.

However, the majority of my interviewees, with hundreds of years of collective experience, advocated for unlocked facilities. I should stress that there was strong sentiment among police respondents and some social workers, who wanted secure places to keep survivors safe.

Diane Redsky maintains that locking up abused youth is only a short-term stopgap measure that can do more damage than good in the long term:

DIANE REDSKY: Right now we're struggling with Tracia's Trust as a community, where there's some differences of opinion on whether you do a secure-care model, which means you lock up kids, or you don't, that there's an alternative approach. And so, we're kind of doing a push-and-pull, currently right now, where we see the community believe that it's ineffective to lock up sexually exploited youth because they're victims of child abuse, and we don't treat any [other] victims like that, why should they be any different?

And that alternative ways, such as secure by location, is a way better investment in the long term, because the current system with StreetReach is a quick fix for everybody else except the young girl herself. We're creating long-term damage and further traumatizing and victimizing her under the guise of child protection, which it will be a process which we will figure out and we will answer and everybody will get right back on track at some point, but that's a current challenge of ours.

According to Ms. Redsky, the best means of keeping youth contained is geographical isolation at a secure location, ensuring they are away from pimps and off the streets. The counter to this argument is that the approach separates youth from their social networks and support systems. This could, on the other hand, be a requirement of the refuge if the young person's entire social network is a gang or a trafficker that is exploiting her.

In general, the view among police officers I interviewed is that secure facilities are needed in order to protect exploited youth from running away and re-exposing themselves to danger. Among interviewees working in NGOs, on the other hand, the consensus is that secure facilities are oppressive and can cause survivors more damage than good. Respondents did agree that more resources should be provided for high-risk youth, with a focus on trust building and developing relationships to encourage survivors to leave the sex industry. But the disagreement about secure youth facilities appears to be intractable, as the views of interviewees are so opposed. Jay Rodgers (Deputy Minister, Department of Families; executive director of Marymound at the time of interview) describes the challenges of finding common ground between the two sides of the debate:

JAY RODGERS: I would share the view that we want not to criminalize these girls and young women, but at the same time we've got to do everything we need to do to keep them safe. We get criticized here, at Marymound, because we have secure facilities so our CSU [Crisis

Stabilization Unit] ... we have the ability to sort of control behaviours of kids. I think for some of these kids and young women that's necessary for the time just to get them stabilized and starting to put them onto something better. So [the solution] gets bounced [around] with philosophical argument. We don't want to criminalize these kids; we don't want to lock them up for any longer than they need to be, but do we need semi-secure facilities? And do we need the police to be involved? For sure, I think it's maybe, there's got to be a better way of just informing the public and informing service providers how everybody works, because we all have the same objective, but we just seem to want to fight over philosophical reasons sometimes.

Despite the difficulty Mr. Rodgers notes in finding common ground between advocates of secure versus unlocked settings, there may be some middle ground. This is an area where mediation and conflict-resolution processes (discussed in chapter 9) could be used to assist both groups to find some form of resolution.

However this debate is resolved, most research participants felt that more safe housing and better resources are required for young sex industry survivors. Some participants have bold visions, among them Kim Trossell, manager of the Dream Catcher Program at Klinic Community Health who works with survivors leaving the sex industry. She envisions a safe house that is more like a village, fully resourced and long term, where survivors would receive a continuum of resources in an inclusive and supportive space to support each other. Here is how she describes this inventive idea:

KIM TROSSELL: The Dream Catcher Village would be created. That's my dream, which would include a centre hub for community services and programming, and the outside would be transitional homes and treatment centres and everything within almost like a city reserve, I guess you would say. So, it would be a one-stop shop, trauma treatment, addiction treatment, all in one reunification of families, working together in that sense. Funding is the number one issue that stands in the way of all of that; yeah, we need to create a sustainable system. Our needs are specialized. Services are in existence; addiction treatment is in existence but not specialized for our needs. When women access services for addiction treatment they're sexually assaulted within the treatment centres, either by other participants in the programs or by the facilitators themselves in the programs because once it's identified that a woman is a sex trade worker, a label and stigma has been attached, so for her to access mainstream services it's not conducive for her healing. It prevented me for years from accessing services because it was always thought, oh well, you need to deal with your addiction before you can deal with your trauma; well, no it's one, I'm one person, I'm a whole being, you need to treat me as a whole being and treat all the parts of me. So, having it under one roof is crucial, so that the specialized services are all together where women aren't fragmented and sent to one agency for one service and across the city for another.

Bringing all the necessary medical, counselling, and other resources together under one roof, Ms. Trossell points out, might naturally resolve some of the challenges survivors face with everyday tasks.

Paige, a survivor, describes how a safe house could be set up here, built on the successful model of Thistle Farms in Las Vegas, Nevada, a large manufacturing company run by sex industry survivors who are employed to produce body-care products:

PAIGE: It would be a house of women who are wanting to get well, and I believe that the women would run the house and would need to manage. But I don't think it needs to be staffed. I think the women would need to be accountable to one another because they're all adults. We would bring them; we would start off with two women, and then in a month or two or three – I'm not sure how it would work – we would bring in two more, and the two older ones would be accountable, and if, say, that third person ends up smoking crack in the bathroom, she's not going to be walking [getting away with it] because they're all going to want to be clean, so she's going to have to do a report and do a time-out. And maybe she could then just be able to live there and there would be karma. Where I get this from is there's a house down in Nevada called Thistle Farms, and it's definitely worth checking it out. This woman who started out, and she's brought tons of women through there, it's a home and they all live together. Thistle Farms is what it's called, they made body products and everything now and they sell it online, and all the stuff is what keeps the house running. It's all made from the thistle plant, and if you study a thistle it is one of the strongest plants there are, and down in Nevada I think it is. Or wherever it was, it says, "Down on track, let's go over here down by the railroad tracks here. Even though it's dirty, it's heavy in weeds, you might see some thistles. All the flowers might die, the grass might die, but the thistle will live. That explains women." It's a home, and after [women] do a couple years there then they go off into the plant and they work, or they go off on their own and they build their lives.

Break Free is another seemingly successful program designed around the concept of providing full service to survivors, including advocacy and direct services such as housing. Established in 1996, in Minnesota, the program is said to help five hundred women per year (Breaking Free, 2018).

Interviewees mentioned that greater coordination of all available resources at the government's disposal is needed to provide a safety net for vulnerable youth. Among other challenges, many young survivors are homeless: they have no "safe space" to escape to. Kelly Holmes (RAY) voiced one innovative idea for creating escape paths for youth who are in danger:

KELLY HOLMES: I think underground railroads need to be set up, for a lack of a better way of putting it. I think we need an underground system for these youth to be able to flee. It [the problem] is constantly changing and moving, very much like an underground railroad. We had one from the north for domestic violence cases. Something similar should be happening here. I think there needs to be more 24/7 and safe spaces in every town, and multiple ones in the city, in different neighbourhoods. I also think, based on our migration of kids coming from the north, from the south, and some of our travellers and stuff, [there should be something], I call it, for lack of a better way of explaining it, is just like a 911 or 311. There should be like an 811 for youth going, "I have no idea where I am, and I don't know where I'm staying tonight." And immediately there's a way for them to get picked up and taken to somewhere safe. So, I feel like those kind of safety nets aren't in place.

Ms. Holmes has worked with homeless and troubled youth for over twenty-five years and has a lot of creative ideas, mainly about how to make the system of resources available to these youth more effective. As well as escape routes, she believes it is important to provide safe places for high-risk youth to live, and suggests that an emergency phone line should be set up by the provincial government, so that practitioners and youth could call for immediate help at any time of day or night. The system doesn't need new resources, she maintains; instead, there must be better coordination of resources that already exist:

KELLY HOLMES: We don't need anything new. We've just got to get smarter at the way we're doing things. And I feel like all of us have our burdens within our own system of why we're not doing that. And often it's time and administration that is garnered up by some intelligent person in a white ivory tower that is figuring this all out for us, and not understanding what we need to do on the street. I don't need to be doing paperwork when there's kids bleeding in my doorway. And I don't know what it's going to, I mean I get accountability, I get all of those things, but I think that there could be a way that we could make sure we're part of that and do the work that we're designed to do.

On the topic of intervention, a final significant theme raised by research participants was changing technology. Several participants mentioned that technological advance is both a modern-day challenge and an opportunity. The internet has connected organized criminals, such as traffickers and pimps, and has also become the new marketplace for the sex industry. At the same time, advances in technology connect law enforcement agencies locally, nationally, and globally, creating a plethora of opportunities for intervention and enforcement against pimps, traffickers, and johns. Technological advances also provide more effective platforms for counter-exploitation, education, and information sharing.

The sex industry in Canada has changed over recent decades. Richardson (2015) wrote that children now have sex for as little as five dollars, while controlled by traffickers who first get them addicted to street drugs to keep them vulnerable. Traffickers often recruit via the internet. Public Safety Canada (2020) reports on their webpage that in February 2009 Canada's National Strategy combatting sexual exploitation on the internet received a total allocation of seventy-one million dollars over five years to support various organizations and strategies, programs and research into child sexual exploitation and human trafficking, including child trafficking. In March 2009, the Royal Canadian Mounted Police National Child Exploitation Coordination Centre (NCECC) coordinated Project Salvo, Canada's largest investigation into child sexual victimization on the internet. Thirty-five police agencies participated and over fifty arrests were made on charges of sexual assault, sexual interference, and possessing, making, and distributing child pornography (Public Safety Canada, 2020). These efforts continue; however, the people I interviewed for this book advised that we are often trailing sorely behind organized crime's use of the internet and technology.

Darryl Ramkissoon (WPS staff sergeant) has observed that much of the sex industry is moving off the street and online, and that is where new investigative resources are essential. Staff Sergeant Ramkissoon describes this new digital terrain as follows:

DARRYL RAMKISSOON: We're falling behind with technology; sex trade has gone online and w'ere seeing it more and more, which is probably contributing to less amount of people, girls, we're seeing on the street. I'd like to say that we're helping them get off the street, but we know some of them have gone online, so as far as keeping up with technology, it is expensive; that's the kind of resources we need to combat, and even with human trafficking it's all online now. Between agencies it's difficult, especially, not with our local prostitution but with human trafficking stuff.

The internet, Staff Sergeant Ramkissoon notes, is making the sex industry invisible. Several of my participants recognized that the internet and social media are a growing risk factor for upcoming generations of youth, who are bombarded by the internet with little control over the content. Sexual predators troll sites looking for naive victims; it is important for government to intervene with school programs to educate young people about the dangers lurking on the internet.

Christina Miller (WPS detective) described the internet as playing a role in normalizing sexual behaviour among young children: "With social media and the influx of access to porn, sexual behaviour has become normalized." She stated that "it's curiosity, it may not have ill intentions to start, but that one picture can go viral and lead to teen suicides and bullying, and we've seen it across the country." Ms. Miller notes that social media is a growing threat because it provides a platform for predators to mask their identity and trick victims into being exploited.

Trevor Bragnalo (WPS constable) relates that the RCMP thought the sex industry had stopped in Thompson until it realized it had just gone online.

TREVOR BRAGNALO: It's done through cellphones, texting, Snapchat, like, Twitter, I don't even know what there is now, Periscope, like, you go on Craigslist and probably find tons, and that's where it is. Or that's where prostitution and sexual exploitation is going, it's going online. You can't fight it anymore. You can't fight online. You're anonymous unless you somehow change laws where providers have to provide subscription information. That's a whole different battle. But with the girls, I don't know how you can combat that online. In Thompson for a while I recall people are like, "Oh yeah, there's no prostitution issues here." And for a while I believed that, I was like, "Yeah, I don't think there is." Like the police involvement, the files, talking to group home workers, and you looked at it and you're like, oh wait, these girls always disappear. Where are they going tonight? And then we actually followed them, we conducted surveillance on these fourteen-year-old girls, where would they go, why are they coming downtown for the TI [Thompson Inn]? Holy shit, this is what's going on, it is a huge issue, it's the dirty underbelly.

Rosemarie Gjerek (Klinic) expands on Bragnalo's comments, noting how increased access to pornography and violence through the internet is affecting gender roles and sexuality and the values that children are learning in modern society.

ROSEMARIE GJEREK: It's about teaching healthy relationships; think about where kids are at. Even supports for families that are experiencing problems, I think, messages that we teach little boys, how do we grow up to be a man that is respectful? We have some very conflicting messages: what is it to be attractive, everything from how to look, and whatever. We have the same messages for boys in terms of how to be a man and what that means. I think the most profound message was listening to a group of young boys just talk about that, what it means to be a man. I think you have to address pornography, and the level of violent pornography. The fact that anyone can access [pornography] on your computer or on your phone, and learn these really wrong messages about human sexuality. I don't think we can discredit or discount the impact that that has, and when you look at that expectation that all kids are doing [sex], because you see it. The prevalence of those messages is pretty profound. The impact of social media, the impact of media, music, and having to have opportunities to talk about that and understand that.

Ms. Gjerek contends that because young people today have increased access to the internet and social media platforms, they need internet awareness and education that much earlier. It seems clear that technology is one of the most pressing challenges that must be tackled by government and the police now and in the future. A more insidious threat is that technology allows people and agencies to claim that sexual exploitation has evaporated because we don't see it in the street.

Several of my respondents mentioned Backpage or "Craigslist as sites of sex trafficking, but didn't suggest ways that law enforcement agencies should intervene to tackle this issue. A number of the NGO workers in my sample spoke of the internet as a growing platform for trafficking and the exploitation of young women. Most of the police officers I interviewed said that government and the general public must focus more on controlling the internet.

Grant (2016b) reports that some American business initiatives are taking up the slack for Canadian law enforcement's perceived lag in tackling internet-based sexual exploitation and trafficking. Sarah Jakiel, chief programs officer for the American anti-trafficking organization Polaris, says, "It's fair to say that Canada is a number of years behind the US." Claudia Ponce-Joly notes that agencies that work with youth need to have technology experts assisting them.

CLAUDIA PONCE-JOLY: When young people are starting to become vulnerable that is when the strategy should start, and it could be information and education. Just as young people are educated on safety and health, they should be educated on what kind of risks are in our communities [and], unfortunately, what kind of people may be attempting to have contact with them. This should be part of education in my view, and especially for children that are vulnerable, involved in the child welfare system or in corrections or any other kind. It's something they should be prepared for because they will encounter some form of it.

Much of it may be online or through friends that they already trust, but much will be encountered through texting, Facebook, and many other kinds of technology-based approaches. I think that would be my first strategy, that I would [start] prevention and education at the youngest age possible. And I do believe that those strategies are occurring, but for those of us that are helping those strategies to be developed, we have to be keeping in mind that we're not necessarily at the cutting edge of technology, and I think that law enforcement, child welfare, and helping organizations need to have people employed with them that *are* on the cutting edge of technology that can help keep us ahead or at least help keep us up to date, so that we can help educate and help combat the luring.

Law enforcement and support practitioners clearly must be savvy about the current technology if they are to keep up with organized criminals, who have the resources, drive, and flexibility to take advantage of it. Ms. Ponce-Joly noted that the whole spectrum of agencies must have people who are competent in using the current technology.

The following seven findings emerged from analysis of my participants' comments about the challenges and opportunities that exist for intervening in and interrupting the sex industry.

First, the system needs more collaboration. My contributors characterized the system as being made up of fragmented pieces, some of which are effective yet address only a small part of any individual survivor's needs. No one agency addresses everything effectively. Better integration of services would more effectively address survivors' needs.

The complex, intersectional, and multilayered challenges that survivors face were outlined above, and it is clear from that discussion that numerous resources must be strategically brought to bear to address the wishes and needs of survivors. Another, related finding is the difficulty that sex industry survivors have in doing what others might deem routine daily tasks; to alleviate this difficulty, services need to be more customer oriented.

Second, no one agency can stand alone. Respondents noted that many organizations work in isolation, without effective joint coordination of their activities, and described how many organizations have effective programs that might be more collectively efficient if they were simply better coordinated. They noted the importance of changing policies and meeting in the middle in order to make better use of existing programs to create win-win scenarios for everyone.

Interviewees advocate for creating regional coordinators with a hands-on operational approach to coordinating data, investigations, and treatment programming. Some participants made specific recommendations for improved provincial, national, and international coordination of data and resources for intervening in the sex industry; resources and programs that are available in each region; and better strategic operational coordination, criminal intelligence, and synchronization of complex organized crime investigations.

Respondents observed that underground railroads and a better safety net should be established to assist young women exiting the sex industry. The provincial government could create a hotline that is connected to a safety net of resources for practitioners and survivors to call at any time of day or night. The creation of an underground railroad by a network of agencies working together on counter-exploitation and intervention could provide pathways for survivors to escape their traffickers and predators. It could furnish a safety net that does not currently exist.

Third, better communication can improve collaboration. Several participants highlight that a lot of inefficiency in the system could be eradicated through better inter- and intra-agency communication. Improved communication could make agency professionals more aware of available programs and resources, and could perhaps also lessen tensions between agencies with differences of opinion over the best means of helping these women.

Interviewees also thought that some inefficiency results from agencies' lack of knowledge of the resources available to survivors. Currently, and tragically, some survivors are left out in the cold because practitioners are not aware of available resources. Some participants stated that most professionals in survivor-oriented programs simply are not aware of all the resources available for their clients. This could be remedied by applying a greater focus on asset mapping and on training practitioners about the resources readily accessible to them. The provincial and federal governments could provide more comprehensive information in public awareness campaigns and websites about the resources at one's disposal to assist young people to leave the sex industry.

Fourth, aging out of the system is a problem. Interviewees asserted that individuals don't change on the day they turn eighteen years of age. They stressed that we currently have a problem wherein people "age out" of the child welfare system: service agencies magically deem them to need fewer resources on the day they turn eighteen. Jay Rodgers pointed out that most agencies have the authority to continue resources for individuals beyond the age of eighteen, yet they choose not to do so. This is a challenge that might be remedied when agency executives gain better awareness of the intersectional challenges that sexually exploited youth and survivors are struggling with.

Fifth, more safe houses are needed. The province's lack of sufficient safe houses to protect young women trying to exit the sex industry was a significant and continuously repeated finding of this research. Several participants noted that there are safe houses for domestic violence victims, but not yet for sex industry survivors. Others advanced compelling arguments for the creation of a fully resourced long-term residential facility that could help survivors escape the sex industry.

Sixth, more youth facilities are needed. My respondents saw it as critical that the province create both secure and open facilities for youth in Manitoba. Young people often get lost in the debate between secured versus open facilities to house young survivors during crisis and subsequent treatment. It could be that there is room to include both types of service, depending on the needs of individual survivors.

Better collaboration between agencies is also required in order to find systemic efficiencies. This could result in increased flexibility in use of available resources. For example, it would be possible to detain a youth for a period of time until she is stable and then move her into a less secure setting. Participants stressed that the current three to seven days of secure custody that is available in Manitoba is not nearly long enough to assist young women recovering from a crisis. Some need one year or more in order to recover from severe addictions, stabilize, and acclimatize back into normal behaviour patterns.

Seventh, we need a greater focus on technology. Interviewees agreed that all of the agencies need to keep up with rapidly ever-changing technology. A significant finding is that we, in law enforcement and social services, lag behind organized crime in mastery of the internet and related social media technology. Interviewees worried about the sex industry becoming invisible. This is disturbing because it makes it increasingly challenging for practitioners to protect survivors and support them, and for law enforcement to intervene. It is also disconcerting because invisibility drives the oppression and violence of the sex industry underground and further from public view.

This chapter is devoted to themes that arose during interviews about specific challenges that survivors and practitioners face and how they might be remedied. Participants made numerous suggestions for areas that could be improved, from broad issues that can translate into policy, such as focusing on building relationships and trust, to more specific resource issues, such as providing more safe houses and transitional housing for young survivors. Yet even these specific issues are laden with conflict about how solutions should be structured and run. For instance, there is an ongoing debate, perhaps the most divisive among the agencies, about whether facilities for high-risk exploited youth should be locked or open, with powerful arguments on either side.

By contrast, there was great consensus amongst almost all interviewees on other issues. Everyone, for example, endorsed the need for better collaboration at every level in creating and utilizing resources around counter-exploitation and prevention, and increased coordination of existing resources. They generally reported that much of the sex industry is moving to the internet and that law enforcement and partnering agencies should keep up with this technology. Police respondents agreed that there is a need to keep up with technological advancements and that organized crime is already way ahead of the curve.

Several participants identified the issue of youths aging out of the child welfare system and proposed solutions. Child welfare agencies in fact have the authority to continue child welfare resources for youth in their care, up to twenty-five years of age, but constricting bureaucratic red tape must be reduced. Some proposals for education and changes of policy/practices seem to have a great deal of merit, such as the Dream Catcher Village suggestion, which would gather multiple resources within one safe place, with a mix of experiential practitioners to assist survivors. Some interviewees suggested creating a safe house with resources located in a geographically secure place in the countryside. This might partially address concerns about placing youth in locked-up facilities.

9 Conflict Transformation, Community Building, and Change

MARIE: I guess just that I think people need to realize when it comes to CFS – not that CFS is always bad, you know what I mean, there's times when kids in care really need to be removed from the home – but if you're talking about kids that are running away from their group home because they don't want to stay there because they could be getting bullied by other kids in the group home, so they run away and they become exploited, that's no reason to lock up a kid in a ten-day facility. 'Cause what happens, they just let them loose and it's a revolving door. There's no fixing their broken souls, so they just keep getting more damaged, more damaged, and every time they get locked up or every time that they're on the street, that's another chance for someone to turn them into a crack head, another chance for someone to shoot them up, or rape or whatever. And I think CFS needs to acknowledge the fact that their practices are creating a second generation of homeless and sexually exploited youth. Forty-six percent become homeless within six months of aging out [of child welfare], and what happens? They do survival sex, right? They enter the sex trade. It's a rock and a hard place, there's no shelters for women who just want to exit, there's only shelters for domestic violence, which is well needed, right? But there needs to be transitional housing, there needs to be a place for these women to go, especially if they're transient, cause then they're going to do survival sex. They're going to do whatever it takes to have a warm place to stay, especially in the winter.

Marie mentions that survivors often engage in selling sex as a means of surviving day to day, and lack of housing can drive them quickly into survival sex just to get out of the cold. The practitioners I interviewed, some of whom are also sex industry survivors, provided rich insights about what could be done to intervene to assist these young survivors. These practitioners are in the trenches, invested in and working on these issues, and are sometimes in conflict with their own organizations as well as practitioners in other agencies who are, ironically, usually also working to help survivors. Daphne Penrose, for example, said that too often youth are lost between agencies as a result of individuals "wearing their ego into the room," thinking they are the expert and more capable than others of providing services. Joy Smith expressed the same concern more strongly when she stated that some people "have egos as big as all outdoors." I look at these dynamics as conflicts that could be overcome through more effective collaboration. Conflict-resolution tools could be useful in dealing with these conflicts and challenges, helping people to overcome difficulties within and between their organizations, and in finding better systemic responses for sex industry survivors.

My respondents identified several seemingly incompatible goals and the issues that lie at the heart of these systemic inefficiencies. One example we have already seen: the debate between agencies over whether youth facilities should be secure or open. Parties on both sides of this argument appear entrenched, with no apparent middle ground (see Boulding, 2000; Deutsch & Coleman, 2000; Kriesberg, 1998). But others identified a potential compromise: making survivors geographically secure by placing them in facilities in the countryside. The conflicted parties might reach this resolution by participating together in conflict-transformation processes.

This book explores conflict and power disparities as they concern sexual exploitation and human trafficking. Scholars in the field of peace and conflict studies (PACS) often apply the descriptions of positive versus negative peace that were developed by Johan Galtung (1996) about post-war societies. Galtung characterizes "positive peace" as involving improved standards of living beyond the absence of war; the mere lack of active war is "negative peace." These ideas can be extended to the phenomenon of crime reduction and victimization in modern-day Canada. While people in mainstream Canada enjoy a high standard of living and positive peace, many survivors in the sex industry do not. This disparity constitutes structural violence (Galtung, 1996; Reimer et al., 2015).

The dynamics I described in previous chapters can be explained using frameworks from various disciplines. For example, the concept of intersectionality from the field of sociology explains the multiple layered challenges facing sex industry survivors. Community building and collective impact models (Chrislip, 2002) describe and provide tools for creating social change. Conflict analysis and resolution techniques and theories can be used to analyse and work out conflict, such as that mentioned above between agencies and individuals (Byrne et al., 2003; Byrne & Senehi, 2012; Kriesberg, 1998; Lowry & Littlejohn, 2003; Rothman & Olson, 2001; Sandole et al., 2009; Saunders, 2003). These can be combined with a multitrack intervention and peace-building process for making inclusive political change (Diamond & McDonald, 1996; Byrne & Keashly, 2000).

Another relevant and important framework for analysing conflict is story or narrative-based peacebuilding, which is an intervention approach that has also grown in popularity within PACS (Reimer et al., 2015; Senehi, 2009). This is of course the framework I employ in these pages: this book gathers a mass of personal stories from survivors and a broad range of other actors and links their statements and observations. This creates a tapestry of insights that form a community narrative regarding the issue, via which I hope to contribute to the growing public discourse and momentum for change around a challenging social issue.

Byrne and Senehi (2009) emphasize that analysing a conflict requires understanding of how it originated, how it escalated or reduced, and the characteristics and values of the parties or groups involved, such as the conflicted parties' goals, intervention styles, and preferred problem-solving strategies. They provide a valuable overview of conflict elements that interplay to varying degrees, and how they are resolved (Byrne & Senehi, 2009). By analysing conflict, or inefficient cooperation and collaboration between agencies, we may facilitate their working better together. The benefits of improved efficiency translate directly to the service recipients – in this case, sex industry survivors.

Byrne et al. (2003) designed a social cube for use in exploring the following six interrelated conflict dynamics: (1) history, (2) religion, (3) demographics, (4) political institutions and non-institutional behaviour, (5) economics, and (6) psycho-cultural factors. These six facets or social forces of conflict can be looked at together to identify patterns of behaviour between groups, and to identify the causes of conflict. We will likely fail in attaining shared goals for multiple stakeholder agencies addressing sexual exploitation if we attempt to analyse their conflicts in terms of only one dimension; we need to consider numerous aspects to understand such complex social issues (Byrne et al., 2003).

Conflicts are not static; they are dynamic and ever-changing, as we have seen, for instance, between agencies. The conflicts can occur where agencies intersect, and result in pointing of fingers or fighting over funding. Service agencies, such as the police, child welfare, health, justice, and political leaders, all have vested interests in the protection and safety of sexually exploited children and adults, yet they all have different mandates for achieving those goals. Knowledge of dynamics such as those identified by Kriesberg can be used to identify the right tools for finding common ground and thus better efficiency, or at least allow participants or mediators to avoid making conflicts worse.

Kriesberg (1998) points out that people undergo changes in identity in response to conflicts in which they are involved, and emphasizes the importance of constructive dialogue addressing the concerns and grievances of conflicted parties so that they do not become more entrenched in their positions. Identity and positionality are crucial elements in conflicts. Rothman and Olson (2001) have contributed significantly to our understanding of the role of identity in conflicts. One method for reconciling positional conflict is interactive conflict resolution (ICR), which Fisher (1997) has described as effective. ICR techniques are facilitated face-to-face activities in communication, training, education, or consultation that promote collaborative conflict analysis and problem solving among parties engaged in protracted conflict, in a manner that addresses the parties' needs and promotes building peace, justice, and equality (Fisher, 1997). ICR processes have been credited with bringing about long periods of cessation of violence between the Israelis and Palestinians (Rothman & Olson, 2001). With such a track record, they might be useful in resolving conflict between agencies that should be working better together, such as police and social workers, different NGOs, or even individuals striving to work better within a given organization.

Rothman and Olson's (2001) ARIA (Antagonistic, Reflexive, Integrative, Action) ICR model delineates key stages of conflicts and their resolution. The stages include (1) the antagonistic frame, in which the conflicted parties' positions are established; (2) the reflexive frame, in which both parties' desired outcomes are discovered; (3) the integrative frame, in which common ground is discovered; and (4) the action plan, in which creative problem solving seeks to achieve the shared goals discovered in the earlier stages. This approach offers structured and workable tools that can be used to address even the most intractable conflicts. In the case of sexually exploited women and youth, their positions (antagonistic frame) may reveal distrust for the authorities as well as the lack of perceived ways to escape their exploitive relationships.

Police, child welfare, and NGO workers often express frustration with the lack of collaboration among agencies and the fragmented interagency resource systems. They may also feel frustration and resentment at being mistrusted or taken advantage of. These antagonistic perspectives need to be brought out honestly, yet respectfully, if the truth about stakeholders' positions is to be known and addressed, as it is only from an honest starting position that sustainable conflict resolution can be achieved. Processes such as ARIA can provide this starting position by having parties lay bare their strongest feelings about the fundamental causes of a conflict.

The factors involved in the sex industry and in conflict between groups – race (Indigenous vs. Europeans), age (young vs. older), government vs. non-government service providers, and other oppositional groups – can be delineated. Understanding the effects of identity, position, and process can assist in the analysis and resolution of such conflicts. Mediators should be aware of cultural values that prohibit working towards shared goals. For example, face-saving is an important value in high-context cultures, ones in which people are highly sensitive to their position in society and often feel shame if they are viewed as disgracing their community. The culture of Canadian Indigenous people is one example (Rice, 2011; Tuso, 2013); another example might be sexually exploited people, who could feel shame due to the social stigma attached to the sex industry. They may be distrustful and feel insecure about leaving the entrenched environment of that industry, where they are confident and competent, albeit manipulated and abused. Face-saving is a critical factor to consider in involving survivors in strategic planning and work that concerns the sex industry. It is counterproductive to engage survivors in program development and other work if the process is judgmental and shaming or risky for them.

It is also important to understand gender-related vulnerability in the analysis of sexual exploitation. Amahazion (2014) notes that society, and the literature on sex workers, often tends to pigeonhole or label them as socially deviant and as undesirable to others. This is a form of oppression that applies primarily to women. (Here we should recall Leslie Spillett's important point, discussed above, that she doesn't see people as "survivors" but as people.) The fear of being labelled a "prostitute" is so strong that it can silence people and prevent them from seeking help.

Sociologist Patricia Hill Collins (2009) wrote about the overlapping forms of oppression that many women face in society. Women involved in the sex industry are continually judged (Amahazion, 2014; Doezema, 1998; Lozano, 2010). They are denied protection and security in their work and lives that others take for granted (Kempadoo & Doezema, 1998). The five top factors indicating vulnerability to being sex trafficked in Canada, as outlined in CWF (2014) research, are: (1) being born female (2) being poor, (3) having a history of violence or neglect, (4) having a history of child sexual abuse, and (5) having a low education level. Of note is that four of these five factors are involve or are linked to poverty.

Sally Engle Merry (2009) suggests that gender violence is rooted in local cultural perceptions of power and gender. Therefore, according to her, human rights should be thought of in terms of local contexts. Regional differences are increasingly salient, as Canada has growing pockets of newcomers, and each of these local contexts and ethnic groups has unique cultures. For example, genital mutilation is a problem among certain cultural newcomer groups that are quickly growing in Canada. How are we helping to protect young girls and women who wish not to be subjected to this? Transgenerational trauma is another social dynamic that is more common among some cultural groups, in particular those with large refugee populations and Canada's Indigenous people.

Boulding (2000) suggests that peacebuilding should also be carried out in local contexts, transforming oppressive structures through "feminist analysis" emphasizing empowerment, replacing "power-over" with "power-with" structures. These perspectives relate to sexual exploitation, as dynamics in exploitation are relevant in all oppressive relationships, and the vast majority of sexual exploitation victims across Canada are female Indigenous Canadians (Department of Justice, 2014). Paterson (2010) further comments that it is important to consider power relationships in the analysis of domestic violence. These same power relationships are relevant in any exploitive scenario – including sex trafficking.

According to Lozano (2010), prostitution exists because of power differentials through which women are objectified and dehumanized. As Delacoste and Alexander (1987) write, "In virtually all countries, men earn more for the same or equivalent work than do women" (p. 190). In most cases, all of the money earned by sex industry survivors goes to traffickers and other people exploiting them, and any money the survivor is allowed to keep for herself often goes towards buying alcohol and street drugs for self-medication, to numb the psychological distress of living with the previously noted social stigmas (Greene et al., 1999). Much has been written on the perspective that prostitution maintains women's oppression in society (Barry, 1995; Delacoste & Alexander, 1987 Lozano, 2010; Murray 1998).

Sensitivity to, and understanding of, cultural norms can be advantageous for mediators, as no model of conflict mediation can be designed to fit all cultural contexts (Lederach, 1996). Every event or process should be approached with sensitivity to diversity and cultural differences and nuances within each group (Tuso, 2013). Jeong (2000) also highlights the significance of group identities in conflict, stating that identity can be used "instrumentally to promote individual or collective interests" (p. 72). Group identity is significant to sexual exploitation, as the sex industry culture that children and women become entrenched in is powerful and exclusive. In general, different elements affect conflicts; therefore, analysis is critical to determining which dynamics are significant and how they may best be addressed.

Othering is another important concept related to understanding positions and perceptions in conflict. Said (1979) described the process by which people develop perceptions of the "other." Such perceptions can hamper any conflict-resolution process and can also be a barrier to collaboration. They can hamper people on the fringes, such as sex industry workers, from coming forward and accepting assistance, out of fear of being labelled and ostracized. And labelling is a significant factor in gender-specific violence. Kempadoo and Doezema (1998) point out that the mere fact that a "prostitute" is distinguished as belonging to a specific group "perpetuates her exclusion from rights to freedom from violence at work" (p. 65). In general, social labels and categories negatively stigmatize women (Lozano, 2010). Lozano (2010) agrees that "othering" occurs in the way modern-day prostitutes are identified as such: they are labelled as bad women as opposed to virtuous, distinguishing them along other dichotomies such as normal versus abnormal, wife versus prostitute, and virgin versus whore (Bell, 1994; Kempadoo & Doezema, 1998). These labels can ruin people's lives in numerous ways; therefore, we must be careful to avoid labelling people.

John Paul Lederach, an international leader in peacebuilding, has taught us that the answers to deep-rooted social problems such as sexual exploitation are already in the community. Local inhabitants understand the context and nuances of the culture and can identify the solutions to problems and conflicts. This approach resonates strongly, as it is common sense that people doing the work and people who have been exploited and trafficked in the sex industry will have insights into the barriers and opportunities that they experienced. They are well positioned to identify where improvements are needed. It is probable that strategies informed by the input of grass-roots stakeholders "envisioning a shared future" are most effective (Lederach, 1997, p. 27). Just as supporting Indigenous people will require looking for answers within that community (Cook & Courchene, 2006, pp. 4–6), the members of which truly understand the impacts of colonialism on Indigenous youth and transgenerationally (see Volkan, 1997), survivors of the sex industry and service providers are likely to know what the system needs.

Several tools can be used to resolve conflicts once the true issues are identified. One method, "sustained dialogue," focuses on getting the right people in the discussion and then keeping them engaged long enough to work through a five-stage problem-solving process: (1) deciding to reach out and create a space for dialogue, (2) coming together and mapping out the problems to be resolved, (3) probing the specific problem, (4) planning interactions, and (5) devising ways to empower people to act on the plans created (Saunders, 2003, p. 86). Saunders considers it important to connect people from diverse groups in the process, not just high-level negotiators.

Saunders (2003) notes that conflict can occur within and between identity groups; therefore, one should avoid the tendency to think of any group as homogenous. People involved in agencies, communities, and groups, including those who have been trafficked and sexually exploited, all have different experiences and perspectives. When analysing policies, strategies, and approaches to issues such as sexual exploitation, we must avoid the temptation to think that all people in any organization or group are the same. Sustained dialogue is one tool for achieving this outcome. It can be a key strategy for developing trust and finding shared goals among stakeholders, including relationships between victims and service providers and between all of the various stakeholder agencies (Saunders, 2003). Unpacking and understanding the nature of the positions of the various stakeholders who work together to help exploited youth might be discovered through the exercise of the antagonistic frame of Rothman and Olson's ARIA model. This is one way to create the starting point for conflict resolution and reconciliation (Rothman & Olson, 2001, pp. 92–7).

The enduring tension between social work and policing professionals could be addressed by utilizing these conflict analysis and resolution (CAR) techniques. Both professions have a responsibility to address sexual exploitation, and both stand to gain from more effective collaboration, yet there is persistent counterproductive tension between them. Inter-agency conflict between NGOs can also be addressed in this same way. Interpersonal conflict is common within and between organizations and can potentially be overcome through appropriate interventions.

The significance of organizational culture is neglected in the literature on sexual exploitation, yet understanding and respecting culture is likely the key to finding common ground in solving conflicts (Engle Merry, 2009). Avruch (1998) notes that there are 150 or more known definitions of culture, and some elements are more salient than others as sources of conflict. If mediators can ascertain which cultural issues are truly relevant to conflicted parties, they may have a better chance of resolving the disagreement.

Culture, according to Avruch (1998), is "a learned shared system of actions, meanings and practices, which are socially and psychologically distributed within a group, and are transmitted laterally and intergenerationally" (p. 17). While individuals embrace culture, it is also shared within groups and communities (p. 17). Conflict exists in every human group, whether between individuals, communities, agencies, or states. Understanding what is important in these cultures can assist in finding shared ground for conflict transformation, gaining better collective outcomes around issues such as sex trafficking and exploitation.

Change resistance is another form of conflict that CAR techniques could be used to address. Most organizations, whether governmental or not, have some natural resistance to organizational change. Research has found that as much as 90 per cent of major corporate strategy changes fail because administrators did not plan to mitigate the psychological impacts the changes would have on people (Cameron & Green, 2004).

Schein (1985) found that preparing people psychologically for changes in their workplace reduces anxiety, making new policies and practices easier and less painful to integrate. In Schein's change management model, management first creates awareness of the need for change among employees (the "unfreezing" stage). Changes are then implemented, after which "refreezing" occurs in the final phase, and then the changes are internalized over time (Schein, 1985). Recommendations that require any form of change – as all recommendations do – are ill fated if those in charge do not consider and plan management of the change.

One form of community building and change that seems particularly suited for counter-exploitation work is collective impact, a contemporary term for collaborative cross-agency team building to affect social issues. Chrislip (2002), a pioneer in collective impact work, writes that collaboration is now a means for "building social capital" and "transforming civic culture" around social problems. Multi-agency systemic change requires work to find a shared vision and goals, and change may be achieved using some combination of CAR strategies. On collective impact work, Chrislip (2002) wrote about the importance of bringing the right parties together to create strategies to address community concerns (in Chrismas & Ponce-Joly, 2015, p. 25). My research identifies opportunities for improved collaborative, multidisciplinary, cross-sectoral approaches to intervene in sexual exploitation and human trafficking.

As we have seen, a broad spectrum of services affect sex industry survivors, yet those services do not always work well together; sometimes they needlessly work against each other. In a study that was character-ized as the first Canadian attempt to analyse the coordinated response to human trafficking in a large urban centre, Kaye et al. (2014) surveyed fifty-three people from various agencies involved in anti-trafficking. They found that "while a criminal justice framework is important for addressing human trafficking, local strategies will benefit from an em-phasis on cross-sector collaboration that emphasizes the rights of the trafficked persons above the needs of law enforcement" (p. 36).

New solutions might involve stakeholders envisioning themselves as equal participants in collective community-based approaches. For instance, Lederach (2005) describes how interventions can work at the community level and must be flexible in order to adapt to changing needs during the peacebuilding process. The same principles apply to community-based collaborative interventions to address sexual ex-ploitation. People in government and non-government agencies alike are continually asked to do more with less. Collaborative, multidisci-plinary, collective approaches may increase the efficiency of systems of existing resources, by reducing policy gaps and redundancy between service providers and by finding shared goals that multi-agency sys-tems can strive for together.

The Boston Gun Project (also known as Operation Ceasefire), men-tioned briefly in chapter 3, is a relevant case study in the potential of collective impact work. In the late 1980s, the City of Boston and sur-rounding municipalities experienced a crisis of shootings in which every month an African American youth (under eighteen) was shot and either injured or killed. Many of these young men were involved in gangs, and most were from impoverished neighbourhoods. Pro-throw-Stith and Spivak are two emergency room doctors who got tired of seeing young black men coming in on stretchers; they saw these youth as an endangered species and framed violence as a public health issue. They involved the medical community, and other service sectors, in preventative rather than reactive approaches, and they motivated collaboration between all of the various stakeholders, changing the culture and the public discourse to one in which violence was gener-ally not acceptable. The Boston Gun Project brought police resources together with other agencies and groups, resulting in a 63 per cent de-cline in youth homicides over three years (Kennedy et al., 2001; Linden, 2012). It involved aggressive enforcement and prosecution strategies combined with increased community partnership, bringing multiple service sectors together with a common goal of reducing violence.

Prothrow-Stith and Spivak (2004) challenged common assumptions about violence-afflicted youth, characterizing them as victims rather than as criminals. They found that the answers are in the community, and people need empowerment to solve problems themselves or with the support of government, rather than solutions being imposed by government. They also found that there is no single best practice; problems that took a long time to develop will take a long time to solve; punishing offenders alone does not fix problems – problems need intervention; violence is not inevitable, but results from social conditions; and poverty in itself does not cause violence, even if it correlates with it. Viewing youth violence as a health problem challenged traditional health care paradigms that historically tolerated high violence rates among African Americans and those in low socio-economic groups (Prothrow-Stith & Spivak, 2004).

Understanding the root causes of violence and how vulnerability leads to victimization can lead to potential solutions for youth exploited in the sex industry. Assumptions about social dynamics, such as that increased crowding in poor neighbourhoods correlates with higher violence rates, have been challenged. For example, in Hong Kong there is more crowding and *less* violence than in the US (Prothrow-Stith & Spivak, 2004). How can we explain this? Nor did theorized biological bases of violent behaviour provide reliable explanations (Prothrow-Stith & Spivak, 2004). As Englander (2006) has emphasized, even close correlations do not provide causal explanations.

The violence reduction programs undertaken in the Boston area focused on interrupting the cycle of violence by humanizing youth, shifting attention away from punitively fixing blame and into supporting the needs of the involved youth (Prothrow-Stith & Spivak, 2004). Pulling relevant disciplines together for better collaboration and viewing perpetrators also as victims achieved astounding results. Prothrow-Stith and Spivak (2004) advocate multiple systems approaches as, they wrote, "In an avalanche, not one snowflake feels responsible" (p. 61). And in addition to multidisciplinary collaboration, they also advocate that the multiple systems involved share a vision of intervention and violence prevention.

The violence reduction achieved in Boston, while effective in the short term, was not sustained in the long term (Linden, 2012), as priorities eventually shifted among partnering agencies. Police and community groups eventually became less engaged, moving resources to new priorities. Nonetheless, the Boston experience contains valuable lessons for successful interventions to help those being exploited in the sex industry. For one, Prothrow-Stith and Spivak (2004) maintain that "demonizing youth" or criminalizing them only exacerbates their problems (pp. 144–5) and causes further oppression. And their success after reframing the issue supports the importance of seeing sexually exploited youth as victims rather than as perpetrators.

The case study presented by the CWF (2014) also illustrates that youth who have been sexually exploited or trafficked experience trauma that most people will never undergo. Therefore, they need unique approaches for intervention and treatment (Richardson, 2015). Canada's laws, as noted above, were recently changed to better reflect the perspective that exploited children, youth, and women are victims rather than criminals. In the twenty-first century, there is growing understanding across society that selling sex involves power disparities and affronts human rights and dignity. Public discourse in Canada has seen increased awareness and debate, in recent years, over economic disparity, the impacts of colonization on Indigenous people, and the status of sex industry workers as victims rather than criminals.

Sexual exploitation is a global as well as a Canadian social problem, tracing economic, social, and power disparities along intersecting lines including gender, race, and class. Dissecting power disparities at the root of such conflicts can shed light on oppression and how it may be reduced. Some scholars have focused their research on this growing discourse, and a "world culture" agrees universally that enslavement and sexual exploitation breaches basic global human rights (Amahazion, 2014). Yet large segments of society are still blind to the extent that sexual exploitation and trafficking goes on.

A significant aspect of public engagement and discourse is often not that the wrong story is told, but that no story is even acknowledged. During a field study in South Africa with a group of PACS students in 2011, I had the great privilege of meeting with Piet Meiring, who sat on South Africa's original, post-apartheid Truth and Reconciliation Commission (TRC) along with Desmond Tutu. Professor Meiring pointed out that people testifying at the TRC generally did not seek money or punishment, even in cases where a police officer or soldier had killed their child; what they really wanted was acknowledgment of what had happened. This is why the Canadian government's acknowledgment of the harm caused to Indigenous peoples by Canada's settlement and assimilation programs was so important.

It seems that if public apathy is reduced and all of the significant elements in society are engaged, any problem is more solvable (Klatt et al., 2014). Lederach (1996) emphasized the need for citizen empowerment so that people can participate more in solving society's problems. The public narrative seems critical in motivating agencies in all aspects, from funding to goal setting. The Missing and Murdered Indigenous Women and Girls movement is a case in point. Advocacy over the past decade has moved the issue of violence against Indigenous women into the public eye, to the point that in September 2016 the federal government initiated a fifty-eight-million-dollar national enquiry. Acknowledging the situation for what it is will, in the end, go a long way towards reconciliation.

The themes arising from this research highlight the need for multidisciplinary partnership, collaboration, and coordination of resources for exploited and trafficked young women, who currently exist in a fragmented system. There are a lot of good services, yet no one can access them all or, without enormous effort, even know what exactly exists. There are also gaps in the various systems. Participants in this research suggest resources and programs that could be added, some of which have been implemented in other countries and were recommended in the existing literature.

Reducing conflict requires an understanding of the conflicted parties' goals, intervention styles, and problem-solving strategies (Byrne & Senehi, 2009). An effective consultation process could ensure input and engagement of the community. Mediation tools, such as I have outlined here, could assist in overcoming any disagreements that occur in the process. I know from personal experience that conflict can also occur during community consultation. I participated in the consultation that the Manitoba Child Protection Branch conducted during development of the StreetReach program in 2008. During those meetings voices were raised, feelings were hurt, and tears were shed; some people walked out on meetings and later refused to participate. A mediation process, such as those outlined in this chapter, could make such processes much more effective and less painful. Such mediation processes could include PACS tools such as sustained dialogue (Saunders, 2003) and Rothman and Olson's ARIA model (Rothman & Olson, 2001).

Moving now to the fifty-thousand-foot view, how do we reduce conflict to make the whole interagency system work better? Diamond and McDonald (1996) provide a framework of multitrack diplomacy that may help achieve this aim. Their nine-track model for achieving peacebuilding objectives considers all of the stakeholders that play significant roles in resolving conflicts and achieving systemic change. The model engages combinations of people from various sectors of society – official government diplomats; unofficial, non-governmental experienced or skilled citizens; private business; citizen-to-citizen cultural or educational exchanges, media; activism or advocacy; faith-based organizations; philanthropy; and peacemaking – via information sharing, such as through media and social movements.

Improved coordination of multitrack intervention approaches may be the key to achieving resolution of some of society's most challenging conflicts and social problems. This multisectoral approach could effectively coordinate all the major elements required to change the public discourse and have an impact on the sex industry (Byrne & Keashly, 2000). Multimodal approaches hold great promise for social change, as they can affect the larger narrative, which I suspect is indispensable in achieving significant progress.

A central challenge in resolving conflicts is understanding that they exist and what the true conflict is. Thus, conflict analysis is needed before we set out to resolve and transform conflicts. The analytical social cube identified by Byrne, Carter, and Senehi (2003) is one model that could be used to analyse and understand the interrelatedness of numerous factors fuelling conflicts. As an example, let us return to the ongoing debate, discussed above, about secure versus open facilities for youth. Marymound has the main secure facilities in the province (the Crisis Stabilization Unit) and would like to work more closely with Indigenous organizations to provide better services for young female survivors. However, it was founded and to this day is run by the Catholic Church. Thus some in the Indigenous community view Marymound as closely associated with the residential school era, which creates a challenge for generating new partnerships.

Tools such as the social analytical cube (Byrne et al., 2003) can help us to understand this troubled history, as well as the psycho-cultural issues at the heart of such conflicts, by allowing us to identify multiple underlying and interrelated causes. The Catholic Health Corporation, for instance, has evolved so that in the present day it is mainly lay and non-sectorial in its service delivery approach. If people opposed to church-run institutions come to understand this new context, they might be more inclined to take advantage of the services Marymound offers.

My interviewees also identified political goals, including devoting more resources to combating sex trafficking and sexual exploitation of young women, and finding ways to collaborate and share information and resources better. These large, systemic political goals seem well suited to being addressed through a version of Diamond and McDonald's (1996) nine-track diplomacy intervention model (see also Byrne & Keashly, 2000). This model may be ideal for making change that allow all of the agencies to be brought together in a coordinated effort to end sex trafficking and sexual exploitation.

As well, the people I interviewed were involved with or working for many different organizations, each with their own unique organizational cultures. The significance of organizational culture is not often acknowledged in research, yet understanding and respecting culture is critical in finding common ground, resolving conflicts, and bringing about social and organizational change (Avruch, 1998; Engle Merry, 2009; Trice & Beyer, 1993). This is why I asked for input from people in a broad range of service sectors with fundamentally different mandates and cultures. Understanding their varied perspectives sheds light on the root causes of inefficiency and conflict. It also helps in making organizational change, which many agencies are naturally resistant to (Cameron & Green, 2004; Schein, 1985).

The collective impact model is designed to address problems such as this, bringing a broad range of actors together to effect social change (Chrislip, 2002). It has been applied in other jurisdictions to tackle the sex industry. Kaye et al. (2014) examined over fifty agencies focused on human trafficking and found that "while a criminal justice framework is important for addressing human trafficking, local strategies will benefit from an emphasis on cross-sector collaboration that emphasizes the rights of the trafficked persons above the needs of law enforcement." Their findings revealed opportunities to bring agencies together to confront the sex industry. Sex trafficking is a complex and multifaceted problem that calls for an amalgamation of numerous local intervention and prevention tools to address it. A collective impact strategy can work by utilizing conflict resolution tools to analyse root causes and address interpersonal and interagency conflicts. The interest groups and actors could be brought together to make political change and affect overall systemic coordination and change, utilizing a multitrack diplomacy intervention model as suggested by Diamond and McDonald (1996).

The main broad recommendation that emerged from this research is the need for greater all-community engagement, coordination, and collaboration. Collective impact approaches and PACS intervention and prevention methods offer some useful tools, but the greatest movement forward, it seems, is through changing the public discourse. Agencies in government and non-government sectors should all strive to develop partnerships and collaborate more with client-centred approaches. We need to find ways to affect the public narrative, reduce society-wide apathy and indifference, and advance the social agenda on reducing sexual exploitation of children and youth in the sex industry.

Informing the public through strategic marketing has been successful in recent decades on issues such as impaired driving, seatbelt use, and the link between smoking and lung cancer, and currently we have campaigns to reduce distracted driving. Sometimes shifting public opinion is a slow process. Many, for instance, are in denial about global warming despite a massive and undeniable body of scientific evidence proving otherwise. The sex industry is similar in that much of the public is in denial, caught up in wilful blindness or apathy unless it is happening to their loved ones or in their own backyard.

However, the time for change around the sex industry is now, with growing public awareness and a developing social movement in Canada concerning the sex industry and missing and murdered Indigenous women and children. Conditions are right in Canada, and there has been much movement around the issue of sex trafficking and exploitation over the past two decades. Perhaps we can cause social change by affecting the public discourse.

Ten salient recommendations arise from this research; all support a multitrack peacebuilding and intervention strategy that engages multiple elements of society in a holistic program to interrupt the oppression of vulnerable women and children in the sex industry. Cook and Courchene (2006) in their "vision for the future" in Manitoba provided a list of the general categories of action needed to reduce sexual exploitation, in eleven broad recommendations: (1) adequate funding, (2) treatment programs, (3) education and awareness, (4) outreach resources and prevention programs, (5) professional counsellors and psychologists, (6) housing and homelessness initiatives, (7) stronger punishments for perpetrators, (8) community policing, (9) partnerships between communities and police, (10) better networking and collaboration between agencies and communities, and (11) stronger support systems and resources for communities (p. 4). My overall findings follow very similar lines and are outlined in the next chapter.

This chapter has described some tools that are necessary to achieve these goals. They include conflict analysis, understanding positionality and culture, finding common ground using conflict transformation tools, and achieving community-wide change through collective impact and multisectoral approaches. The key to achieving these goals lies in understanding that conflict is a natural aspect of human nature, as well as of every organization and system of organizations. This is why I have dedicated an entire chapter to conflict resolution.

10 Key Findings, Recommendations, and Future Research

ASHLEY: If money was no object the best thing that could be done is to have more voluntary long-term rehabilitation centres for women and girls who have been exploited, where they can learn life skills, boundaries, healthier relationships, and learn how to believe in themselves again. It can take a long time to learn from the trauma and they need reliable support ... A safe place for these women to live so that they can start to rebuild their lives, so that they could have someone to support them and to plant the seeds and to believe in them so that they could believe in themselves and, you know, show them that they can do new things and be a safe place for them to live, like offer a one-year or two-year program, right? Until they're on their feet.

Ashley points out one of the key findings of my research, that the trauma that survivors endure causes damage that can take a very long time to undo, and this recovery takes unique resources. This chapter outlines the most significant findings as well as recommendations that flow from the data, as well as issues for future research. The stories I gathered present a resounding consensus among experts on some issues, mixed views on others, and in some cases sharply diverging views. For example, respondents had conflicting positions on whether facilities for housing high-risk youth should be secure or open. On this issue, as well as other topics that found strong consensus among interviewees, I found saturation, wherein I believe no further new ideas would come forth no matter how many more interviews I completed. The insights gained are outlined here.

My respondents explored the problematic question of whether participation in the sex industry is a legitimate career choice or occurs more as a result of coercion, threats, and manipulation by pimps and traffickers. People took different positions, some arguing that anyone selling their body for money is a victim and others that women have agency over their bodies and should be free to choose that life if they so wish. At the outset, I anticipated each side of this debate would have a large number of adherents, possibly equal numbers. I found, however, that interviewees strongly feel that working in the sex industry is not a choice children make – that young people wind up in the sex industry as a result of lack of resilience in the face of predators who manipulate, coerce, and threaten them. This lack of resilience stems in part from oppressed living conditions, often in tandem with a history of childhood physical, sexual, and emotional abuse, impoverishment, and lack of economic and educational opportunities. In short, it results from a lack of hope. These observations all present a bleak picture of the conditions that survivors endure.

Youth are often recruited and groomed into the sex industry at the tender age of thirteen years or younger, targeted by predators who are experts in the psychology of vulnerability and human frailty. These youth become profoundly and emotionally entrenched in the sex industry subculture by the time they reach adulthood. The subculture is so seductive and all-encompassing that young women often succumb to a form of Stockholm syndrome, which is a phenomenon in which hostages eventually fall in love with their captors (Westcott, 2013). As part of this entrenchment, a survivor often refuses to work with authorities and is convinced that selling sex is a career choice and that the man who beats her when she fails to earn enough money is her friend and lover. Service providers such as police, social workers, and treatment staff therefore have the unique challenge of striving to help people who think or say they don't want to be helped.

Sex industry survivors are victims of structural violence (Burton, 1997; Foucault, 2010; Galtung, 1996). These youths are often victims of childhood sexual abuse, leading to substance abuse and severe behavioural problems, and they frequently end up becoming wards of the state. As mentioned above, poverty and lack of opportunities are factors in these outcomes, as they underlie young people's lack of resilience, their lessened ability to resist predators who excel at spotting and exploiting vulnerable people (Brock, 1998; Lowman, 1987). As for direct violence, my research confirms the observations of Cullen-DuPont and other researchers, including Farley (2003), who writes that women and children in the sex industry are most often trapped in violent exploitive relationships, suffering brutal assaults as part of their daily experience.

The risks for Indigenous youth are even higher, compounded by "transgenerational traumas" (Volkan, 1997) as well as poor living conditions (also see CBC, 2008, 2011; Cook & Courchene, 2006; Galley, 2009;

Lauwers, 2012). The dangers for Indigenous youth are further exacerbated by structural issues, such as having to leave their home communities for schooling in larger urban centres, where organized criminal predators are always looking for new recruits to enslave in the sex industry.

One finding of this research was the challenges that sex industry survivors face in performing what many would consider basic tasks. My respondents detail how simply asking a survivor to attend a doctor's appointment or pick up a prescription can be a substantial barrier due to the multiple daily coping challenges that some individuals struggle with. This new insight should have implications for building survivor-oriented treatments as well as program and policy development.

The general conclusions of this study are consistent with previous findings of the struggles that sex industry survivors experience with trauma and post-traumatic stress, negative self-image, and the fear of being discovered and labelled (Wong et al., 2011; Sanders, 2004). These often contribute to self-medicating and numbing through substance abuse, and risk-taking behaviour such as inconsistent condom use, which increases their likelihood of contracting sexually transmitted diseases and AIDS (Hong et al., 2007; Lau et al., 2010). A smaller body of research has highlighted the survival skills and positive psychological coping mechanisms that survivors develop in the face of the unspeakable degradation, humiliation, and mental and physical torture that accompanies their activities in the sex industry (see Aspinwall & Tedeschi, 2010; Choudhury, 2010; Kong, 2006; Sossou et al., 2008; Wood & Tarrier, 2010). My respondents also described the vulnerability and lack of resilience that led to their becoming entrapped in the sex industry, often as young children. They displayed extreme courage and tenacity in overcoming some of the most oppressive degradations that humanity has to offer. The survivors I interviewed are much like the thistle that thrives in harsh desert conditions, where other vegetation have shrivelled up and died (see Paige's comments, chapter 8).

As my respondents described youth vulnerability, it became clear why children in the care of the state are particularly vulnerable. This is not an indictment of the child welfare system, which has substantial challenges in Manitoba, with the highest number of children in care per capita of any of Canada's provinces and territories (Puxley, 2014). Rather, it underscores that social workers in Manitoba are up against steep challenges in their work assisting youth who are living the effects of impoverishment and low resilience. Chief Ron Evans made it clear that this situation points to governments' responsibilities to help reduce poverty among Indigenous people and provide better educational and employment opportunities for them. At the same time, the high numbers of children in care call for more action from frontline service providers, including social workers, police, and the broad spectrum of caregivers, to intervene earlier and prevent sex industry recruitment.

Additionally, my participants highlighted the need for a paradigm shift in child welfare, suggesting that the child should not, unless absolutely necessary, be removed from the family home and support systems; when possible, the offending adult should be the one who is removed. Too often, respondents stressed, the child is taken to a group or foster home rather than resources being brought into the home to assist the family. Some respondents, who have many years of experience both as clients and as practitioners in the child welfare system, asserted that the system needs to be more child centred; it should do what is best for the child, not what is most convenient for service agencies.

My respondents made it abundantly clear that practitioners should have more training in intervention, so that they are fully aware that they are working with sexually exploited youth and know what to do for them. We need more awareness training for teachers and parents, who are in a position to see the signs of trafficking and intervene, and we need education for children at all levels, so that they understand and can resist the approaches of sexual predators who troll social media and shopping malls for victims. Previous research has been relatively clear on how troubled youth are sexually exploited; however, the literature contains less on effective interventions and clinical care (Berckamns et al., 2012; Richardson, 2015). My hope is that the practical recommendations that resulted from my research fill in some of those gaps.

This research also provides insights into how organized the activity of sex trafficking and exploitation is in Manitoba and the rest of Canada (CWF, 2014; Richardson, 2015). Previous literature has noted components of organized crime, but my research provides a first-hand perspective on how it operates on the ground in targeting, grooming, and trafficking our children. These accounts make clear how calculating, brutal, and oppressive the tactics of traffickers are.

My participants expressed near-unanimous agreement that there is a need for more anti-trafficking education and awareness for people at all levels, including greater public awareness to combat broad societal apathy about this issue. Participants endorsed greater awareness and education of the general public, including campaigns in schools to target younger audiences. They believe education also needs to be enhanced within the community to teach children how to recognize predatory overtures and avoid being groomed into the sex industry, and to teach johns about the psychological and physical damage that sex purchasing inflicts on children. Although there is, as mentioned above, some research about the efficacy of mass media campaigns in curbing behaviour, as yet there is no research specifically on the effectiveness of public media campaigns dealing with the sex industry. More evidence of the impact of such media campaigns is needed to justify increased spending in this area.

Another finding was the need for more specialized anti-trafficking training for the broad spectrum of service agencies that have contact with sexually exploited people. Some social workers and police officers observed that in past cases they could have intervened early in the process if they had recognized the signs that the child was being trafficked and had known how to react. These observations were driven home by compelling survivor stories describing how women were trafficked and exploited while adults all around them did nothing, presumably because they did not recognize what was going on or know how to address the issue. Clearly, more training is needed for people who work with sex industry survivors, as well as those who come in contact with them.

My interviewees were unanimous in supporting the new trust-building approach to young sex industry survivors that is currently being adopted by the police and the justice system, in light of recent changes in the laws. Across the board, respondents agreed that sex industry survivors should be viewed as victims and should not be criminalized. Beyond this broad consensus, however, there is still debate on particular tactics, such as whether the police should have the ability to apprehend survivors in order to assist them when they cannot assist themselves, by forcing them into counselling and drug rehabilitation programming.

A large number of police respondents felt they still need to be able to apprehend survivors, and because that ability has been removed by a change in the law, they are less able to assist vulnerable people. Buttressing their case, some survivors said the only reason they were able to escape the sex industry, and in some cases to remain alive, was that the police had arrested them and placed them in jail or a program. They needed that measure at that time, to forcefully extricate themselves from the grasp of the sex industry subculture, as well as the accompanying substance abuse and multiple other intersectional life challenges. Some middle ground might be found here so that social workers, police, and other service providers can walk with survivors and support them even when they aren't reaching out for assistance.

Interviewees were generally less interested in the type of laws that exist than in how the laws are used. Most felt that there should be stiffer penalties for sex purchasers that would act as a deterrent, and that the police and the justice system should be going after customers, traffickers, and pimps aggressively. Almost no participants commented on the effects of international treaties or even national programs; they were interested in what is available locally, at their fingertips, and how it affects them directly. There is a strong need for more coordination at all levels of enforcement, including across jurisdictions. There was a resounding call among interviewed police officers and prosecutors for better sharing and use of intelligence in the prosecution of sex industry offenders.

My participants described the myriad of challenges that survivors face in trying to escape the sex industry, noting that many women struggle their whole lives to stay free, always on the verge of being triggered into relapse and old trauma patterns even twenty years after exiting the sex industry. Several respondents said that it takes most survivors seven relapses or more before they finally escape the sex industry for good. Supporters and caregivers must be non-judgmental and compassionate and understand that setbacks are to be expected. A significant number of those who leave the sex industry then work in helping professions, assisting other women to escape and remain free of the industry.

One theme that attracted strong support was the need for flexibility in the system. Everyone is different and their requirements shift, so we need to "meet them where they are at," as several respondents noted. Sex industry intervention and prevention must be flexible and adaptive to respond effectively to the unique and changing needs of each individual. This requires collaboration and coordination amongst all of the partnering agencies to make better collective use of existing resources in a focused, holistic, and targeted fashion.

Participants asserted that many agencies, programs, and resources exist, each with their strengths and focus, yet they often operate in isolation from each other. Much greater efficiency could be achieved by coordinating available resources. Survivors are often lost in the gap, struggling to gain support among numerous disconnected organizations that are strangled by bureaucracy.

Practitioners reported that some programs are not available when they are needed. They either close at 5 p.m. each day – when all the action happens at night – or have long wait lists. A person with a severe addiction problem who is told to wait two weeks might as well be told to wait two years. These services need to be more client centred, with immediate access, focused on the needs of the survivors rather than the convenience of the agencies.

These systemic inefficiencies often arise because organizations deferred or refused responsibility for extreme-risk, high-liability sexually exploited youth, leaving clients caught between agencies, like children between fighting parents. An example is the conflict mentioned by Michael Richardson above, wherein when it comes time to pay for assisting youth in care to become school ready, the education system says it is a child welfare responsibility and the child welfare system says it is an education system problem.

We cannot address and resolve these conflicts and begin to collaborate unless we understand the conflicts, and this can be achieved through the use of conflict analysis tools. Byrne and Senehi (2009) write that conflicts that occur in different contexts, and at the interpersonal, intergroup, organizational, or even international levels, are often due to incompatible goals. They also point out that analysing conflicts requires an understanding of how they originated and progressed as well as the characteristics and values of the parties or groups involved. There are shared goals that these agencies could all identify with. For example, what would happen if funding was tied to the requirement that vulnerable youth have positive outcomes, and that agencies that do not play well together will not meet funding requirements? This type of approach might address conflicts as described by Shannon McCorry when she stated, "Sometimes it almost feels like, from a person who is sitting back and looking at all these resources, like sometimes they're competing with one another, and they're not necessarily working together." She suggested that the government look at the whole picture and fund programs in such a way as to ensure that all the required services are offered. It should look at the big picture.

It seems very clear from my research that potential solutions can be found within the community. This finding connects with the lessons from Lederach (1996), who claims that deep-rooted problems in the community are often understood and resolved by grass-roots individuals who know the nuances of local culture. In addition, McNiff and Whitehead (2005) emphasize the importance in research of the practitioner's hands-on insights. My research participants, interestingly, suggested many of the same recommendations as Cook and Courchene (2006, p. 4; listed at the end of the previous chapter). Below I summarize the recommendations that interviewees put forth, with key findings and recommendations further condensed within a table that follows the final chapter.

Recommendations

First, provide adequate funding. In Manitoba, funding for counter-exploitation is relatively robust. Tracia's Trust has a ten-million-dollar annual budget, plus a lot of police, social work, and program money invested. However, there is room for more targeted funding; for instance, my respondents stressed that the private sector has not been adequately engaged. There is a price tag for the increased training of front-line practitioners that they believe is badly needed, and there are some costs to set up the coordination hubs that were suggested. The following recommendations are worth considering:

1 Multitrack intervention could bring together multiple elements of society to tackle the issues and create opportunities for the private business sector to engage to a greater extent.
2 Collective impact round tables should be established, and should include survivor voices, to create change in the public discourse.
3 We need increased focus on collaboration and coordination that reduce inefficiency within the existing systems of resources. We might find a shared vision to reduce violence and oppression through these peacebuilding tools, as well as reducing economic disparity and improving social justice for some of our most oppressed citizens, survivors of the sex industry.

Second, improve treatment programs. Several of my study participants saw a need for more training in and research into establishing effective intervention and treatment programs and improving accessibility of those that currently exist. These services are often inaccessible to people when they need them because they are closed at night or have long waiting lists. Some services are also inaccessible because people don't know they exist or how to access them. One of the aims of this book is to illuminate the intersectional challenges of survivors of all ages in the sex industry, as well as the structural issues they face. Anti-trafficking and counter-exploitation-related programs, including treatments for addictions and trauma, and job readiness programs need to be client centred, designed around the needs of the service users. Several recommendations follow:

1 Increase anti-trafficking training in awareness and service delivery skills for practitioners, as well as sensitivity to issues such as the structural problems described above.
2 Improve coordination and collaboration among agencies to wrap a holistic, protective blanket of services around survivors of all ages,

and also to enable working collectively on prevention as well as intervention processes.

3 Create triage within a one-stop shop, one central location that practitioners can call for resources at any time.

4 Make addictions, trauma, and other survivor-oriented treatments more accessible and needs based. These programs must be open 24/7 or close to it, with no lengthy wait times for services that are needed urgently. The appropriate cultural programming must also be available to people when they need it.

If agencies work together to streamline and create more client-centred treatment programming, they could reduce the level of suffering these women face and perhaps decrease the number of relapses back into addiction and the sex industry. Reducing relapses and making treatment more effective equates to reduced costs to the system. Survivors should also be at the table designing improvements in these intervention processes.

Third, enhance education and awareness. A strong theme emanating from this research was the need to make the public, youth, and purchasers of sex aware of the dangers and pitfalls that young women face on the streets in Manitoba, as well as increasing training for those who work in anti-trafficking and service provision. Successful existing campaigns and programs must be expanded upon. Here are several recommendations to consider:

1 Improved and increased training should be developed and delivered for all practitioners and people such as teachers and parents who have contact with young people at a higher risk of exploitation. For example, youth who have been sexually assaulted and are now placed in group homes, or those who have relationship issues, should be surrounded by social workers and caregivers who are trained to recognize the signs of exploitation and how to intervene.

2 More in-school programs for all ages are needed to raise awareness and build children's resistance to exploitation at early ages. Parallel programs are needed for teachers and caregivers, to enable them to recognize the signs of exploitation and how to intervene.

3 The number of public awareness campaigns might need to be increased to affect public discourse on sex trafficking and exploitation, as well as on young survivors' fundamental human rights. This measure was highly recommended by my respondents. However, more research is required on the efficacy of such campaigns before significant funding is allocated.

There needs to be increased awareness and prevention for youth who must leave their rural homes to attend school in larger urban centres; the rural-urban trafficking pipeline must be closed down. Building resilience among youth, giving them better support, and removing traffickers' opportunities to use the pipeline are critical.

Survivors should be involved in designing training and awareness campaigns, primarily to ensure that the messaging does not retraumatize survivors. Consideration should be given to how Indigenous communities in rural areas can be exposed to educational materials. For example, some of the highest-risk communities, and therefore the ones most in need of awareness materials (e.g., rural reserves in northern Manitoba), have no internet or even cell phone coverage; messages in broader campaigns must be delivered in person, verbally or by printed material.

Fourth, deliver more outreach resources and prevention programs. Training and awareness campaigns must reach into families and schools, to parents and teachers who have the most exposure to children and are best positioned to intervene if needed. Training should also be provided for medical staff in hospitals and any other adult groups that have exposure to children. The following are several recommendations to consider:

1 Workshops should be developed, utilizing trained mediators and techniques such as sustained dialogue and ARIA, where agency boards and directors feel that collaboration between police, social service agencies, and CFS could be improved.
2 More practitioners within all of the relevant service agencies should receive intervention and prevention training regarding sexually exploited youth.
3 More research is required into early childhood intervention, to assess early warning signs of sexual assault and abuse and design appropriate and effective interventions. This training must be available to parents, teachers, police, social workers, and medical staff.

Fifth, train and hire more specialized counsellors and psychologists. It became clear during this research that sex industry survivors face numerous unique challenges. Numerous practitioners interviewed discussed the complex multilayered, intersectional challenges that sex industry survivors struggle with. Patently, more expert resources are required to work with survivors who are dealing with complex issues that include trauma and PTSD, addictions, and mental health issues. Practitioners working with survivors are often themselves survivors with extensive personal experience; they serve as role models providing support and guidance for other survivors. Many survivors also need clinical, highly trained support, and these resources must be available immediately when they are required, not after lengthy waits for appointments. The following recommendations address these shortfalls:

1 The government should provide more advanced training for counsellors, psychologists, social workers, and medical staff.
2 The province should provide more advanced trauma specialists and make them accessible to survivors.

The provision of the specialized assistance needed by survivors with complex multilayered problems associated with their enslavement in the sex industry could become a training stream in universities and colleges that could be expanded in the psychology, psychiatry, and social work fields in Manitoba.

Sixth, focus on housing and homelessness initiatives. The government must provide new safe houses and adequately resourced transitional housing for sex industry survivors. My contributors emphasized that there are too few safe houses for sex industry survivors, yet victims of domestic violence have direct access to such houses. This need for safe houses and transitional housing is a key finding. Following are several recommendations:

1 The government must provide multiple treatments and services for survivors in safe housing, with design input from survivors.
2 The government should consider creating the Dream Catcher Village.
3 The government should consider developing a program designating places of safe refuge and community safety nets.

Seventh, implement stronger interventions for perpetrators. Most of my interviewees argued that we, as a society, should be targeting and attempting to diminish the demand side, or the market drivers, for the sex industry by holding traffickers, pimps, and johns more accountable. They put forth a variety of practical suggestions. Some recommended stiffer penalties that would act as a deterrent, while others feel that harsh court sentences are not effective and that more education for johns is the answer. The following are several recommendations that flowed from my findings:

1 We, as a society, should implement a multitrack intervention process, bringing community stakeholders from multiple perspectives together to respond better to sex industry market drivers.

2 More research is needed into the benefits and the diminishing returns of prosecuting and punishing sex purchasers.
3 More research is necessary, in the Canadian context, to explore the drivers of and most successful interventions for people purchasing sex; we need more research into the most effective balance of enforcement and education to affect deterrence.
4 More early childhood education can teach young boys about sexuality and about not objectifying girls. These education goals could be incorporated into the recommended early childhood counter-exploitation awareness training for all young children in schools.

Eighth, augment community-oriented policing. My respondents noted that community-oriented policing approaches are best. Two recommendations emerge from their interviews:

1 It is vital to ensure the use of multitrack intervention, collective impact approaches, and ever-increasing collaboration and coordination so that community-oriented policing remains a priority for the police and the communities they partner with.
2 The government should implement collective impact round tables and service hubs, with these including the police. Continuous attention should be paid and conflict resolution and transformational processes should be devoted to ensuring that the boundaries between agencies are continually negotiated and conflicts are not allowed to fester.

Ninth, facilitate collaboration between agencies and communities. Collaboration and coordination were key needs identified in the interviews, both between and within organizations, to reduce overlap and interagency gaps and to improve communication. The following are several recommendations that should be considered:

1 Stakeholders should come together to develop safety nets for survivors.
2 PACS tools, such as ARIA and sustained dialogue, and collective impact approaches should be employed to improve collaboration and coordination between agencies and units within organizations, as well as with communities.
3 Provincial and national governments should create triage hubs and should coordinate safe centres and make them accessible to survivors.

4 It is critically important that all agencies involved in working with and supporting sex industry survivors collaborate and coordinate with each other. Services often operate in isolation due in part to structural or bureaucratic impediments, and sometimes practitioners are not even aware that certain services exist. In some cases these problems might be resolved through improved communication; in others, change is required to make the services more unified. Change management processes within organizations should be well thought out, and managers in partnering agencies should plan to mitigate resistance to organizational change and the impact change has on employees (Schein, 1985).

Tenth, develop stronger support systems for communities and outside resources. My research participants argued that there is a need for central coordination: governments should create centralized hubs for one-stop shopping at the local provincial, federal, and international levels. Some participants discussed several initiatives that are underway; the effectiveness of these, however, cannot yet be determined.

The fundamental challenge, it seems, is to move the focus of responsibility for these pressing social issues into the centre, between all of the stakeholders. At the moment, there is competition, both financial – where agencies fight for perceived scarce resources – and philosophical – agencies have fundamental differences of opinion that create barriers to collaboration. Often these conflicts could be resolved through better communication and sharing, and through using PACS intervention and prevention peacebuilding tools. Finding closure in some cases requires a paradigm shift among partnering agencies.

Several broader recommendations emerged from the findings. For example, a number of participants talked about the need to engage the private corporate sector more in the conversation and in strategies for preventing sexual exploitation. Gord Mackintosh (former MLA) mentioned the vital role that the private sector plays, in sex trafficking and exploitation, by providing hotel rooms, taxis, and the internet. It is clear, from the interviews, that the private sector could play a significant role in combating the sex industry, for instance by bringing the hotel industry on board in the crusade against pimps and johns. But there is room for much more partnership on this issue.

A significant and growing feature of the sex industry is the internet. It seems evident that we need to invest more in technological resources to ensure that anti-trafficking agencies and police keep up with organized crime. My research participants mentioned the importance of developing specialized teams that could tackle online luring and exploitation and be a centralized resource within the sex industry.

As well, a centralized hub of culturally appropriate resources is something that all of the agencies could draw upon. This idea might reduce gaps by making resources available to every agency, rather than the ineffective random nature of the current system of available resources. It is a model that is worth investigating.

Several areas for future research were identified throughout this study. Sex trafficking and exploitation are social and economic as well as political problems that are affected by social dynamics. They are an issue that crosses multiple service sectors and can be looked at from different perspectives, from economic, legal, and political to psychological, social, and cultural. People's awareness of the issue is growing and attitudes and approaches are now beginning to change, so the opportunities and need for further research are significant. Below I present some of the broad areas for future research.

First, more research is required into prevention and early childhood abuse as an indicator of later sex industry involvement. Previous literature indicates strong correlations between early childhood sexual abuse and trauma, and later involvement in the sex industry (McIntyre, 2012). This research confirms that early childhood abuse and early teenage promiscuity and substance abuse tend to correlate with later vulnerability. There is room for much more research to create early warning systems and supports that could prevent these issues from manifesting in continuing trauma and victimization of people abused as children. Future research could examine how police services and child welfare agencies can create better supports, interventions, and follow-up for youth identified as having been subjected to sexual abuse and trauma.

Second, the impacts of recent changes in the provincial and national laws need to be studied. Convictions for trafficking and pimping in Canada are low. Thus, there is much room for research on the impacts of changes to Canada's law and affected strategies. Several of my contributors mentioned that we might sometimes be using the wrong tools in prosecuting johns and pimps; for example, in cases where there is insufficient evidence for conviction under human trafficking laws, there might be ample evidence of crimes long on the books such as forcible confinement, sexual assault, and other related charges. More research could reveal which of these laws are most effective and how they may be adjusted for more expedient prosecutions.

Third, we need to explore the invisible sex industry and the internet. The sex industry has moved to the internet and social media, and we need research into changing technology and how to cope with that move. Previous literature highlighted the need for more research on the less visible aspects of the sex industry (Cook & Courchene, 2006). While experts I interviewed said that they are aware of massive and growing use of social media and the internet in the sex industry, it is still mostly uncharted territory for law enforcement agencies. Children and women are selling themselves in this emerging digital domain, and that domain may also be affecting our growing newcomer communities, whose children can be lured by predators into selling their bodies online.

My respondents stated that current systems and agencies are lagging in technological competence compared to the nimbler organized crime syndicates, which do not face the same law enforcement constraints of operating within the law and jurisdictions, of limited budgets, and of bureaucratic constraints. Research is needed to analyse the role that technology plays in the sex industry, as well as how law enforcement and partner agencies can keep up with those changes. Social media itself provides the police with a massive opportunity to tackle the sex industry, yet organized criminals may be using it to its fullest advantage; this needs to be reversed.

Fourth, research on the demand side of the market is badly needed. Existing knowledge about traffickers, pimps, and purchasers of sex is sadly lacking. Sex purchasers acknowledge the harms caused by sexual exploitation once they are educated about them, yet research in this area is somewhat limited. McIntyre (2012) wrote that she realized during her research with survivors that "if we were ever going to successfully disrupt and adjust the supply of young persons involved in the sexual exploitation field we needed to address the demand" (p. 64). New research must examine both the supply and the demand side of the equation, and what effect evolving laws and intervention and prevention strategies are having on the sex industry. Deterrence is also an essential element in any crime reduction strategy (Linden, 2012), and especially crucial now that the political landscape has changed so that, in Canada, we generally treat sellers of sex as victims and purchasers as the driving force in the market. Although the demand side of the equation was beyond the scope of this book, most of my participants mentioned that johns must become the focus of future strategies to eliminate the sex industry. Some said that if traffickers, pimps, and johns were removed, there would be no supply market and the problem would evaporate. Of course, it is not that simple. The question of whether to "criminalize" or educate the purchasers of sex, or strike an efficient balance between education and punishment, is an issue for further research.

Fifth, mental health issues and their impacts on survivors as well as practitioners need investigation. The mental health of exploited survivors is an important correlate of their vulnerability to exploitation, and demands interdisciplinary research in its own right. There is room for much research on mental health challenges faced by sex industry survivors and special considerations in preventing and reducing sexual exploitation, and also in how the system might best assist sex industry survivors with mental health challenges to exit the sex industry. Laws and the courts should be considered in conjunction with mental health issues, because raping or trafficking a developmentally delayed young girl is a common occurrence in the sex industry and is a particularly despicable danger to the community that should be considered as such in the courts.

Sixth, the literature on effective interventions with sexually exploited youth is lacking. My research has noted the need for better training and education for front-line service professionals across the board. There is space for research on prevention, youth and adult interventions, and holistic intervention resource strategies, as well as on systemic issues that allow this plague on humanity to persist. There is also room for research on the role of sex industry survivors working in the field to support other survivors. This work may be part of their journey of healing. However, it can also be traumatic: several survivor-practitioners interviewed for this research stated outright that it is difficult work for them, as events or stories often trigger them to feel depression and distress. What is the impact on survivor-practitioners of doing this type of work, and what is their effectiveness in the field compared to that of non-experiential practitioners?

Overall, my impression is that the sex industry is a continuously changing social phenomenon with new aspects constantly being discovered by researchers. Tragically, there is so much that is unknown about this industry, even as its effects on society and survivors are so immense. However, it presents an excellent opportunity for meaningful research that can make lasting contributions to ending this violence against children, young women, and Indigenous people, in the process protecting an oppressed group of people living on the margins of our community.

Epilogue

Survivor's guilt is a real and persistent danger for peacekeepers and community builders. It was not an issue for me until I learned of the phenomenon through my graduate studies in PACS; then it made sense. Compassion allows us to be more aware of and sensitive to the pain and suffering of others; however, it predisposes us to take on their pain. Peacebuilders, soldiers, police officers and support staff, nurses, doctors, paramedics, and other emergency services personnel know this instinctively, and have to guard against becoming jaundiced and insensitive as a defence mechanism in response to the suffering they are exposed to, day in and day out for decades of their careers. They must be open to emotional connections with people who are suffering, in order to assist them. They bottle their distress up to get their job done, suppressing until they find another release, sometimes in the form of PTSD, substance abuse, and depression.

My colleagues and I in policing walk this tightrope, much like the survivors I interviewed who are drawn into the helping professions despite its potential to trigger a relapse into depression, alcohol and drug abuse, and the treacherous allure of the sex industry subculture. I wanted to contribute to the knowledge and practices that might be a lifeline for struggling sex industry survivors. I knew from my thirty-five years-plus experience in law enforcement, and in particular through my work with exploited people, that the difference between a life saved and a life ruined can sometimes be as simple as someone picking up a phone and calling a colleague in another agency. It could be as simple as asking for help, or taking the time to listen for two minutes and learn how to assist someone in need. It could be a police officer or social worker taking notice and doing something in a seemingly innocuous situation when a child is in fact in danger. Working in law enforcement, we become acutely aware of how fragile a life is, and that the life of someone performing survival sex can be changed by not getting in that next car with a john.

Hearing these stories from survivors and helpers was both depressing and inspiring for me. The unfairness of life's lottery that places some people in desperate, abused circumstances is bound to be disheartening; however, hearing about their resilience and tenacity in overcoming unbelievable degradation and pain is uplifting. The stories of professional practitioners from all sectors and their dedication to the vulnerable were also incredibly heartening. Many are devoted to helping at high personal costs to themselves. In some cases they could be doing less stressful and disturbing work for more money, yet they remain true to their compassion for these most vulnerable survivors.

This exploratory case study gathered the experiences and perceptions of a wide range of stakeholders engaged in fighting the significant social scourge of the sex industry in Manitoba. Their narratives and stories were presented prominently, utilizing their own words at every opportunity. In a way, this book is written as a narrative of participants' stories interlaced with connecting thoughts, the whole organized into a structure that makes some sense of such a complex social phenomenon.

Conducting the interviews and writing this book was an emotional journey for me, as the passion and pain that participants have all experienced bleeds through in every quote. The survivors' stories in particular are excruciatingly honest and gave me an idea of the hell they have gone through. However, one cannot fully understand that kind of anguish unless one has walked in those shoes.

This book has highlighted the stories of people who work hard to make a difference in the lives of those who suffer so much because of the greed and abuse of others. My participants' compelling and engaging stories shed light on a dark subject, hopefully contributing, even in a small way, to the ultimate elimination of sex slavery, trafficking by sexual predators, and sexual exploitation of young people in Canada. This book is dedicated to these brave, warm-hearted, and talented people who survive and go to work every day to make a difference in the lives of our most vulnerable citizens, our children.

By taking the time to read this book, you have shown an interest in and commitment to improving the lives of vulnerable people in our communities, and as such, like Ulysses in the *Odyssey* (Homer, 1909), you are a hero in your own story. We all have something to contribute, whether as a survivor acting as a role model and mentor for others seeking the same path, or as a practitioner striving to do what we can for our fellow human beings. Equally significant are the unsung heroes, the average citizens who decide to speak up about social injustice and for people who have less voice in the system. There is a role for all of us to play, and in that way each of us is the hero in our own story.

Findings and Recommendations

Vulnerability and the sex industry	Recommendations
Survivors are victims, not perpetrators	Research the efficacy of public awareness campaigns
No child chooses willingly to enter the sex industry	Focus on education for younger children, beginning in elementary school
Children are targeted for trafficking and exploitation at younger ages	
Childhood sexual assault and abuse correlates with later sex industry involvement	Create early warning systems based on cases of child abuse
Children seek in the sex industry the love they are missing in their families	Include child's needs for love and belonging in training for service providers
Getting out takes a critical event	Include in practitioner training that crisis events are opportunities for intervention
Getting out takes many attempts	Include in practitioner training that exiting often takes many tries and that non-judgmental support is crucial
Everyone has different needs	
Survivors are one trigger from relapse	Ongoing trauma support is needed for survivor-practitioners
Many survivors become helpers	

Indigenous needs	Recommendations
The majority of sex industry survivors in Manitoba are of Indigenous descent	Continue focus on resources and programs for First Nations, Métis, and Inuit people
Poverty and lack of opportunities are more salient among Indigenous peoples	Governments should consider supporting minimum incomes, improved standards of living conditions for Indigenous people
There is a trafficking pipeline from rural reserves into urban centres	More education, support, and safety measures for youth coming into large urban centres for school or any other reason

Intersectionality and prevention	Recommendations
Indigenous people need more control over their healing resources There are not enough resources for non-Indigenous groups	More input from community members on funding and resource development and deployment
Survivors are intersectionally challenged and need multilayered support	Practitioner training must recognize and address intersectional challenges
Vulnerable youth are often lost between services	Focus on coordination and collaboration of services
Many exploited youth suffer mental health issues	Research mental health among exploited youth
Children in care are at higher risk of exploitation	Mandatory training and policies for youth workers regarding identifying and intervening in exploitation
Need more early investment in families, violence prevention, & child welfare Lack of opportunities due to poverty makes youth vulnerable to exploitation	Government should focus on investing in early childhood and family resilience and well-being

Collaboration and coordination	Recommendations
There is much room for collaboration between stakeholder agencies	Government should make collaboration a funding requirement
Many organizations work in isolation, lacking coordination	
Poor communication is at the root of much inefficiency	Improve information sharing about available programming
Some inefficiency results from opposing philosophies	Conflict analysis and mediation for improved inter-agency collaboration
Need regional coordinators	Establish more operational provincial and federal coordination hubs

New resources	Recommendations
The cultural hub innovation	Consider creating a cultural hub
Need safe housing: Dream Catcher Village	Consider developing a large community safe house, the Dream Catcher Village
Need better resources for adults	
Need to keep up with technology	Increase focus on technology infrastructure and skills development for police and partner agencies to keep up with organized crime
Need underground railroads and a better safety net	Develop a safety net for at-risk youth

Training and education	Recommendations
Culturally sensitivity training often does not coexist with other effective resources	More intense consideration of cultural aspects in all programming
People are forced into cultural programs based on the colour of their skin	Increase sensitivity to women and youths' choices regarding cultural programming
People need choices, so programming is there when they are ready for it	

Training and education	Recommendations
Need more public awareness campaigning	Government should explore the efficacy of increased funding for public awareness campaigns, and make sex industry survivor input in messaging a funding requirement
Need more awareness campaigns targeting purchasers of sex	
Education must be delivered in an accessible way	Increase training for practitioners, specialists, teachers, parents, anyone who has contact with children
Survivors must be included in designing public awareness campaigns	Ensure input from people with lived experience in the development of training
Need more training for service providers	
Need more training for specialists	
Need more training for parents and educators	

Policy	Recommendations
International laws and global programs are not of interest in the local context	Increase focus on training and awareness at all levels on federal resources and laws
Police and other practitioners need to ask more questions	Training for practitioners on specialized trafficking investigations
Awareness of international trafficking is lacking	Training for practitioners and awareness campaigns for the public on the scope of the problem
Mixed opinions on forcing treatment on people	More research into the existing laws and programs for supporting survivors
People like the new police approach of trust building and support	
Need to deter sex purchasers	Increase police awareness of and priority attached to investigating sex trafficking
We could use existing laws that are easier to prosecute and have stiffer penalties	Consider focusing on enforcement of established laws where new ones are difficult or not as useful

Policy	Recommendations
Boundaries of authority for police and social workers could be adjusted	Government should consider police and social worker authorities for investigating sex trafficking and possibly adjust same

More of what is already effective	Recommendations
More education is required for children at younger levels in schools	Early childhood awareness programs appropriate for all age levels
People don't change the day they turn 18	Create policy for child welfare agencies to continue existing services for youth aging out of the system
Resources must be accessible when needed	Reduce waiting lists and ensure services are available at the time they are needed; make services client centred and not tailored to the convenience of agencies
Need both secure and open youth facilities	Mediation to improve collaboration
There is no one-size-fits-all approach People make the difference, not programs	More survivor input in programming development and steering Consider mentorship in treatment development

References

Allison, G. (1999). *Essence of decision: Explaining the Cuban Missile Crisis.* Pearson.

Amahazion, F. (2014). Global anti-sex trafficking: State variance in implementation of protectionist policies. *Human Rights Quarterly, 36*(1), 176–209. https://doi.org/10.1353/hrq.2014.0015

Aspinwall, L.G., & R.G. Tedeschi. (2010). The value of positive psychology for health psychology: Progress and pitfalls in examining the relation of positive phenomena to health. *Annals of Behavioral Medicine, 39*(1), 4–15. https://doi.org/10.1007/s12160-009-9153-0

Avruch, K. (1998). *Culture and conflict resolution.* United States Institute of Peace Press.

Ayers, J.W., J.L. Westmaas, E.C. Leas, A. Benton, Y. Chen, M. Dredze, & B.M. Althouse. (2016). Leveraging big data to improve health awareness campaigns: A novel evaluation of the Great American Smokeout. *JMIR Public Health Surveill, 2*(1), e16. https://doi.org/10.2196/publichealth.5304

Badgley, C. (1984). *Sexual offences against children in Canada: Summary.* Supply and Services. https://www.attorneygeneral.jus.gov.on.ca/inquiries/cornwall/en/hearings/exhibits/Nicolas_Bala/pdf/Badgley-1.pdf

Bales, K. (2004). *Disposable people: New slavery in the global economy* (2nd edition). San Francisco: University of California Press.

Barry, K. (1995). *The prostitution of sexuality: The global exploitation.* New York University Press.

Bell, S. (1994). *Reading, writing & rewriting the prostitute body.* Indiana University Press.

Berckamns, I., M. Velasco, B. Tapia, & G. Loots. (2012). A systemic review: A quest for effective interventions for children and adolescents in street situations. *Children and Youth Services Review, 34*(3), 1259–72. https://doi.org/10.1016/j.childyouth.2012.02.014

Bishop, A. (1994). *Becoming an ally: Breaking the cycle of oppression in people.* Fernwood.

Bill C-36. (2014). "An Act to amend the Criminal Code in response to the Supreme Court of Canada decision in Attorney General of Canada v. Bedford and to make consequential amendments to other Acts. Library of Parliament, Ottawa, Canada, publication no. 41-2-C36-E.

Blumer, H. (1969). *Symbolic interactionism: Perspective and method.* Prentice Hall.

Bonokoski, M. (2012, 14 October). Police recognizing PTSD scourge. *Toronto Sun.* https://torontosun.com/2012/10/12/police-recognizing-post-traumatic-stress-disorder-scourge/wcm/f90918dc-0121-4d9f-afd9-1d835fcbfece

Boulding, E. (2000). *Cultures of peace: The hidden side of history.* Syracuse University Press.

Breaking Free. (2018). https://breakingfree.net/facts-and-stats

Broadbent Institute. (2014). *The wealth gap: Perceptions and misconceptions in Canada.* https://www.broadbentinstitute.ca/the_wealth_gap

Brock, D. (1998). *Making work, making trouble: Prostitution as a social problem.* University of Toronto Press.

Burton, J. (1990). *Conflict: Resolution and prevention.* St Martin's Press.

Burton, J. (1997). *Violence explained: The sources of conflict, violence and crime and their prevention.* Manchester University Press.

Buttigieg, F. (2014). *Human trafficking, other forms of exploitation and prevention policies.* National Crime Prevention Centre, Government of Canada. https://www.publicsafety.gc.ca/lbrr/archives/cnmcs-plcng/cn000043841343-eng.pdf

Byrne, S., N. Carter, & J. Senehi. (2003). Social cubism and social conflict: Analysis and resolution. *Journal of International and Comparative Law, 8*(3), 725–40. https://nsuworks.nova.edu/ilsajournal/vol8/iss3/1/

Byrne, S., & L. Keashly. (2000). Working with ethno-political conflict: A multimodal and multi-level approach to conflict intervention. *International Peacekeeping, 7*(1), 97–120. https://doi.org/10.1080/13533310008413821

Byrne, S., & J. Senehi. (2009). Conflict analysis and resolution as a multidiscipline: A work in progress. In D.J. Sandole, S. Byrne, I. Sandole-Staroste, & J. Senehi (Eds.), *Handbook of conflict analysis and resolution* (pp. 3–16). Routledge.

Byrne, S., & J. Senehi. (2012). *Violence: Analysis, intervention, and prevention.* Ohio University Press.

Cameron, E., & M. Green. (2004). *Making sense of change management: A complete guide to the models, tools and techniques of organizational change.* Kogan Page.

Canada (AG) vs. Bedford. (2013). 2013 SCC 72, [2013] 3 S.C.R. 1101. http://scc-csc.lexum.com/scc-csc/scc-csc/en/item/13389/index.do

Canadian Women's Foundation (CWF). (2014). *From Heartbreaking to Groundbreaking: Stories and strategies to end sex trafficking in Canada.* https://

www.canadianwomen.org/wp-content/uploads/2017/09/CWF-TraffickingReport-Donor-EN-web.pdf

Cattapan, A., C. Hanson, J. Stinson, L. Levac, & S. Paterson. (2017). The budget's baby steps on gender analysis. *Policy Options.* https://policyoptions.irpp.org/magazines/march-2017/the-budgets-baby-steps-on-gender-analysis/

CBC. (2008, 16 May). A history of residential schools in Canada. http://www.ainlay.ca/datafiles/Ourdeva/CBCAhistoryofresidentialschoolsinCanada.pdf

CBC. (2011, 16 May). A timeline of residential schools, the Truth and Reconciliation Commission. https://www.cbc.ca/news/canada/a-timeline-of-residential-schools-the-truth-and-reconciliation-commission-1.724434

CBC. (2014a, 17 August). Tina Fontaine, 15, found in bag in Red River. https://www.cbc.ca/news/canada/manitoba/tina-fontaine-15-found-in-bag-in-red-river-1.2739141

Cederborg, A.C., & M.E. Lamb. (2008). Interviewing alleged victims with intellectual disabilities. *Journal of Intellectual Disability Research, 52*(1), 49–58. https://doi.org/10.1111/j.1365-2788.2007.00976.x

Charmaz, K. (2005). Grounded theory in the 21st century: Applications for advancing social justice studies. In N.K. Denzin & Y.S. Lincoln (Eds.), *The SAGE Handbook of Qualitative Research* (3rd ed., pp. 507–35). Sage.

Child and Family Services Act, Province of Manitoba. (2020). https://web2.gov.mb.ca/laws/statutes/ccsm/c080e.php#

Cho, S-Y, A. Dreher, & E. Neumayer. (2013. Does legalized prostitution increase human trafficking? *World Development* Vol. 41, pp. 67–82, 2013. http://dx.doi.org/10.1016/j.worlddev.2012.05.023

Choudhury, S.M. (2010). As prostitutes, we control our bodies: Perceptions of health and body in the lives of establishment-based female sex workers in Tijuana, Mexico. *Culture, Health & Sexuality, 12*(6), 677–89. https://doi.org/10.1080/13691051003797263

Chrislip, D.D. (2002). *The collaborative leadership fieldbook: A guide for citizens and civic leaders.* Jossey-Bass.

Chrismas, R. (2012). The people are the police: Building trust with Indigenous communities in contemporary Canadian society. *Canadian Public Administration, 55*(3), 451–70. https://doi.org/10.1111/j.1754-7121.2012.00231.x

Chrismas, R. (2013). *Canadian policing in the 21st century: A frontline officer on challenges and changes.* McGill-Queen's University Press.

Chrismas, R. (2017). *Modern day slavery and the sex industry: Raising the voices of survivors and collaborators while confronting sex trafficking and exploitation in Manitoba, Canada* [Doctoral dissertation]. University of Manitoba. http://hdl.handle.net/1993/32586

Chrismas, R., & C. Ponce-Joly. (2015). Multi-disciplinary collaboration: An essential tool and skill of responsible public service in high risk service provision. *Justice Reports, 30*(2), 25–30

CISC (Criminal Intelligence Service of Canada). (2008). *Organized crime and domestic trafficking in persons.* https://www.unicef.ca/sites/default/files /imce_uploads/DISCOVER/OUR%20WORK/CHILD%20SURVIVAL /sib_web_en.pdf

Clawson, H.J., N. Dutch, A. Solomon, & G. Goldblatt. (2009). *Human trafficking into and within the United States: A review of the literature.* US Department of Health and Human Services.

Collins, P.H. (2009). Emerging intersections: Building knowledge and transforming institutions. In B.T. Dill and R.E. Zambrana (Eds.), *Emerging intersections: Race, class, and gender in theory, policy, and practice* (pp. vii–xiv). Rutgers University.

Comack, E., L. Dean, L. Morrisette, & J. Silver. (2009). If you want to change violence in the 'hood, you have to change the 'hood: Violence and street gangs in Winnipeg's inner city. Canadian Centre for Policy Alternatives; https://www.policyalternatives.ca/publications/reports/if-you-want -change-violence-hood-you-have-change-hood

Cook, R., & D. Courchene. (2006). *Preventing and eradicating abuse of our children and youth: Regional team development.* Manitoba Association of Friendship Centers. https://www.gov.mb.ca/fs/traciastrust/pubs/eradicating_abuse. pdf

Cool, J. (2004). Prostitution in Canada: An overview. Library of Parliament: PRB 04-43D. http://publications.gc.ca/collections/Collection-R/LoPBdP /PRB-e/PRB0443-e.pdf

Council of Canadian Academies. (2014). *Policing Canada in the 21st century: New policing for new challenges.* https://cca-reports.ca/reports/policing -canada-in-the-21st-century-new-policing-for-new-challenges/

Creary, P., & S. Byrne. (2014). Youth violence as accidental spoiling?: Civil society perceptions of the role of sectarian youth violence and the effect of the peace dividend in Northern Ireland. *Nationalism and Ethic Politics, 20*(2): 221–43. https://doi.org/10.1080/13537113.2014.909160

Creswell, J. (2007). *Qualitative inquiry & research design: Choosing among five approaches* (2nd ed.). Sage.

Cullen-DuPont, K. (2009). *Global issues: Human trafficking.* Infobase.

Czarnecki, K.D., L.E. Vichinsky, J.A. Ellis, & S.B. Perl. (2010). Media campaign effectiveness in promoting a smoking-cessation program. *American Journal of Preventive Medicine, 38*(3S), S333–S342. https://doi.org/10.1016 /j.amepre.2009.11.019

Dandurand, Y. (2017). Human trafficking and police governance. *Police Practice and Research, 18*(3), 322–36. https://doi.org/10.1080/15614263.2017 .1291599

Dedel, K. (2006). *Juvenile runaways*. Center for Problem-Oriented Policing. http://www.popcenter.org/problems/runaways

Dehn, K. (2009, 11 November). Police change tactics to help chronic runaways. *CTV News*. https://winnipeg.ctvnews.ca/police-change-tactics-to-help -chronic-runaways-1.453367

Delacoste, P., & P. Alexander. (1987). *Sex work: Writing by women in the sex industry*. Cleis.

Department of Justice. Canada. (2014). Youth Criminal Justice Act (YCJA). www.justice.gc.ca/eng/cj-jp/yj-jj/ycja-1sjpa/back-hist.html

DeRiviere, L. (2005). An examination of the fiscal impact from youth involvement in the sex trade: The case for evaluating priorities in prevention. *Canadian Public Policy, 31*(2), 181–206. https://doi.org/10.2307 /3552628

Deutsch, M., & P. Coleman. (2000). *The handbook of conflict resolution: Theory and practice*. Jossey-Bass.

Diamond, L., & J. McDonald. (1996). *Multi-track diplomacy: A systems approach to peace*. Kumarian.

Doezema, J. (1998). Forced to choose: Beyond the voluntary vs. forced prostitution dichotomy. In K. Kempadoo & J. Doezema (Eds.), *Global sex workers: Rights, resistance, and redefinition* (pp. 34–51). Routledge.

Drescher, S. (2009). *Abolition: A history of slavery and antislavery*. Cambridge University Press.

Eckberg, G. (2004). The Swedish law that prohibits the purchase of sexual services: Best practices for prevention of prostitution and trafficking in human beings. *Violence Against Women, 10*(10), 14. https://doi.org /10.1177/1077801204268647

Englander, E.K. (2006). *Understanding violence*. Lawrence Erlbaum Associates.

Engle Merry, S. (2009). *Gender violence: A cultural introduction*. Blackwell.

Estes, R., & N. Weiner. (2001). *The commercial sexual exploitation of children in the US, Canada and Mexico*. University of Pennsylvania Press.

Farley, M. (2003). *Prostitution, trafficking, and traumatic stress*. Haworth.

Farley, M., A. Cotton, J. Lynne, S. Zumbeck, F. Spiwak, M.E. Reyes, D. Alvarez, & U. Senzgin. (2003). Prostitution and trafficking in nine countries: an update on violence and posttraumatic stress disorder. *Journal of Trauma Practice, 2* (3–4), 33–74. https://doi.org/10.1300/J189v02n03_03

Ferguson, R.A. (2005). Racing homonormativity: Citizenship, sociology, and gay identity. In P.E. Johnson & M. Henderson (Eds.), *Black queer studies: A critical anthology* (pp. 52–68). Duke University Press.

Fisher, R. (1997). Interactive conflict resolution. In I. William Zartman and J. Lewis Rasmussen (Eds.), *Peacemaking in international conflict: Methods and techniques* (pp. 239–72). United States Institute of Peace Press.

Five charged in Winnipeg as part of nationwide sex-trade sweep. (2016, 20 October). *Winnipeg Free Press*.

Foucault, M. (2010). Truth and power. In P. Rabinow (Ed.), *The Foucault Reader* (pp. 51–76). Vintage.

Frankl, V.E. (1959). *Man's search for meaning*. Simon and Shuster Inc.

Freeze, C., & I. Bailey. (2011, 9 November). A female RCMP officer's damning indictment of her employer. *Globe and Mail*. https://www.theglobeandmail.com/news/british-columbia/a-female-rcmp-officers-damning-indictment-of-her-employer/article4181592/

French, R., K. Wellings, & P. Weatherburn. (2014). An exploratory review of HIV prevention mass media campaigns targeting men who have sex with men. *BMC Public Health, 14*, art. 616. https://doi.org/10.1186/1471-2458-14-616

Friesen, J. (2014, 5 December). Winnipeg police told to stress protection of Indigenous women. *Globe and Mail*. https://www.theglobeandmail.com/news/national/winnipeg-police-told-to-stress-protection-of-indigenous-women/article21980626/

Galley, V. (2009). Reconciliation and the revitalization of Indigenous languages. In G. Younging, J. Dewar, & M. DeGagné (Eds.), *Response, responsibility, and renewal: Canada's truth and reconciliation journey* (pp. 241–58). Indigenous Healing Foundation.

Galtung, J. (1996). *Peace by peaceful means: Peace and conflict, development and civilization*. Sage.

Giroday, G. (2009, 21 November). Police want tougher law on harbouring minors. *Winnipeg Free Press*. https://www.winnipegfreepress.com/local/police-want-tougher-law-on-harbouring-minors-70690107.html

Giroday, G. (2010, 7 May). Trafficking in city targeted: Smith organizes awareness march. *Winnipeg Free Press*.

Glaser, B. (1992). *Basics of grounded theory analysis: Emergence vs. forcing*. Sociology Press.

Glaser, B.G., & A.L. Strauss. (1967). *The discovery of grounded theory: Strategies for qualitative research*. Aldine De Gruyter.

Grace, D. (2014). *Intersectionality-informed mixed method research: A primer*. Institute for Intersectionality Research & Policy. https://ktpathways.ca/system/files/resources/2019-09/Intersectionality-informed_Mixed_Method.pdf

Grant, T. (2016a, 10 February). The trafficked: How sex trafficking works in Canada. *Globe and Mail*. https://www.theglobeandmail.com/news/national/the-trafficked-how-sex-trafficking-works-in-canada/article28700689/

Grant, T. (2016b, 23 February). U.S. groups to offer tech expertise to help thwart traffickers. *Globe and Mail*. https://www.theglobeandmail.com/news/national/us-groups-to-offer-tech-expertise-to-help-thwart-traffickers/article28846634/

Greene, J.M., S.T. Ennett, & C.L. Ringwalt. (1999). Prevalence and correlates of survival sex among runaway and homeless youth. *American Journal of PublicHealth, 89*(9), 1406–9. https://doi.org/10.2105/AJPH.89.9.1406

Guaranteed $20K income for all Canadians endorsed by academics. (2014, 30 June). *CBC.* https://www.cbc.ca/news/canada/guaranteed-20k-income-for-all-canadians-endorsed-by-academics-1.2691847

Guy, J. (2008). *Report of the Provincial Court of Manitoba on the Fatality Inquiries Act Inquest into the suicide of Tracia Owen.* http://www.manitobacourts.mb.ca/site/assets/files/1051/tracia_owen.pdf

Halek, K., M. Murdock, & L. Fortier. (2005). Spontaneous reports of emotional upset and health care utilization among veterans with posttraumatic stress disorder after receiving a potentially upsetting survey. *American Journal of Orthopsychiatry, 75*(1), 142–51. https://doi.org/10.1037/0002-9432.75.1.142

Hallett, B., N. Thornton, & D. Stewart. (2006). *Indigenous people in Manitoba.* Manitoba Indigenous Affairs Secretariat.

Ham, J. (2014). *Hope, healing, and the legacy of Helen Betty Osborne: A case study exploring cross-cultural peacebuilding in northern Manitoba* [Unpublished master's thesis]. University of Manitoba.

Ham, J., & A. Gerard. (2014). Strategic in/visibility: Does agency make sex workers invisible? *Criminology & Criminal Justice, 14*(3,) 298–13. https://doi.org/10.1177/1748895813500154

Hamilton, A.C., & M. Sinclair. (1991). *Report of the Indigenous Justice Inquiry of Manitoba: The justice system and Indigenous people.* Queen's Printer.

Hankivsky, O. (2011). *Health inequities in Canada: Intersectional frameworks and practices.* University of British Columbia Press.

Hayward, J. (2014, 4 July). Prostitution is a legitimate form of work. *Canadian Press.*

Heckman, J., S.H. Moon, R. Pinto, P.A. Savelyev, & A.Q. Yavitz (2010). The rate of return to the HighScope Perry preschool program. *Journal of Public Economics, 94*(1–2), 114–28. https://doi.org/10.1016/j.jpubeco.2009.11.001

Hedges, C. (2002). *Missing you already: A guide to the investigation of missing persons.* http://research.org.uk/search_papers/hedges_missing_you_already.pdf

Holroyd, E.A., W.C. Wong, A. Gray, & D.C. Ling. (2008). Environmental health and safety of Chinese sex workers: A cross-sectional study. *International Journal of Nursing Studies, 45*(6), 932–41. https://doi.org/10.1016/j.ijnurstu.2006.04.020

Homer. (1909). *The Odyssey.* (S.H. Butcher & A. Lang, Trans.). P.F. Collier & Son.

Hong, Y., X. Li, X. Fang, & R. Zhao. (2007). Correlates of suicidal ideation and attempt among female sex workers in China. *Health Care for Women International, 28*(5), 490–505. https://doi.org/10.1080/07399330701226529

hooks, b. (2000). *Feminist theory from margin to center.* South End.

Huey, L., and E. Berndt. 2008. "You've gotta learn how to play the game": Homeless women's use of gender performance as a tool for preventing victimization. *Sociological Review, 56*(2): 177–94. https://doi.org /10.1111/j.1467-954X.2008.00783.x

Huey, L., and M. Quirouette. 2010. "Any girl can call the cops, no problem": The influence of gender on support for the decision to report criminal victimization within homeless communities. *British Journal of Criminology, 50*(2): 278–95. https://doi.org/10.1093/bjc/azp078

Hunting, G. (2014). *Intersectionality-informed qualitative research: A primer.* The Institute for Intersectionality Research & Policy. Public Health Agency of Canada. https://www.ifsee.ulaval.ca/sites/ifsee.ulaval.ca/files /b95277db179219c5ee8080a99b0b91276941.pdf

Jeong, H.W. (2000). *Peace and conflict studies: An introduction.* Ashgate.

Jootun, D., G. McGhee, & G.R. Marland. (2009). Reflexivity: Promoting rigour in qualitative research. *Nursing Standard, 23*(23), 42–6. https://doi.org /10.7748/ns2009.02.23.23.42.c6800

Jorm, A.F., C.M. Kelly, & A.J. Morgan. (2007). Participant distress in psychiatric research: A systematic review. *Psychological Medicine, 37*(7), 917–26. https:// doi.org/10.1017/S0033291706009779

Kaestle, C.E. (2012). Selling and buying sex: A longitudinal study of risk and protective factors in adolescence. *Prevention Science, 13*(3), 314–22. https:// doi.org/10.1007/s11121-011-0268-8

Karnieli-Miller, O., R. Strier, & L. Pessach. (2009). Power relations in qualitative research. *Qualitative Health Research, 19*(2), 279–89. https://doi .org/10.1177/1049732308329306

Kaye, J., J. Winterdyk, & L. Quarterman. (2014). Beyond criminal justice: A case study of responding to human trafficking in Canada. *Canadian Journal of Criminology and Criminal Justice, 56*(1), 23. http://dx.doi.org/10.3138 /cjccj.2012.E33

Kelly, L., M. Coy, & R. Davenport. (2009). *Shifting sands: A comparison of prostitution regimes across nine countries.* Child & Women Abuse Studies Unit, London Metropolitan University.http://citeseerx.ist.psu.edu/viewdoc /download?doi=10.1.1.467.3126&rep=rep1&type=pdf

Kempadoo, K., & J. Doezema. (1998). *Global sex workers: Rights, resistance, and redefinition.* Routledge.

Kennedy, D., A. Braga, A. Piehl, & E. Waring. (2001). *Reducing gun violence: Boston Gun Project's Operation Ceasefire.* National Institute of Justice.

Kirkup, K. (2014, 8 December). Stop criminalizing sex work. *Winnipeg Free Press.*

Klaine, E. (1999). *Prostitution of children and child-sex tourism: An analysis of domestic and international responses.* National Center for Missing & Exploited Children, US Department of Justice. https://www.ncjrs.gov/pdffiles1 /Digitization/189251NCJRS.pdf

Klatt, T., D. Cavnerb, & V. Eganc. (2014). Rationalising predictors of child sexual exploitation and sex-trading. *Child Abuse & Neglect, 38*(2), 252–60. https://doi.org/10.1016/j.chiabu.2013.08.019

Kluber, S.A. (2003). *Trafficking in human beings: Law enforcement response* [Unpublished master's thesis]. University of Louisville.

Kong, T.S.K. (2006). What it feels like for a whore: The body politics of women performing erotic labour in Hong Kong. *Gender, Work & Organization, 13*(5), 409–34. https://doi.org/10.1111/j.1468-0432.2006.00315.x

Kriesberg, L. (1998). *Constructive conflicts: From escalation to resolution.* Rowman & Littlefield.

Lalor, K., & R. McElvaney. (2010). Child sexual abuse, links to later sexual exploitation/high-risk sexual behavior, and prevention/treatment programs. *Trauma, Violence & Abuse, 11*(4), 159–77. https://doi.org/10.1177/1524838010378299

Lau, J.T., H.Y. Tsui, S.P. Ho, E. Wong, & X. Yang. (2010). Prevalence of psychological problems and relationships with condom use and HIV prevention behaviors among Chinese female sex workers in Hong Kong. *AIDS Care, 22*(6), 659–68. https://doi.org/10.1080/09540120903431314

Lauwers, B. (2012, 24 April). Unpublished presentation about Third World conditions on Canada Indigenous reserves, First Nations Managers and Practitioners Conference, Montreal.

Lavoie, F., C. Thibodeau, M. Gagné, & M. Hébert. (2010). Buying and selling sex in Québec adolescents: A study of risk and protective factors. *Archives of Sexual Behavior, 39*(5), 1147–60. https://doi.org/10.1007/s10508-010-9605-4

Lederach, J. (1996). *Preparing for peace: Conflict transformation across cultures.* Syracuse University Press.

Lederach, J.P. (1997). *Building peace: Sustainable reconciliation in divided societies.* United States Institute of Peace Press.

Lederach, J.P. (2005). *The moral imagination: The art and soul of building peace.* Oxford University Press.

Lee, M. (2011). *Trafficking and global crime control.* Sage.

Legerski, J.P., & S.L. Bunnell. (2010). The risks, benefits and ethics of trauma-focused research participation. *Ethics & Behavior, 20*(6), 429–42. https://doi.org/10.1080/10508422.2010.521443

Levasseur, K., N. Arierom, and S. Paterson. (2016). Assessing the implications of basic income for gender. Paper presented at the North American Basic Income Guarantee (NABIG) Congress, Winnipeg, Manitoba,, 12–15 May May. https://www.researchgate.net/publication/303252462_Assessing_the_implications_of_basic_income_for_gender

Levy, J., & P. Jakobsson. (2013). Abolitionist feminism as patriarchal control: Swedish understandings of prostitution and trafficking. *Dialectical Anthropology, 37*(2): 333–40. https://doi.org/10.1007/s10624-013-9309-y

Linden, R. (2012). *Criminology: A Canadian perspective*. 7th ed. Nelson Education Ltd.

Lowman, J. (1987). Taking young prostitutes seriously. *Canadian Review of Sociology and Anthropology, 24*(1), 99–116. https://doi.org/10.1111/j.1755 -618X.1987.tb01073.x

Lowman, J. (2000). Violence and the outlaw status of (street) prostitution in Canada. *Violence Against Women, 6*(9), 987–1011. https://doi.org/10.1177 /10778010022182245

Lowry, C., & S. Littlejohn. (2003). Dialogue and the discourse of peacebuilding in Maluku, Indonesia. *Conflict, 23*(4), 409–26. https://doi.org/10.1002/crq.147

Lozano, S. (2010). *Theoretical reading on "trafficking" in Women for the purpose of sexual exploitation in prostitution: Case of study: Colombia* [Unpublished master's thesis]. Central European University.

Mac Ginty, R., & A. Williams. (2009). *Conflict and development*. Routledge.

Macleod, J. (1995). *Ain't no makin' it: Aspirations and attainments in a low-income neighborhood*. Westview.

MacQueen, K. (2011, 18 November). A royal Canadian disgrace. *Macleans*. https://www.macleans.ca/news/canada/a-royal-canadian-disgrace/

Mandel, C. (2016, 8 March). Indigenous girls face tough hurdles, new report on women in Canada states. *National Observer*. https://www .nationalobserver.com/2016/03/08/news/indigenous-girls-face-tough -hurdles-new-report-women-canada-states

Manitoba Children's Advocate says her office notified of 166 child deaths. (2014, 17 December). *Thompson Citizen*. https://www.thompsoncitizen.net /manitoba-children-s-advocate-says-her-office-notified-of-166-child -deaths-1.1685589

Manitoba Family Services and Housing. (2008). *Front Line Voices: Manitobans Working Together to End Child Sexual Exploitation*. https://www.gov.mb.ca /fs/childfam/pubs/tracias_trust_en.pdf

Maslow, A.H. (1954). *Motivation and personality*. Harper and Row.

McCall, L. (2005). The complexity of intersectionality. *Signs, 30*(3), 1771–1800. https://doi.org/10.1086/426800

McCracken, M., & C. Michell. (2006). *Literature review of post-secondary education skills training and Aboriginal people in Manitoba*. Canadian Center for Policy Alternatives.

McIntyre, S. (2012, November). *Buyer beware: A study into the demand side of the sexual exploitation industry*. http://www.hindsightgroup.com /resources/documents/Final%20Report%20Nov%2015%20-%20FINAL%20 %28with%20TC%29.pdf_%3B

McIntyre, S., D. Clark, N. Lewis, & T. Reynolds. (2015). The role of technology in human trafficking: A white paper prepared for Microsoft. http://www .hindsightgroup.com/resources/Human%20Trafficking%20White%20 Paper_Revised%20Draft.pdf_%3B

Mcniff, J., & J. Whitehead. (2005). *All you need to know about action research.* Sage.

Meyers, D.T. (2014). Feminism and sex trafficking: Rethinking some aspects of autonomy and paternalism. *Ethic Theory Moral Practice, 17*(3), 427–41. https://doi.org/10.1007/s10677-013-9452-1

Mizus, M., M. Moody, C. Privado, & C.A. Douglas. (2003). Germany, U.S. receive most sex-trafficked women. *Off Our Backs, 33*(7–8), 4. www.jstor.org/stable/20837856

Morris, J.S. (2009). The truth about interviewing elites. *Politics, 29*(3), 209–17. https://doi.org/10.1111/j.1467-9256.2009.01357.x

Muftic, L., & M. Finn. (2013). Health outcomes among women trafficked for sex in the United States: A closer look. *Journal of Interpersonal Violence, 28*(9), 1859–85. https://doi.org/10.1177/0886260512469102

Murray, A. (1998). Debt-bondage and trafficking: Don't believe the hype. In K. Kempadoo & J. Doezema (Eds.), *Global Sex Workers: Rights Resistance, and Redefinition* (pp. 51-64). Routledge.

Native Women's Association of Canada. (2010). *What their stories tell us: Research findings from the Sisters in Spirit initiative.* https://nwac.ca/wp-content/uploads/2015/07/2010-What-Their-Stories-Tell-Us-Research-Findings-SIS-Initiative.pdf

Nebbitt, V., T. Tirmazi, M. Lombe, Q. Cryer-Coupet, & S. French. (2013). Correlates of the sex trade among African-American youth living in urban public housing: Assessing the role of parental incarceration and parental substance use. *Journal of Urban Health: Bulletin of the New York Academy of Medicine, 91*(2), 383–93. https://doi.org/10.1007/s11524-013-9839-2

Nelson, J. (2014, 20 May). Modern-day slavery generates billions: UN report. *Globe and Mail.* https://www.theglobeandmail.com/report-on-business/international-business/modern-day-slavery-generates-billions-according-to-new-report/article18768332/

Norris, M.J., D. Kerr, & F. Nault. (1995). *Summary report on projections of the population with Aboriginal identity, Canada, 1991–2016.* Population Projections Section, Demography Division, Statistics Canada, prepared for the Royal Commission on Aboriginal Peoples. Canada Mortgage and Housing Corporation.

O'Brien, E., S. Hayes, & B. Carpenter. (2013). *The politics of sex trafficking: A moral geography.* Palgrave Macmillan.

Oppal, W. (2012). *Forsaken: The report of the Missing Women Commission of Inquiry.* Library and Archives Canada Cataloguing in Publication, British Columbia. http://www.bcsolutions.gov.bc.ca/opc/

Ostroff, J. (2015, 4 July). Manitoba First Nation's solution to foster care crisis: Remove parents, not kids. *Huffington Post Canada.* http://www.missingwomeninquiry.ca/wp-content/uploads/2010/10/Forsaken-ES-web-RGB.pdf

Outshoorn, J. (2004). *The politics of prostitution: Women's movements, democratic states and the globalisation of sex commerce.* Cambridge University Press.

Palys, T.S., & C. Atchison. (2008). *Research decisions: Quantitative and qualitative perspectives.* 4th ed. Thomson Nelson.

Paperny, A.M. (2009, 27 August). Latest deaths of native women may be linked to crack-for-sex case. *Globe and Mail.* https://www.theglobeandmail.com/news/national/latest-deaths-of-native-women-may-be-linked-to-crack-for-sex-case/article4195211/

Parrot, A., & N. Cummings. (2008). *Sexual enslavement of girls and women worldwide.* Praeger.

Paterson, S. (2010). "Resistors," "helpless victims," and "willing participants": The construction of women's resistance in Canadian anti-violence policy. *Social Politics, 17*(2): 159–84. https://doi.org/10.1093/sp/jxq001

Patton, M. (1980). *Qualitative evaluation and research methods.* Sage.

Paul, A. (2012, 23 June). First Nations suicides reflect youth despair. *Winnipeg Free Press.* https://www.winnipegfreepress.com/local/first-nations-suicides-reflect-youth-despair-160105405.html

Perrin, B. (2010). *Invisible chains: Canada's underground world of human trafficking.* Penguin.

Phillips, L. (1996). Difference, indifference and making a difference: Reflexivity in the Time of Cholera. In S. Cole & L. Phillips (Eds.), *Ethnographic feminisms: Essays in anthropology* (pp. 22–36). Carleton University Press.

Phillips, S., & K. Levasseur. (2004). The snakes and ladders of accountability: Contradictions between contracting and collaboration for Canada's voluntary sector. *Canadian Public Administration, 47*(4), 451–74. https://doi.org/10.1111/j.1754-7121.2004.tb01188.x

Prest, A. (2016, 29 July). Four arrested for purchasing sex services. *Winnipeg Free Press.* https://www.winnipegfreepress.com/local/four-arrested-for-purchasing-sex-services-388695661.html

Prothrow-Stith, D., & H. Spivak. (2003). *Murder is no accident: Understanding and preventing youth violence in America.* John Wiley & Sons.

Public Safety Canada. (2020). *Child sexual exploitation on the internet.* https://www.publicsafety.gc.ca/cnt/cntrng-crm/chld-sxl-xplttn-ntrnt/index-en.aspx

Puxley, C. (2014, 18 November). Manitoba wants fewer kids in care put up in hotels. *Global News.* https://globalnews.ca/news/1678529/manitoba-wants-fewer-kids-in-care-put-up-in-hotels/.

Rabson, M. (2013, 9 May). City has highest Indigenous population, First Nations, Métis numbers growing rapidly. *Winnipeg Free Press.* https://www.winnipegfreepress.com/special/census2011/City-has-highest-aboriginal-population-206745721.html

RCMP. (2013). *Missing and murdered Indigenous women: A national operational overview.* http://www.rcmp-grc.gc.ca/en/missing-and-murdered-aboriginal-women-national-operational-overview

RCMP. (2014). *Human Trafficking National Co-ordination Center.* http://www.rcmp-grc.gc.ca/ht-tp/index-eng.htm

Reimer, L., C. Schmitz, E. Janke, A. Askerov, B. Strahl, & T. Matyók. (2015). *Transformative change: An introduction to peace and conflict studies.* Lexington.

Rice, B. (2011). Relationships with human and non-human species and how they apply toward peacebuilding and leadership in Indigenous societies. In T.S. Matyok, J. Senehi, & S. Byrne (Eds.), *Critical issues in peace and conflict studies: Theory, practice and pedagogy* (pp. 199–216). Lexington Books.

Richardson, J. (2015). Unpublished master's thesis proposal, researching clinical interventions for sexually exploited youth. Faculty of Social Work. University of Manitoba.

Ripsman, N., & J. Blanchard. (2003). Qualitative research on economic interdependence and conflict: Overcoming methodological hurdles. In E.D. Mansfield & B. Pollins (Eds.), *Economic interdependence and international Conflict* (pp. 310–23). University of Michigan Press.

Robertson, M., & A. Sgoutas. (2012). Thinking beyond the category of sexual identity: At the intersection of sexuality and human-trafficking policy. *Politics and Gender, 8*(3), 421–29. https://doi.org/10.1017/S1743923X12000414

Roe-Sepowitz, D.E., K.E. Hickle, M. Loubert, & T. Egan. (2011). Adult prostitution recidivism: Risk factors and impact of a diversion program. *Journal of Offender Rehabilitation, 50*(5), 272–85. https://doi.org/10.1080/10509674.2011.574205

Rogers, J., & U.A. Kelly. (2011). Feminist intersectionality: Bringing social justice to health disparities research. *Nursing Ethics, 18*(3), 397–407. https://doi.org/10.1177/0969733011398094

Rössler, W., U. Koch, C. Lauber, A.K. Hass, M. Altwegg, V. Ajdacic-Gross, & K. Landolt. (2010). The mental health of female sex workers. *Acta Psychiatrica Scandinavica, 122*(2), 143–52. https://doi.org/10.1111/j.1600-0447.2009.01533.x

Rothman, J., & M.L. Olson. (2001). From interests to identities: Towards a new emphasis in interactive conflict resolution. *Journal of Peace Research, 38*(3), 289–305. https://doi.org/10.1177/0022343301038003002

Rugaber, C.S. (2014, 27 January). Wealth gap: A guide to what it is, why it matters. *Business Insider.* https://www.businessinsider.com/wealth-gap-a-guide-to-what-it-is-and-why-it-matters-2014-1

Runeson B., & J. Beskow. (1991). Reactions of survivors of suicide victims to interviews. *Acta Psychiatrica Scandinavica, 83*(3), 169–73. https://doi.org/10.1111/j.1600-0447.1991.tb05518.x

Said, E. (1979). *Orientalism.* Random House.

Sanders, T. (2004). A continuum of risk? The management of health, physical and emotional risks by female sex workers. *Sociology of Health & Illness,* 26(5), 557–74. https://doi.org/10.1111/j.0141-9889.2004.00405.x

Sandole, D., S. Byrne, I. Sandole-Staroste, & J. Senehi. (2009). *Handbook of conflict analysis and resolution.* Routledge.

Saunders, H. (2003). Sustained dialogue in managing intractable conflict. *Negotiation Journal, 19*(1), 85–95. https://doi.org/10.1111/j.1571-9979.2003 .tb00282.x

Schauer, E., & E. Wheaten. (2006). Sex trafficking into the United States: A literature review. *Criminal Justice Review, 31*(2), 146–69. https://doi .org/10.1177/0734016806290136

Schein, E.H. (1985). *Organizational culture and leadership: A dynamic view.* Jossey-Bass.

Schwartz, D. (2014, 12 December). New prostitution laws unlikely to be challenged soon, legal experts say. *CBC News.* https://www.cbc.ca/news /politics/new-prostitution-laws-unlikely-to-be-challenged-soon-legal -experts-say-1.2870523

Senehi, J. (2009). Building peace: Storytelling to transform conflicts constructively. In D. Sandole, S. Byrne, I. Sandole-Staroste, & J. Senehi (Eds.), *Handbook of conflict analysis and resolution* (pp. 201–15). Routledge.

Sethi, A. (2007). Domestic sex trafficking of Aboriginal girls in Canada: Issues and implications. *First Peoples Child & Family Review, 3*(3), 57–71. https:// fpcfr.com/index.php/FPCFR/article/view/50

Sex workers' groups decry new prostitution bill. (2014, 6 December). *Toronto Sun.* https://torontosun.com/2014/12/06/sex-workers-groups-decry -new-prostitution-bill/wcm/9ceec300-43d6-4b51-968f-674c9902da15

Shively, M., S. Kuck Jalbert, R. Kling, W. Rhodes, P. Finn, C. Flygare, L. Tierney, D. Hunt, D. Squires, C. Dyous, & K. Wheeler. (2008). *Final report on the evaluation of the first offender prostitution program.* Office of Research and Evaluation, National Institute of Justice, Washington, DC. https://www .ncjrs.gov/pdffiles1/nij/grants/222451.pdf

Siskin, A., & L. Sun Wyler. (2010). *Trafficking in persons: U.S. Policy and issues for Congress.* Congressional Research Service. https://fas.org/sgp/crs /row/RL34317.pdf

Smith, H. (2014). *Walking prey: How America's youth are vulnerable to sex slavery.* New York, NY: Palgrave McMillan.

Smith, J. (2014a). Connecting the dots: A proposal for a national action plan to combat human trafficking. https://ccrweb.ca/en/connecting-dots-proposal -national-action-plan-combat-human-trafficking

Smith, J. (2014b). *The tipping point: Tackling the demand for prostituted/trafficked women and youth.* http://wunrn.com/wp-content/uploads/tipping.pdf

Sossou, M.A., C.D. Craig, H. Ogren, & M. Schnak. (2008). A qualitative study of resilience factors of Bosnian refugee women resettled in the southern United States. *Journal of Ethnic and Cultural Diversity in Social Work, 17*(4), 365–85. https://doi.org/10.1080/15313200802467908

Stittle, M. (2007, 20 July). Project Kare: How a missing women's task force works. *CTV News.* https://www.ctvnews.ca/project-kare-how-a-missing-women-s-task-force-works-1.249420

Taylor, J. (2015, 12 March). Domestic trafficking an issue for aboriginal women and girls, says Canadian author. *CBC News.* https://www.cbc.ca/news/canada/manitoba/domestic-trafficking-an-issue-for-aboriginal-women-and-girls-says-canadian-author-1.2992043

Totten, M. (2009). Aboriginal youth and violent gang involvement in Canada: Quality prevention strategies. *IPC Review, 3* (March), 135–56. http://www.tottenandassociates.ca/wp-content/uploads/2015/03/Totten-2009-Aboriginal-Youth-and-Violent-Gang-Involvement.pdf

Trice, H.M., & J. Beyer. (1993). *The cultures of work organizations.* Prentice Hall.

Tuso, H. (2013). Unpublished lecture on culture, nature, and gender, presented in seminar titled Culture and Conflict, fall term, Arthur V. Mauro Center, University of Manitoba.

UNESCO. (2014). *The slave route.* http://www.unesco.org/new/en/culture/themes/dialogue/the-slave-route/modern-forms-of-slavery/

United Nations. (1979). Convention on the Elimination of All Forms of Discrimination against Women. UN Women. www.un.org/womenwatch/daw/cedaw/text/econvention.htm#intro

United Nations. (2000). Protocol to prevent, suppress and punish trafficking in persons, especially women and children. United Nations Treaty Collection. https://treaties.un.org/pages/viewdetails.aspx?src=ind&mtdsg_no=xviii-12-a&chapter=18&lang=en

UNODC (United Nations Office on Drugs and Crime). (2014). *Global report on trafficking in persons 2014.* https://www.unodc.org/unodc/en/data-and-analysis/glotip_2014.html

United States, Department of State. (2014, June). "Trafficking in Persons Report." Office to Monitor and Combat Trafficking in Persons. www.state.gov/j/tip/rls/tiprpt/2014/?utm_source=NEW+RESOURCE:+Trafficking+in+Persons+R

Valentine, D. (2007). *Imagining transgender: An ethnography of a category.* Duke University Press.

Valentini, C., & D. Kruckeberg. (2012). New media versus social media: A conceptualization of their meanings, uses, and implications for public relations. In S. Duhe (Ed.), *New media and public relations* (pp. 3–12). Peter Lang..

Vanwesenbeeck, I. (2005). Burnout among female indoor sex workers. *Archives of Sexual Behavior, 34*(6), 627–39. https://doi.org/10.1007/s10508-005-7912-y

Venkatraman, B.A. (2003). Human trafficking: A guide to detecting, investigating, and punishing modern-day slavery. *Police Chief, 70*(12), 1–8. https://www.policechiefmagazine.org/human-trafficking-a-guide-to -detecting-investigating-and-punishing-modern-day-slavery/

Vidal-Ortiz, S. (2006). Sexuality discussions in Santería: A case study of religion and sexuality negotiation. *Sexuality Research and Social Policy, 3*(3), 52–66. https://doi.org/10.1525/srsp.2006.3.3.52

Volkan, V.D. (1997). *Bloodlines: From ethnic pride to ethnic terrorism.* Farrar, Strauss and Giroux.

Welch, M.A. (2014, 24 January). New database lists 824 murdered, missing native women in Canada. *Winnipeg Free Press.* https://www.winnipegfreepress. com/local/grim-number-jumps-in-study-241776001.html

Westcott, K. (2013, 22 August). What is Stockholm syndrome? *BBC News Magazine.* https://www.bbc.com/news/magazine-22447726

Wheaton, E., E. Schauer, & T. Galli. (2010). Economics of human trafficking. *International Migration, 48*(4), 114–41. https://doi.org/10.1111 /j.1468-2435.2009.00592.x

Wilson, S. (2008). *Research is ceremony: Indigenous research methods.* Fernwood.

Winterdyk, J., & P. Reichel. (2010). Introduction to Human trafficking: Issues and perspectives [Special issue]. *European Journal of Criminology, 7*(1), 5–10. https://doi.org/10.1177/1477370809347894

Wiseman, J. (1970). *Stations of the lost: The treatment of skid row alcoholics.* Prentice-Hall.

Wong, W.C., E. Holroyd, & A. Bingham. (2011). Stigma and sex work from the perspective of female sex workers in Hong Kong. *Sociology of Health & Illness, 33*(1), 50–65. https://doi.org/10.1111/j.1467-9566.2010.01276.x

Wong, W.C., Y.T. Wun, K.W. Chan, & Y. Liu. (2008). Silent killer of the night: A feasibility study of an out-reach well-women clinic for cervical cancer screening in female sex workers in Hong Kong. *International Journal of Gynecological Cancer, 18*(1), 110–15. https://www.ncbi.nlm.nih.gov/pubmed /17466035

Wood, A.M., & N. Tarrier. (2010). Positive clinical psychology: A new vision and strategy for integrated research and practice. *Clinical Psychology Review, 30*(7), 819–29. https://doi.org/10.1016/j.cpr.2010.06.003

Wrede, K., & R.B. Stiftung. (2013). Anuradha Koirala – The woman who fights human trafficking in Nepal and beyond. *Human Dignity Forum.* http:// www.human-dignity-forum.org/2013/04/anuradha-koirala-the-woman -who-fights-human-trafficking-in-nepal-and-beyond/

Younging, G. (2009). Inherited history, international law, and the UN Declaration. In G. Younging, J. Dewar, & M. DeGagné (Eds.), *Response, responsibility, and renewal: Canada's truth and reconciliation journey* (pp. 323–8). Aboriginal Healing Foundation.

Yuen, W., W. Wong, E. Holroyd, & C. Tang. (2014). Resilience in work-related stress among female sex workers in Hong Kong. *Qualitative Health Research, 24*(9), 1232–41. https://doi.org/10.1177/1049732314544968

Zimmerman, C., M. Hossain, & C. Watts. (2011). Human trafficking and health: A conceptual model to inform policy, intervention and research. *Social Science & Medicine, 73*(2), 327–35. https://doi.org/10.1016/j.socscimed.2011.05.028

Index